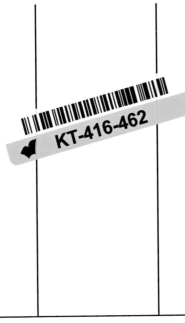

KT-416-462

04500017

Bradt

The Peak District

Slow down and discover the rich and diverse character of The Peak District with its moorland wilderness, pastoral uplands, deep-cut dales, limestone edges, stone villages and historical mill towns.

1 'England's green and pleasant land' – Monsal Dale from Monsal Head. 2 Relaxing on the River Derwent, Matlock Bath. 3 Winster is crammed with handsome stone, mullion-windowed town houses and attractive mining cottages. 4 Street entertainment at the Tideswell Food Festival.

EXPLORING WILD PLACES

Windswept moorland, lonely dales and rocky edges – it's not difficult to find peace and solitude in the Peak District.

1 Peveril Castle at Castleton with Mam Tor and the Great Ridge behind. 2 Fingers chalked up and ready to go – climbing on the Roaches. 3 Mam Tor, the so-called 'shivering mountain'. 4 Derwent Edge with its strange and wonderful rock formations. 5 An early purple orchid. Wild flowers thrive in the lime-rich White Peak soil. 6 Water voles frequent the riverbanks of the White Peak dales.

1 The mysterious chasm of Lud's Church, shrouded in mythology and history. 2 Kinder Scout – where the mass trespassers fought the battle that paved the way for open access to England's uplands. 3 Carsington Water – a great place for birdwatching, boating, walking and cycling. 4 Cycling the Tissington Trail, a former railway line. 5 The mountain hare grows a winter coat to camouflage itself on those rare snowy days! 6 The red grouse is a common sight on the Dark Peak moors.

WWW.WALKINGENGLISHMAN.COM

CHRIS JENNER/SS

STEVEN GILLIS/AGE FOTOSTOCK/SS

HISTORY IN THE PEAK DISTRICT

Bronze Age stone circles, Roman lead mines and impressive Victorian engineering vie for your attention alongside more recent history.

1 The debris from the 1948 Superfortress crash still lies strewn across Bleaklow Moor. **2** The Edwardian Opera House in Buxton. **3** Take a city tram in deepest rural Derbyshire at the National Tramway Museum. **4** The tragic Riley Graves on the edge of Eyam, the 'Plague Village'.

V8

AUTHOR

Helen Moat is a freelance writer, linguist, teacher and traveller. She grew up in Northern Ireland, moved to England as a young adult, with spells in Germany and Switzerland before settling down in the Peak District, her adopted home. When she's not cycling along Europe's rivers to Istanbul, camping in the East African bush or trekking in the Thai rainforest, she's likely to be found wandering on the Peak moorland or spinning her wheels through the dales.

AUTHOR'S STORY

When I moved to the Peak District in 1999, I swapped the flatlands of East Anglia for the hills and dales of Derbyshire. It was a good exchange, although I didn't see it initially. My love for the Peak District was a slow burner, but I soon realised I'd been truly blessed – being able to put down roots in this exceptionally beautiful corner of England: my sons have grown up here and are *raight* Derbyshire lads and I've no reason to *chunter*. The Peak District has shaped our lives, just as it's shaped the lives of so many who live and work here. It's allowed us as a family to spend much of our free time in the outdoors: to cycle, walk and scramble on the edges; to be within touching distance of the Peak District's wildlife. There's nothing to beat that.

I thought I knew the Peak District fairly well when I started writing this book. As a family of music lovers, we'd hunted out village festivals and tucked-away pubs with great music sessions. Loving the outdoors too, we'd spent many days poring over maps, translating contours, blue lines and blobs into fine waterside, dale and ridge walks. And after 15 years of uncovering hidden vales and ravines, some within striking distance of my own doorstep, I've realised you could live a lifetime in the Peak District and still not cover every bridleway, packhorse route or public footpath. This book is only a taster – and hopefully an inspiration for your own exploration.

Writing *Slow Travel Peak District* has allowed me to engage with the Slow philosophy as never before; to look up, look down and catch the detail; to stand and stare and ponder; to wander down hidden dells or jitties. I've learned to stop and chat with strangers: National Trust volunteers, foodies, twitchers, ramblers, climbers and river swimmers, to name but a few – and found them eager to share their knowledge of and passion for the Peak District. I've learned to read the landscape, from the ruin on the hilltop to the tell-tale rise of an Iron Age hillfort or an abandoned mill. I've learned the songs of birds and to scan the hillsides for signs of life. It has been a life-enriching experience.

First edition published February 2016
Bradt Travel Guides Ltd
IDC House, The Vale, Chalfont St Peter, Bucks SL9 9RZ, England
www.bradtguides.com
Print edition published in the USA by The Globe Pequot Press Inc,
PO Box 480, Guilford, Connecticut 06437-0480

Text copyright © 2016 Helen Moat
Maps copyright © 2016 Bradt Travel Guides Ltd includes map data © OpenStreetMap
contributors
Photographs copyright © 2016 Individual photographers (see below)
Project Managers: Anna Moores & Katie Wilding
Series design and cover research: Pepi Bluck, Perfect Picture

ISBN: 978 1 78477 007 5 (print)
e-ISBN: 978 1 78477 152 2 (e-pub)
e-ISBN: 978 1 78477 252 9 (mobi)

British Library Cataloguing in Publication Data
A catalogue record for this book is available from the British Library

Photographs
Photographs (c) individual photographers credited beside images & also those from picture
libraries credited as follows: Alamy.com (A), Dreamstime.com (D), David Preston (www.
davidpreston.com), Shutterstock.com (S), Superstock.com (SS), Visit Buxton (VB),
Visit England (VE), Visit Peak District (VPD)

Front cover Millstones on Stanage Edge (robertharding/A)
Back cover Well dressings at Tissington (eye35/A)
Title page Winster at dawn (Jim Dixon)

Maps David McCutcheon FBCart.S and Liezel Bohdanowicz

Typeset by Pepi Bluck, Perfect Picture
Production managed by Jellyfish Print Solutions; printed in Turkey
Digital conversion by www.dataworks.co.in

ACKNOWLEDGEMENTS

Thanks to all the people of the Peak District whose passion for the area has been a constant source of inspiration in writing this book. There are too many to single out, but I'd like to mention Chris Gilbert, Chris Millner, Colette Dewhurst, Gill Shimwell, Ian Howells and Lorne Chadwick for giving up so much of their precious time to chat to me and take me out on the job.

I'd also like to thank my long-suffering husband Tom for his invaluable support, guidance (and expertise as a Natural England conservationist), as well as taking on the role of proofreader. Thanks are also due to Jamie, my eldest son, who accompanied me on walks and cycles and assisted with the map work, and to Patrick, my youngest, just for being there and making me laugh.

Thanks also go to everyone at Bradt who helped, encouraged and supported me throughout the process: Rachel Fielding, Katie Wilding, Anna Moores, Tim Locke, along with my fellow Slow Travel writers, Donald Greig, Kirsty Fergusson and Marie Kreft. Without them, this book would never have happened.

DEDICATION

This book is dedicated to my husband Tom who has always
encouraged me 'to fly' and to my much-loved sons, Jamie and Patrick.
And in memory of my mother, a constant source of love and encouragement,
and my father who passed on his love of the outdoors to me.

Helen Moat

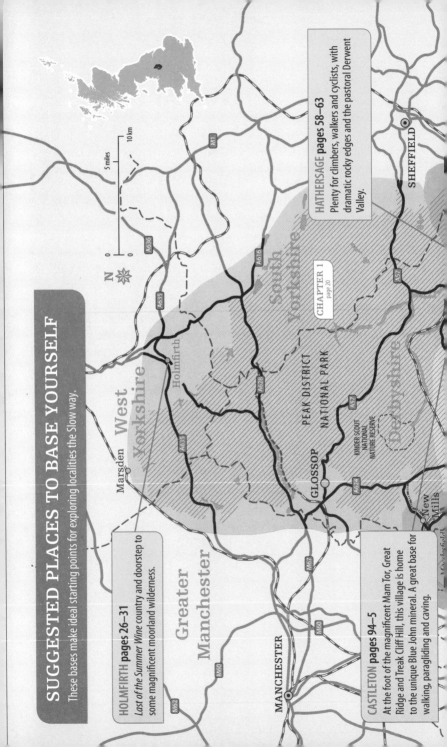

SUGGESTED PLACES TO BASE YOURSELF

These bases make ideal starting points for exploring localities the Slow way.

HOLMFIRTH pages 26–31
Last of the Summer Wine country and doorstep to some magnificent moorland wilderness.

CASTLETON pages 94–5
At the foot of the magnificent Mam Tor, Great Ridge and Treak Cliff Hill, this village is home to the unique Blue John mineral. A great base for walking, paragliding and caving.

HATHERSAGE pages 58–63
Plenty for climbers, walkers and cyclists, with dramatic rocky edges and the pastoral Derwent Valley.

CHAPTER 1
page 20

N

0   5 miles
0   10km

West Yorkshire

South Yorkshire

Derbyshire

Greater Manchester

PEAK DISTRICT NATIONAL PARK

KINDER SCOUT NATIONAL NATURE RESERVE

Marsden

Holmfirth

GLOSSOP

New Mills

MANCHESTER

SHEFFIELD

M62

M60

M67

M60

M1

A636

A635

A635

A616

A628

A57

A57

A624

A636

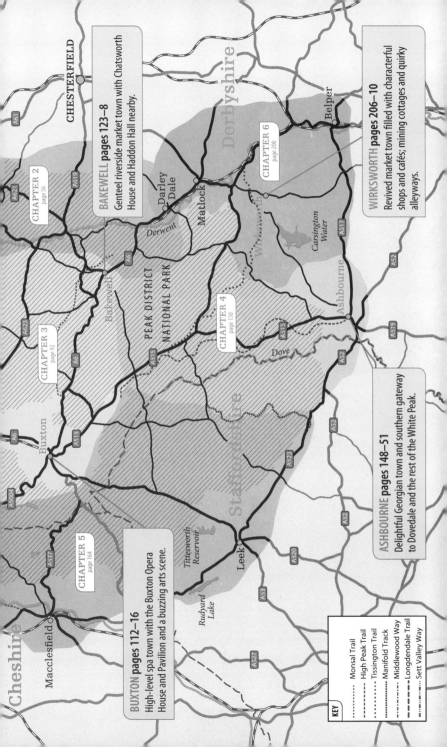

CHAPTER 2
page 56

BAKEWELL pages 123–8
Genteel riverside market town with Chatsworth House and Haddon Hall nearby.

CHESTERFIELD

Derbyshire

CHAPTER 6
page 200

WIRKSWORTH pages 206–10
Revived market town filled with characterful shops and cafés; mining cottages and quirky alleyways.

Belper

Darley Dale

Matlock

Derwent

Wirksworth

Carsington Water

CHAPTER 3
page 92

PEAK DISTRICT

NATIONAL PARK

Bakewell

CHAPTER 4
page 130

Ashbourne

Dove

ASHBOURNE pages 148–51
Delightful Georgian town and southern gateway to Dovedale and the rest of the White Peak.

Buxton

Staffordshire

CHAPTER 5
page 164

BUXTON pages 112–16
High-level spa town with the Buxton Opera House and Pavilion and a buzzing arts scene.

Tittesworth Reservoir

Leek

Rudyard Lake

Macclesfield

Cheshire

KEY
.... Monsal Trail
.... High Peak Trail
.... Tissington Trail
▬▬▬▬ Manifold Track
▬ ▬ ▬ Middlewood Way
▬ ▬ ▬ Longdendale Trail
▬▪▬▪ Sett Valley Way

CONTENTS

THE PEAK DISTRICT ONLINE

For additional online content, articles, photos and more on the Peak District, why not visit
🖉 www.bradtguides.com/peak.

THE PEAK DISTRICT

Said to be the second most visited national park in the world after Mount Fuji, the Peak District is an area of spectacular natural beauty. Most visitors (usually day-trippers), however, rarely stray into the park by more than a few miles from their nearest entry point – or head straight for the honeypots. So it isn't difficult to find an empty dale or an unfrequented edge. In the northern reaches of the Dark Peak, you can walk across moorland wilderness for hours without seeing anyone, while scores of villages and hamlets, tucked into dales and upland, see only a handful of visitors. Up and down the Peak District, characterful pubs, mostly frequented by local people, are known for their hand-picked ales and good locally sourced food, and are often alive with music sessions and events. Cafés and restaurants off the beaten track are a little bit more difficult to reach but are worth the effort, along with forgotten dales and woodland gardens. Stopping to chat with the shopkeeper, café owner, ranger, farmer, gamekeeper, birdwatcher or photographer, with their wealth of local knowledge, can greatly add to the richness of the Peak District experience. Likewise, it's worth visiting the park across the seasons, at dawn or dusk or even after dark. Finally, this is not a definitive guide to the Peak District, but a personal one. It's shaped by my own voyage of discovery over 15 years – many of the places happened upon or checked out after a casual but enticing mention in conversation. That's the beauty of Slow Travel: it takes you off in unexpected directions.

THE PEAK DISTRICT

So what is the Peak District? The name can be misleading, as there is little in the way of distinctive peaks. The word 'peak' is actually derived from the Saxons, the Pecsaetan, who settled the 'pecs' or hills in the Dark Ages. Nowadays, two terms are used to describe the area: the White Peak

THE SLOW MINDSET

Hilary Bradt, Founder, Bradt Travel Guides

> We shall not cease from exploration
> And the end of all our exploring
> Will be to arrive where we started
> And know the place for the first time.
>
> T S Eliot, 'Little Gidding', *Four Quartets*

This series evolved, slowly, from a Bradt editorial meeting when we started to explore ideas for guides to our favourite country – Great Britain. We wanted to get away from the usual 'top sights' formula and encourage our authors to bring out the nuances and local differences that make up a sense of place – such things as food, building styles, nature, geology, or local people and what makes them tick. Our aim was to create a series that celebrates the present, focusing on sustainable tourism, rather than taking a nostalgic wallow in the past.

So without our realising it at the time, we had defined 'Slow Travel', or at least our concept of it. For the beauty of the Slow movement is that there is no fixed definition; we adapt the philosophy to fit our individual needs and aspirations. Thus Carl Honoré, author of *In Praise of Slow*, writes: 'The Slow Movement is a cultural revolution against the notion that faster is always better. It's not about doing everything at a snail's pace, it's about seeking to do everything at the right speed. Savouring the hours and minutes rather than just counting them. Doing everything as well as possible, instead of as fast as possible. It's about quality over quantity in everything from work to food to parenting.' And travel.

So take time to explore. Don't rush it, get to know an area – and the people who live there – and you'll be as delighted as the authors by what you find.

and the Dark Peak. These two distinctive landscapes are shaped by the underlying rocks. In the centre and south, the White Peak, with its softer hills and dales, occasionally reveals its white limestone foundations in rocky outcrops. To the north, with arms wrapping around the west and east of the White Peak, lies the Dark Peak – higher and bleaker and underlain by tougher gritstone – so-called because of the moorland's dark peat. Within the two, there are the many stories that make up the landscape and its people.

It's difficult to summarise this small area of wonderful diversity in a few words. It's the skylark fluttering high above the moorland on a summer's day, filling the air with sweet song, or the low melancholy call of the curlew from somewhere in the peat channels. It's the symmetrical lines of the dry stone wall that spread out across pasture like an abstract painting; the tumble of stone settlements on hill or in dale. It's the land shaped by wind and weather and prehistoric ice ages: the misshapen rocky towers and crinkled ridges. It's the millstones that scatter the edges, a memorial to an industry that harnessed the power and energy of rivers like the Derwent and Wye. It's the people who lived and worked in this landscape, and continue to do so. Indeed, the biggest surprise in researching this book was the people I met along the way. All of them talked about the Peak District with passion. Tough men who go out in all weathers to build a wall or mend a fence or down-to-earth and practical northern women who work diligently to make the Peak District a better experience for all those who visit. In chatting with them, I was struck by the poetic language they've used to describe this place. It does that to you – for there is so much poetry in the landscape itself.

> *"It's the symmetrical lines of the dry stone wall that spread out like an abstract painting; the tumble of stone settlements; the land shaped by wind and weather..."*

FOOD, BEER & SONG

Apart from Derbyshire oatcakes and Bakewell pudding, the Peak District is not known for its distinctive local dishes, but the area is foodie heaven. With cattle-grazing lowland pastures and flocks of sheep on the hill farms, the Peak District is not short on quality butchers, farm shops and farmers' markets – supplying organic beef and lamb along with great local cheeses, farm-produced ice cream and crusty pies. I was greatly encouraged when chatting to local businesses (cafés, pubs and restaurant owners) to discover that many of them source local produce wherever they can, whether it's flour, beef, lamb, dairy products, fruit or vegetables. Although some of the big-brand coffee shops are sneaking into Peak towns, local tea rooms and cafés continue to thrive, while pubs resist big corporations or closure by buying in local, handpicked ales or starting their own micro-breweries. A few of them have their own in-house bakeries or make their own cheese, concentrating on preparing quality, locally produced dishes. Many of the pubs combine good food and beer with home-spun entertainment – resurrecting ancient customs or holding mini-festivals and weekly music sessions, some of the best in the country.

CAR-FREE TRAVEL

While most trains stop short of the national park, or skirt around its border (the Hope Valley line being the exception), a regular bus service cuts across the Peak District along the A6, linking Derby and Manchester. To visit more isolated areas by public transport takes patience and forward planning, but it pays off. There's no better way to experience the Peak countryside than from the elevated seat of a local bus. For walkers and cyclists, the public footpaths and back lanes that connect these settlements give you a truly Slow experience. For car users, combining road journeys with walking and cycling is the best way to experience the more inaccessible, and the more beautiful parts, of the Peak District.

TRAIN

Northern Rail (𝄞 www.northernrail.org) operates trains from Manchester Piccadilly to **Glossop** and **Hadfield**, while the Trans-Pennine Huddersfield to Manchester line stops at **Marsden, Diggle, Saddleworth** and **Greenfield**. The Sheffield to Manchester Piccadilly line makes its way through the 'green and pleasant' Edale Valley, stopping in **Grindleford**, **Hathersage**, **Bamford, Hope,** and **Edale** before continuing on to **New Mills** and **Marple**. It's a wonderful way to approach the Dark Peak.

For something different, and terrific fun, take the **Hope Valley Line Folk Train** either from Manchester to Hathersage or Sheffield to Edale 𝄞 www.hvhptp.org.uk/folktran). You can also take advantage of the station-to-station guided walks (advance booking required: 𝄞 01298 28400 𝄞 www.transpeakwalks.co.uk). If preferred, you can create your own walks between railway stations with the help of the Peak District OS maps. The pleasant riverside walk between Hathersage and Grindleford station is just one of many possibilities.

Further southwest, **Macclesfield**, on the Stafford to Manchester line, is well served by trains. From its station there's direct access on to the **Middlewood Way** with further halts at **Middlewood Railway Station** on the Stockport to Buxton line and at **Marple** at the other end. New Mills has two railway stations: **New Mills Central** on the Hope Valley Line, linking Manchester and Sheffield, and **New Mills Newtown** on the Manchester to Buxton line. Marple and New Mills railway stations also link the **Peak Forest Canal**.

WELL DRESSINGS & OPEN GARDENS

Well Dressing Week (varying from place to place) is the perfect time to visit a participating Peak District village, with displays by springs, fountains, churches, schools and other significant landmarks.

These colourful flower-head and seed mosaics are found across the Peak District over the summer, adding colourful interest to the mellow stone-built settlements.

No-one knows for sure the origins of well dressings in the Peak District. It's thought they stem back to pagan times and were created to give thanks for the region's plentiful springs of water. For dates, check ⊘ www.welldressing.com as well as www.peakdistrictonline.co.uk.

Also showing off Peak villages and towns at their best are the open gardens that take place from June to September. It's a great way to explore the nooks and crannies of lanes, backstreets and jitties – from the garden woodlands, valley streams and cliff-backed plots of country houses to the pocket-sized gardens and hillside patios of small cottages, all offering a potpourri of colour and design. The upcoming dates for the garden open days can be found at ⊘ www.opengardens.co.uk.

The best way to approach the southern fringes of the Peak District by train is on the picturesque **Derwent Valley Line** from Derby to the terminal station of Matlock. For more information, go to ⊘ www.eastmidlandstrains.co.uk.

BUS

While the towns and villages bordering the Peak District National Park are reasonably well served with buses, especially those with rail links, the roads inside the park are not always on bus routes, particularly in the northern reaches of the Dark Peak. The 184 **Huddersfield** to **Oldham** bus service, linking Marsden and Greenfield, skims the park at the northeastern end with stops that give access to open moorland and the wonderful Pennine Way.

One of the most stunning bus journeys in the Peak District is the 200 service from **Chapel-en-le-Frith** to **Castleton**, taking in the glorious **Edale valley**. A word of warning: it offers a very limited service on schooldays only. Equally scenic, Hulley's 272 bus service from **Sheffield** to **Castleton** halts at Longshaw Estate, Fox House, Burbage Bridge and Hathersage, all surrounded by prime walking country.

Hourly buses also run from Sheffield Interchange to Chatsworth with TM travel (which offers a discount for the stately home) and from

Matlock in the opposite direction, while **Hulleys of Baslow** provides a frequent bus service from Chesterfield too, but only as far as Baslow. The pleasant mile through the park from Goose Green to Chatsworth House isn't a hardship though. Hulleys of Baslow also serves many of the surrounding Peak villages. These bus routes epitomise the 'Slow' philosophy, crawling up hill and down dale and on into isolated settlements before reaching their final destination – what a way to see the Peak District. Check the Hulleys timetables for details: ⊘ hulleys-of-baslow.co.uk/timetables.html.

Less dawdling, the **High Peak** buses plough the Ashbourne to Buxton road, taking in Fenny Bentley and Tissington. A more limited service connects the villages straddling the A53.

Another main artery into the Peak Park is the A6, well-served by the **Transpeak** service linking Manchester and Derby. The route takes in Ashford-in-the-Water, Bakewell, Haddon Hall and Rowsley. Alternatively, take the 6.1 to Bakewell from Derby. **Trentbarton** (⊘ www.trentbarton.co.uk/peakdistrict) is advertised as the 'scenic sixes', and scenic these buses are. The buses pass through a UNESCO World Heritage Site, the **Derwent Valley Mills** (page 201), leaving the A6 briefly at Belper to divert to Wirksworth before re-joining it again at Cromford. With Trentbarton's unlimited travel zigzag card, you can hop on and off wherever you fancy between Derby and Bakewell. Further west, still on the fringes of the park, the B5053 has about half a dozen buses ploughing the road each day from Matlock to Ashbourne, stopping off at Wirksworth and Carsington.

THE PEAK DISTRICT ONLINE

There is a wealth of websites to help you plan your visit to the Peak District, run by organisations that seek to preserve and enrich the landscape and enhance the visitor's enjoyment. Apart from providing useful information, they offer everything from events, walks and courses to audio guides.

ONLINE RESOURCES

Peak District Online ⊘ www.peakdistrictonline.co.uk
Peak District National Park Authority ⊘ www.peakdistrict.gov.uk
Peak District and Derbyshire ⊘ www.visitpeakdistrict.com

National Trust ⌀ www.nationaltrust.org.uk
Moors for the Future ⌀ www.moorsforthefuture.org.uk
RSPB ⌀ www.rspb.org.uk
Southern Trent Water ⌀ www.stwater.co.uk/leisure-and-learning
Yorkshire Water ⌀ www.yorkshirewater.com/walks-and-leisure.aspx
Cheshire East Council ⌀ www.cheshireeast.gov.uk (select 'leisure and culture')
Staffordshire Peak District ⌀ www.enjoystaffordshire.com
Yorkshire Peak District ⌀ www.yorkshire.com (search for 'Peak District')
Oldham Peak District ⌀ www.visitoldham.com
Slow Travel Peak District ⌀ www.bradtguides.com/peak
Slow Travel Peak District online accommodation ⌀ www.bradtguides.com/peaksleeps

HOW THIS BOOK IS ARRANGED

I've loosely divided the book by its **National Character Areas** (NCAs). These share distinct characteristics of wildlife, geology, culture and landscape, as used by planners, conservationists and heritage groups throughout Britain. The Peak District covers four main National Character Areas: the **Derbyshire Peak Fringe and Lower Derwent**; the **Dark Peak** (including the Eastern Peak Moors), the **White Peak** (which I've divided into north and south) and the **South West Peak**. In an area where the Midlands meet 'the North', and spans four counties with natural links to four cities, the NCAs are by far the best way to navigate and to appreciate the Peak District's natural and manmade beauty.

While the national park is clearly defined, what constitutes the wider Peak District is open to debate. Some of the locations outlined in this book sit on its fringes and are outside the four main NCAs. I have included those that I feel are marked by a distinctive 'Peak District' character and are of particular interest.

FOLLOW BRADT

For the latest news, special offers and competitions, subscribe to the Bradt newsletter via the website ⌀ www.bradtguides.com and follow Bradt on:

 www.facebook.com/BradtTravelGuides @BradtGuides
 @bradtguides www.pinterest.com/bradtguides

PRACTICAL INFORMATION

Telephone numbers are given where possible and are marked with the symbol ✆ along with websites marked ⌂. Opening periods (and, if necessary, times) are indicated by the symbol ◷; opening details can of course change so it's always worth checking ahead if you can. Many of the Peak District's attractions are open all year round, but some of the stately homes and rural cafés are closed during the winter, and the latter may only open at weekends out of season. It's best to check opening times before setting off. Postcodes are included to help locate destinations, and where they're not so easily identified, particularly on walks, I've included grid references (indicated by the ♀ symbol) with possible bus and train links.

ACCOMMODATION, EATING & DRINKING

The accommodation in this guide has been chosen for its value for money, scenic location, historical interest or unique features – but most of all because it fits in with the Slow approach. It includes characterful hotels, B&Bs, self-catering accommodation, youth hostels and campsites run by people who care about the Peak District and its landscape. The same goes for the listed cafés, pubs and restaurants – businesses that employ sustainable methods and seek to make as little impact on the environment as possible, producing their own ingredients or sourcing local products. All of them serve good food in places that have been chosen for their ambience, character or lovely surroundings – and sometimes all three. Hotels, B&Bs and self-catering options are indicated by ♠ and are listed under the heading for the area in which they are located. Campsites are indicated by ▲. For further accommodation reviews and additional listings, go to ⌂ www.bradtguides.com/peaksleeps.

MAPS

You'll find a map of the Peak District with suggested places to base yourself on pages 4–5, while heading each chapter is a numbered map of the area that corresponds to the numbered place headings in the text. On the area maps, you'll also find a ♀ symbol showing the location of the walks outlined in the chapter. While some of the walks come with a sketch map, it's worth investing in the two Peak District Ordnance Survey Explorer maps: ❀ The Peak District Dark Peak Area, OL1, and ❀ The Peak District White Peak Area, OL24.

They cover most of the Peak District and are an invaluable aid. Recommended maps are always flagged with the ❀ symbol.

CYCLING

These are exciting times for off-road cyclists in the Peak District. The ultimate aim is to connect the surrounding cities to the Peak District with a spoked wheel of cycle paths that will connect existing cycle trails. The White Peak route will link the **Monsal** and **High Peak** trails into Matlock and Buxton, while the Little Don Link will skirt the edge of the Peak District from Sheffield along a disused railway to join the **Trans Pennine Trail** in Barnsley. Meanwhile the Staffordshire Moorlands Link will use the Caldon Canal towpath and signed on-road routes to link Stoke on Trent with the **Manifold Track** and the Roaches,

TRESPASSERS ON KINDER

On Sunday 24 April 1932 a group of Manchester ramblers and supporters of the growing 'Right to Roam' movement set off to Kinder to carry out a mass public trespass in a bid to allow free access for everyone to the open countryside.

As they scrambled up to the Kinder plateau, some of the Duke of Devonshire's gamekeepers were ready and waiting for the 400 or so protesters. A scuffle ensued with belts, stones, sticks and bare hands all enthusiastically employed. Despite the fracas, only one gamekeeper was slightly hurt, and the protesters continued on to the top where they met up with another Right to Roam group from Sheffield. The two groups of protesters shook hands triumphantly, but their elation was short-lived. Back in Hayfield, a small number of protesters were arrested and detained by the police, who'd been waiting with the gamekeepers. The next day, six of the ramblers were charged at New Mills Police Court with unlawful assembly and breach of the peace. The ramblers pleaded not guilty, but five of the six were found guilty and jailed. This outcome only strengthened the determination of the Right to Roam groups, now garnering support from the wider public. A few weeks later, 10,000 ramblers gathered in Winnats Pass near Castleton, demanding access to the forbidden moorlands, hills and dales of the Peak District.

It was to be another 17 years before the National Parks and Access to the Countryside Act in 1949 opened up the countryside to the public. Even then, large tracts of land were out of bounds for ramblers until the Countryside and Rights of Way Act came into force in 2000, with its final implementation as recently as 2005. Today, walkers enjoy open access to most of the open ground of the magnificent Peak landscape, many of them unaware that their freedom to roam was initially hard won by a group of determined working-class city dwellers.

while the Hope Valley Link will complement the **Little John Route**, a Sustrans-signed Sheffield to Manchester route across the national park. Some of this work has begun, but it will take years if not decades for it to be completed. In the meantime, the Peak District has more than its fair share of off-road trails (some of which have been highlighted above) that can be linked with quiet back lanes.

WALKING

There's no better way to see the Peak District than on foot. Many of the scenic dales have no roads running through them, while the open moorland often stretches out far beyond the nearest highway or lane. The same goes for most of the magnificent ridge and edge walks across the Peak District. If heading out into more exposed areas, take an Ordnance Survey map with you and make sure you are kitted out with suitable footwear and waterproofs as the weather can change quickly, particularly on the moors. If you don't have the confidence to try more challenging routes independently, you can join a guided walk. The National Trust, Peak District National Park Authority and a host of other local organisations (see *The Peak District online*, pages 12–13) offer themed walks which can include everything from geology, archaeology and history to crash sites, wildlife and foraging. For those who prefer an easy amble, many of the Peak District villages and towns have created heritage walk leaflets and information boards. Pick up a pamphlet from the nearest information point. The dismantled railways offer flat easy walking with great views and are well facilitated with car parks, kiosks offering snacks and drinks, and picnic benches along the way. It may be slightly more demanding, but you can make the dismantled railway walks more interesting by climbing the stiles on to the uplands. Route-finding becomes more fiddly and you will need a map, but it's worth the effort.

HORSERIDING

The Peak District offers countless opportunities for the horserider: quiet country lanes, traffic-free trails and bridleways. There are 65 miles of off-road trails alone, while the Pennine Bridleway is a 268-mile National Trail that crosses rugged Peak terrain along the high ground of northern England, a challenge for the experienced rider. Apart from the dismantled railways, Macclesfield Forest, Carsington Water and the

THE BEST OF QUIRKY PEAK DISTRICT

The Peak District is full of quirky character and oddities. Here are some of the best.

Quirkiest town

With its maze of jitties and puzzle gardens set into the hillside, it's not without reason that Prince Charles named **Wirksworth** Quirksworth. Come during the Wirksworth Festival to see it in all its idiosyncrasy (page 206).

Quirkiest church

The Cathedral in the Peak, **Tideswell** has a superb collection of individual wood-carvings. Check out the organist carved into the wood by the pipes, and the mythical creatures along with a nest of fledgling birds in the chancel (page 111).

Quirkiest museum

Bakewell Old House Museum must be in the running with its rat skeleton and buttons, along with the shoe of a runaway boy and the foot of a runaway elephant (pages 124–6).

Quirkiest pub

If you think time travel isn't possible, visit the **Barley Mow at Kirk Ireton**. It will take you back to a time when ale and cider was served from a jug and beer was poured straight from barrels behind the counter (page 205).

Quirkiest café

There's strong competition, but the prize goes to **Scarthin Café** at **Scarthin Books**, **Cromford**. There's something Beatrix Potter-esque about a café hidden behind a curved bookcase, not forgetting the old stove, quirky posters and assortment of curios (page 219).

Quirkiest festival

There are so many to choose from, but the **Saddleworth Rushcart Festival** has one of the most bizarre ancient traditions to be recently revived. Where else would you get a drunken morris man on a mountain of rushes with a copper kettle full of ale in his hand as he's wheeled through the parish in a cart (page 35)?

Quirkiest competition

No question, it has to be the **World Champion Hen Racing** held by the **Barley Mow**, **Bonsall** – the ultimate in silliness (page 225).

Quirkiest building

There are many, but the **Istrian Kažun at Parsley Hay**, a dry-stone Croatian dwelling on the **High Peak Trail**, is a hot contender (page 144).

Quirkiest landmark

Rowtor Rocks, **Birchover** has to be one of the strangest (and least-known) landmarks in the Peak District. Along with the prehistoric rock art, there are carved-out rooms, staircases and seats – all the work of a playful vicar (pages 87–8).

Quirkiest landscape

Lud's Church, not a church but a deep chasm hidden away in a quiet area of woodland and shrouded in mythology and mystery (page 193).

Upper Derwent Valley have riding routes, while the perimeter track of Carsington Water is open to horseriders and has wonderful views over the reservoir.

Useful information is provided by the Peak District National Park Authority at ⌀ www.peakdistrict.gov.uk (search for 'horseriding').

ACCESSIBLE PEAK DISTRICT

For a comprehensive list of accessible sites, visit the Peak District website ⌀ www.peakdistrict.gov.uk/visiting/accessible-places-to-visit/access4all and view the map. There are a good number of scenic walks beyond the Peak District towns and villages that are wheel-friendly. The best of these accessible paths are found by reservoirs such as Langsett, Dovestone, Derwent Valley, Carsington Water and the Goyt Valley, but be aware of some gradients. For flat accessible paths, look no further than the dismantled railways: the Manifold Track and the Monsal, High Peak, Tissington, Longdendale and Sett Valley trails. Some riverside walks are at least partially accessible and include Dovedale, Tideswell, Lathkill and Bradford dales. For accessible forest trails, visit Macclesfield Forest. Short panoramic upland paths include Tegg's Nose close to Macclesfield or Surprise View near Hathersage, while nearby Baslow and Curbar Edge (accessed from Curbar Gap car park) have paths that are fairly flat, if somewhat uneven.

FEEDBACK REQUEST & UPDATES WEBSITE

We've worked hard to ensure information is accurate and up-to-date, but in the face of 90,000 words and countless hours of research, errors are bound to occur. Nothing stands still: businesses and attractions are constantly evolving, changing hands or closing down. We would welcome your updates and suggestions. Contact us on ✆ 01753 893444 or ✉ info@bradtguides. com. We will forward emails to the author who may post updates on the Bradt website at www.bradtupdates.com/peakdistrict. Alternatively you can add a review of the book to www.bradtguides.com or Amazon.

19

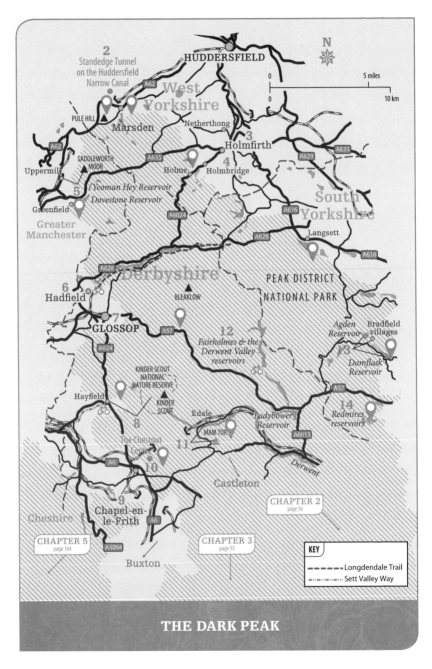

THE DARK PEAK

1

THE DARK PEAK

On the map, the Dark Peak with its underlying gritstone and dark peat moorland stretches out as a thrilling expanse of wilderness with just the occasional road cutting across it, along with the wriggly blue and orange lines of streams and contours. This area of upland isn't really empty of course, but teems with all manner of non-human life – from buzzards and peregrines to golden plover, curlew and grouse, while the moorland is packed with bog mosses, lichens and cottongrasses – and the insects and animals that inhabit it. Here you'll encounter real wilderness walking and the opportunity to slow down and clear your head of all the noise that comes with modern life. Views extend in every direction, only interrupted by rocky tors and wooded cloughs.

Gathered around the moorlands, just outside the national park border, are the old mill towns and villages of **Marsden**, **Holmfirth**, **Greenfield**, **Uppermill** and **Glossop,** reinvented as tourist destinations. They still retain their northern grit and long-established traditions while catering for visitors with boutique shops, welcoming tea rooms and delightfully low-key tourist attractions.

The map is daubed with the blue blobs of the reservoirs that pad out the valleys and stretch out along the fringes of the national park. The reservoirs were created to feed the insatiable mills and industries of the towns and villages that surround the Peak Park, and to quench the thirst of the growing populations. There are 34 reservoirs in the Peak District, the vast majority situated in the Dark Peak. Not only do they provide clean drinking water but they double up as a watery playground, offering everything from sailing, canoeing and cycling to rambling and birdwatching. Some of them receive hundreds of thousands of visitors every year (like the **Derwent Valley reservoirs**),

> *"There are 34 reservoirs in the Peak District, the vast majority situated in the Dark Peak."*

ℹ **TOURIST INFORMATION**

Edale – The Moorland Centre Fairhead, Edale, Hope Valley S33 7ZA ✆ 01433 670207

Glossop Information Point The Grouse Inn, SK13 6JY

Holmfirth 49–51 Huddersfield Rd, Holmfirth HD9 3JP ✆ 01484 222444

Marsden Marsden Library and Information Centre, Peel St, HD7 6BW ✆ 01484 222555

Upper Derwent Visitor Centre Fairholmes S33 0AQ ✆ 01433 650953

---

while others like Damflask and Agden around the Bradfields are less accessible with little or no amenities, and see only the occasional walker. As with the empty moorland, these quiet expanses of water are great places to reconnect with nature.

WALKING & CYCLING

The Dark Peak offers some of the most exciting and demanding walking in the Peak District. Exposed moorland, with heights reaching over 2,000 feet on Bleaklow and Kinder, requires the walker to come well equipped with OS maps, sturdy footwear and layers of clothes suitable for changeable weather. Walking the Dark Peak section of the Pennine Way is an excellent way of seeing the wild beauty of this windswept landscape. The approach to Edale is particularly thrilling, passing a series of remarkable weathered rock outcrops. For those who enjoy a more gentle form of exercise (and at least one warming pub along the way), there are plenty of pleasant reservoir and valley walks along the Goyt Valley and the Derwent Valley reservoirs.

Along with walking, cycling is one of the most popular outdoor pursuits in the Dark Peak. After the heady success of the **2014 Tour de France** culminating in the newly created **Tour de Yorkshire**, the Dark Peak is choc-a-bloc with lean cyclists pushing themselves on steeply graded roads. You can follow the Peak District section of the 2014 Tour de France with its switchbacks and punishing gradients – or you can seek out one of the dismantled railways, requiring less energy but still offering exceptional views along the way. **Longdendale Trail** passes five reservoirs flanked by moorland, while the shorter **Sett Valley Trail** to the south extends from the foot of the Kinder Massif to New Mills. East of Hayfield, the **Derwent Valley Reservoirs Trail** takes you on a scenic waterside ride.

SADDLEWORTH MOOR & THE FAR NORTH

Nowhere else in the Peak District feels quite as wild as the northern reaches of the Dark Peak. Heading this area of upland, Saddleworth Moor rolls out across the South Pennines, a sea of undulating blanket bog, cottongrass, mosses, heathers and bilberry, before halting short of conurbations such as Oldham and Huddersfield. Despite the surrounding urbanisation, it's virtually an empty landscape. A few country roads leak a handful of miles into the national park, usually accessing the reservoirs before being swallowed up by the uplands, while the A635, the only artery cutting across the national park at this point, sees little in the way of roadside settlement. Most human activity is confined to the reservoirs, the sprinkling of public footpaths and the **Pennine Way**, one of England's most popular long-distance walking trails. Skirting the moors and reservoirs, northern towns such as **Marsden**, **Holmfirth** and **Uppermill** offer a host of festivals, events and attractions full of local character.

1 MARSDEN

With the sweeping backdrop of Marsden Moor and the gentler Colne Valley at its feet, Marsden just outside the northern tip of the national park is a magnet for artists and visitors. Bit by bit this traditional mill settlement is becoming gentrified with cafés, boutiques and galleries while retaining its northern grit. Enjoy a rummage on Peel Street, where most of the village's independent shops are located, and a waterside amble along Weir Side and Market Place – all at the village's heart.

To experience the village at its most vibrant, come during one of its many festivals. The season begins in February with the **Imbolc Fire Festival** (on the years the festival is running – check tourist information) with a stand-off between the Green Man (spring) and Jack Frost (winter). The Green Man wins, of course, and the end of winter is celebrated with a torchlit procession, drumming, a light show, juggling and giant puppets. In April, **Cuckoo Day** celebrates the return of the cuckoo with music, clog dancing, processions and a cuckoo walk. This tradition began when the good people of Marsden noticed that spring and sunshine came with the return of the cuckoo. They reckoned if they imprisoned the bird, winter would be kept at bay. So the locals built a tower around the cuckoo, but just as they added the last layer, it flew away – so the story goes. In October, Marsden tries to keep those winter blues at bay again by putting on an excellent **Jazz Festival**. From ragtime and blues to fusion and trad jazz, Marsden's pubs and clubs are alive with music. Most events are free.

Exploring the Marsden Moor Estate

South of Marsden a line of reservoirs leads up into the Dark Peak: **Butterley, Blakeley, Wessenden** and **Wessenden Head**. The **Pennine Way** follows the reservoirs, a soul-restoring walk up through moorland, until the rough, stone path emerges at the junction of **Wessenden Head Road** just off the A635. Here you'll find a large metal frame on an 'easel stand', created by Yorkshire artist Ashley Jackson as part of his **Framing the Landscape** project. Jackson says, 'To see the spirit of Yorkshire and its moor through your eyes is one thing; many people will look but only a few will see and feel its very soul.' I could see what he meant as I gazed through the frame to the blues of Wessenden Reservoir with the yellows and browns of the moorland behind it. The frame focuses the eye on this inspirational landscape, the captured detail making it all the more impressive. Just above the Jackson frame, there's a roadside memorial to 12-year-old Keith Bennett, one of the Moors Murders victims from the 1960s. It's hard to comprehend the darker side of humanity in these beautiful surroundings.

If you are planning to walk from Marsden to Wessenden Head, note the A635 is not on a bus route. From here, you must backtrack to your starting point, call a taxi, take in a wider circular walk or continue on the Pennine Way to the Manchester Road on the A62, which is served by buses.

A Moors for the Future (an organisation promoting the recovery of moorland) **audio trail** covers a seven-mile walk from Marsden Railway Station that includes Pule Hill, Black Moss and Swellands reservoirs. The audio trail focuses on the human footprint on the moors, from the Mesolithic people of 9000BC to the present day National Trust, which owns and manages the moorland. To download the guide, follow the links on ⊘ www.moorsforthefuture.org.uk/audio-trails. If you prefer your guides to be flesh and blood rather than virtual, the National Trust offers a range of **guided walks and activities** on the moors, departing from Marsden Railway Station. Check its website for details.

On the Marsden Moors the weather can change quickly. Bring a detailed OS map and wear suitable clothing.

Pule Hill

For an alternative walk, catch the bus southwestwards on the A62 bus route from Marsden and disembark at the **Carriage House** pub. If using your own car, park in one of the lay-bys on **Mount Hill**. From the end of Mount Hill road, follow the little path that winds its way to the summit of **Pule Hill** and continue along the ridge before dropping down to **Pule Hill Quarry**. Here you'll find a **Simon Armitage Stanza Stone**, part of the Ilkley Literature Festival Stanza Stones, and the only one on the edge of the Peak District. The views from Pule Hill are extensive, taking in Colne Valley and the plains beyond. It's an exposed spot, so brace yourself for the winds that blow across it.

2 STANDEDGE TUNNEL ON THE HUDDERSFIELD NARROW CANAL

Standedge Tunnel & Visitor Centre, Waters Rd (off Reddisher Rd), Marsden HD7 6NQ
✐ 01484 844298 ⊘ www.canalrivertrust.org.uk/standedge-tunnel; ⊙ 30-minute boat trips Mar–Nov; 2-hour trip alternate Sat Apr–Oct; refreshments at Wateredge Café.

From Marsden railway station, a towpath along the Huddersfield Narrow Canal leads to Standedge Tunnel, a construction over three miles in length, and more than 600 feet below the ground. It took 17 years of engineering hiccups and hard graft to complete the structure. Ironically, after all that blood and sweat, the canal was only used for 40 years, made redundant by the railway. For all of that, the engineers and navvies have left behind a wonderful legacy: Standedge Tunnel is the longest, highest and deepest canal tunnel in Britain.

Before leaving the station car park, take time to drop into the **National Trust Visitor Centre** to find out about the Trust-owned Marsden Moor Estate above town (page 24). From there, it's a short 15-minute

"Standedge Tunnel is the longest, highest and deepest canal tunnel in Britain."

walk along the canal, a pleasant moor-side approach to the tunnel (or you can take the water taxi service that runs on weekends in the season). There's also a car park right beside the visitor centre.

The interpretive boards at **Standedge Visitor Centre** give a comprehensive history of the tunnel: a story of endurance, hardship – and a good pinch of bloody-mindedness. While the centre (free of charge) tells you everything you need to know about the tunnel's history, you can't really appreciate its scale without taking one of the boat trips. Inside the tunnel, you begin to appreciate what it was like for the professional 'leggers' to propel the narrowboats through the dark, claustrophobic tunnel with nothing more than the strength of their legs. 'Strong in't arm and thick in't head, as they used to say around these parts,' Chris, our guide laughs. The men were paid one shilling and sixpence to leg each boat through the tunnel, taking anything from one and a half to three hours, depending on the boat's load. The 30-minute guided boat tour only goes a short way into the tunnel, but it's enough to give you an idea of their working lives. Otherwise, the fortnightly Saturday boat trip takes in the entire length of the tunnel. The trip lasts two hours, with visitors returned to their starting point by taxi. You can start from the Marsden or Diggle end, with a taxi service at both ends.

As I stood on the bridge above the canal tunnel, an intercity train thundered out of the hillside where ancient packhorse trails cross the moors above. Here, traces of ancient travel and the dizzying speed of modern life cross paths.

¶¶ FOOD & DRINK

Crumbals on the Corner 17 Peel St, HD7 6BR ✐ 01484 847082. A varied and imaginative menu – check out the beetroot and white chocolate, or ginger and lime cake.
Riverhead Brewery Tap and Dining Room 2 Peel St, HD7 6BR ✐ 01484 844324. With its own micro-brewery in the basement, the pub is known for its hand-crafted beers. Quality food served upstairs with riverside views.

📷 SHOPPING

Peel Street is lined with individual shops, boutiques and cafés. If you like good design, look out for **Roobarb Gifts** selling home accessories made by textile artist Sarah Foster and other local designers, while **Cubecure** offers an eclectic mix of gifts and designer clothing.

3 HOLMFIRTH

🏠 **Sunny Bank Boutique Guest House** (page 240), **Cross Farm** (page 241)

Little Hollywood, *Last of the Summer Wine* and yellow bicycles – they're all part of Holmfirth in the **Holme Valley**. This little Yorkshire town, tucked into a wooded dale on the eastern fringe of the Peak District, couldn't be more removed from the bright lights of Hollywood – but it does share a history in movie making. Most people have heard of *Last of the Summer Wine* (Britain's longest-running television sitcom), portraying an old-fashioned if slightly barmy idyll. But not many know that Holmfirth was home to one of the earliest film studios in the world, with **Bamforth & Co** producing comedy films here as early as 1898. Son of a Holmfirth painter and decorator, James Bamforth continued the family tradition in painting – but pictures rather than houses. He went on to produce painted lantern slides, eventually replacing them with photographs. It was a natural

> *"It was the cheeky seaside postcard, not the silent movies, that made Bamforth's name."*

progression for Bamforth to move from photography to film, grabbing unsuspecting townspeople to star in a string of successful movies. You can see the site of the original studio on **Station Road**.

It was the cheeky seaside postcard, not the silent movies, that made Bamforth's name, however. By 1960, the company led the market in comic postcards. **Holmfirth Library** on Huddersfield Road displays a small collection of the naughty postcards on its stairway, with their double entendres, out-sized women and hen-pecked men. The schoolboy humour and barely veiled sexism seems somewhat old-fashioned now, but the cards were hugely popular in their heyday.

In the **Information Centre** next to the library, you can pick up the Holmfirth Blue Plaque Trail and a *Last of the Summer Wine* leaflet to guide you around town. The *Last of the Summer Wine* legacy is more visible than the Bamforth one and includes everything from **Ivy's Café** (Sid's Café) at **Towngate** and **Nora Batty's Steps** (a holiday cottage)

CIDER WITH ROB

I'm standing in the dimness of the old stable block surrounded by the unfamiliar equipment of cider-making: a scratter, press of wood-slatted racks and vats of juices. Cider maker and owner of **Pure North** Rob North releases a cap on one of the casks and it emits a slow hiss: the cider is not yet ready. This is a purely organic process from the layering and pressing of apple 'cakes' (the mulched apples) in hessian cloths, through to the long, slow fermentation and maturation of the cider. It's not difficult to get caught up in Rob's enthusiasm. His small commercial enterprise started out as a hobby when he bought an old farm with a handful of apple trees. There are now over 340 trees and 20 odd varieties of eating, cooking apples and perry pears. After the tour of the orchard and cider house, I get down to the pleasurable business of cider tasting. From the Deanhouse Dry to the light and subtle Katy; from the Valley Oak with its sweet, full farmhouse flavour to the Spiced Cider (tasting of Christmas) – I'm in cider heaven. See page 31 for details.

to the **Wrinkled Stocking Tea Room** on **Huddersfield Road** and the **Last of the Summer Wine Exhibition** on **Scarfold**, filled with photographs, *Summer Wine* paraphernalia – and some of Compo, Clegg, Foggy and Seymour Utterwaithe's daft inventions. For real devotees, the **Summerwine Magic Tour** starts from Sid's Café (⏱ www.summerwine.tv), winding ten miles through hill and dale to various film locations.

A five reservoirs walk in the Holme Valley

❋ OS Explorer map OL1; start Digley north car park, ♥ SE110072; 5 miles; fairly easy with uneven sections above Ramsden Reservoir & the odd short climb

The five reservoirs walk from Holmbridge takes in part of the **Kirklees Way**, the traditional Yorkshire villages of Holme and Holmbridge and the reservoirs of **Digley, Bilberry, Brownhill, Ramsden** and **Riding Wood**. You can walk some or all of them together or separately. I did all five on a day of warm sunshine following one of sleet, wind and rain; a soul-restoring ramble with the long muted upward call of the curlew accompanying me all along the Kirklees Way. Refreshments available at at **Fleece Inn** and the attached **Pantry** (Holme HD9 2QG ✆ 01484 683449 ⏱ fleeceinnholme.co.uk ☺ closed Mon), or at **The Bridge** (Holmbridge HD9 2NQ ✆ 01484 687652 ☺ closed Mon).

Digley & Bilberry reservoirs

1 From **Digley Reservoir north car park**, a well-defined track leads down **Gibriding Lane** (eventually disappearing into the reservoir). After crossing between Digley and Bilberry reservoirs, turn left and continue on along the south bank. If you're just doing a lap of Digley (a little over one mile) continue on the path to **Fieldhead Lane** and head back to your starting point along **Digley Royd Lane**.

Kirklees Way & Holme

2 If you plan to continue on to the next set of reservoirs, look out for the **Kirklees Way** signpost part way along Digley Reservoir on the south bank. (Warning: Kirklees Way no longer veers off from the dam head as the OS map suggests.) From the signpost turn right up the grassy pathway, over a series of stiles through fields to **Holme**.

3 To detour for a bite to eat, turn right again up the main street of this lovely little village to visit **The Pantry** or **The Fleece Inn** next door. Aim to arrive at The Pantry for breakfast, brunch or lunch: the breakfast-in-a-roll, pastries, pies and pasties are delicious and excellent

Otherwise, just potter through the streets, taking a random left or right. Holmfirth is not just a film set, but a traditional northern working-class town. Standing side by side with the boutiques and cosy tea rooms are old-fashioned shops, such as the hardware and cobbler's store, little changed since Holmfirth's mill days.

It's not just the larger-than-life *Summer Wine* characters that have left their mark on Holmfirth; the yellow bicycles, synonymous with the

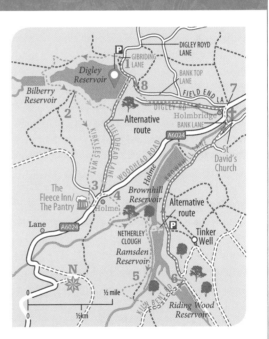

value for money. I've never seen such a posh and versatile village store in such a tiny space. There's a small amount of pleasant seating outside the pantry – a little suntrap on cloudless days.

Brownhill, Ramsden & Riding Wood reservoirs
You can start your walk from **Holme** if you plan just to take in Riding Wood, Ramsden and Broomhill reservoirs only. From **The Fleece Inn**, walk downhill along **Woodhead Road** (the A6024).

4 Take the first fingerpost on the right (just below Underhill House) on Woodhead Road, signed **Kirklees Way**. The path heads down through a meadow to a ravine. Cross the bridge above a tumbling waterfall and continue on the path, the ravine now on your other side. As the path heads towards the head of the dam between Brownhill and Ramsden reservoirs, you have a choice: you can continue downhill to cross between the reservoirs and on down Brownhill Lane to Holmbridge, or you can take a right ▶

A five reservoirs walk in the Holme Valley (Continued...)

◄ fork just before the little wooden Kirklees Way post and continue along the hillside on to a broader path that follows parallel to the shoreline of **Ramsden Reservoir**.

5 Bear right on the track and head down to **Netherley Clough** and a little footbridge. Cross it and head uphill with the stream now on your left. The path leads steeply up into woodland, eventually coming out at the Yorkshire Water access track. Turn left here on to **Kiln Bent Road** and follow the road that passes over the head of **Riding Wood Reservoir**.

6 Turn left on to **Brownhill Lane**. Further along, there's a small picnic area next to a tumbling stream and the car park near **Tinker Well** if you need a break, but the end of the walk is in sight. From here the road continues to run alongside **Brownhill Reservoir**, turning into **Bank Lane** before it hits the A6024 at **Holmbridge**. Keep right and follow the curve of the road round **St David's Church**.

7 Take the left turn up **Digley Road**, a delightfully leafy cul-de-sac lane that follows **Digley Brook**. Climb the steps (aided by a handrail) on the right at the end of the lane, and follow the way through a copse as it veers left and out on to more open land until you reach **Bank Top Lane**.

8 Keep left, following the short stretch of road that turns into **Digley Royd Road**. One last left turn takes you into **Gibriding Lane** and your starting point. If you started from Holme, follow the first part of the walk (outlined on page 28), or take the direct route along **Fieldhead Lane** that crosses the head of Digley Reservoir.

2014 Tour de France, still hang brightly above shop windows, and even though the Yorkshire *Grand Départ* is fast becoming a distant memory, the buzz in town remains with the yellow bicycles. Holmfirth now gears itself up for the thrills and spills associated with the world's greatest cycle race in the form of its very own **Tour de Yorkshire**. Cycling enthusiasts should look out for possible routes taking place in this northeast corner of the Peak District at the end of April/beginning of May.

As with Marsden, Holmfirth has its share of excellent festivals, from the **Festival of Folk** (with music and dancing) and **Film Festival** in May to the **Arts Festival** in June and Holmfirth **Art Week** and **Duck Race** in July.

Just north of Holmfirth at **Netherthong**, you can find a real little gem: a small orchard, cider press and café, tucked away on the fringe of the village and popular with visitors, cyclists and ramblers in the know.

¶¶ FOOD & DRINK

The choice of cafés, restaurants and pubs in Holmfirth itself can be confusing. Check out **Nick's Kitchen** (5 Victoria Sq, HD9 2DN ☎ 01484 685734 ⊙ closed Tue & Wed), a small, intimate establishment that's a firm favourite with visitors and locals alike. **The Toad and Tatie** (38 Woodhead Rd, HD9 2PR ☎ 01484 689635) is less 'toad and tattie' and more tasty seafood and steak, and has its own smokehouse. **The Wrinkled Stocking Tearoom** (30 Huddersfield Rd, HD9 2JS ☎ 01484 681408 ⊙ closed Wed & Sun) takes its name from the brush-weilding battleaxe *Summer Wine* character Nora Batty. For tea lovers, there are more than 20 loose leaf varieties to choose from, along with home-baked cakes. Hot and cold lunches are served, with most of the ingredients locally sourced.

Phone Rob at the **The North Cider and Juice Company and Pure North Cider Press café** (Deanhouse, Netherthong HD9 3TD ☎ 07720 398706 ⊘ www.purenorthciderpress. com ⊙ closed Mon (apart from bank holidays) & Tue) to arrange a tour of the orchard and press here (see box, page 27) followed by cider tasting. Alternatively, head straight for the shop and café with its little wooden balcony (blankets and heaters provided for cooler days), and cosy dining room complete with wood-burner. Try the Ploughman's Platter accompanied by one of Rob's organically grown ciders.

▣ SHOPPING

Holmfirth is a rewarding little town to peruse, with plenty of old-fashioned stores and trendy boutiques and craft shops. Regarded local artist Ashley Jackson has a shop in town (⊘ www.ashley-jackson.co.uk) on **Huddersfield Road**, where you can also enrol on one of his art courses that take place on the moors. On the same road you'll find **Holmfirth Fair Trade Shop** stocking ethical gifts that are sourced locally and from abroad. **Silver Dream Studio** (⊘ www.silverdreamstudio.co.uk) in Hollowgate offers handcrafted contemporary jewellery produced onsite by silversmith Jacqui Laithwaite-Rawes, while **The Chocolate Box** (Hollowgate) tempts its customers with rows of old-fashioned sweet jars and English and Continental chocolates. Bibliophiles should look in at **Daisy Lane Books** (Towngate), a secondhand bookshop in one of Holmfirth's most historic buildings. Several markets offer good rummaging: the **General Market** takes place on Thursday, and there's a **Saturday Craft and Food Market**. The **Farmers' Market** is held on the first and third Sundays of the month.

4 HOLMBRIDGE

In 2014, the Tour de France cyclists raced through Holmbridge before tackling the climb up to **Holme Moss,** and the route still draws road racers. Holmbridge is a pretty village beside the **River Holme** with remnants of the mill industry around **St David's Church**.

There's some great walking around Holmbridge, including the Holme Valley reservoirs. If you are arriving by bus in Holmbridge, head up Digley Road to Gibriding Lane (page 28), leading to Digley Reservoir – the first of five beautiful reservoirs.

Holmfirth Vineyard

Holmfirth Vineyard, Woodhouse Lane, Holmfirth HD9 2QR ✆ 01484 691861 🖰 www.holmfirthvineyard.com. Daily guided tours with wine tasting (advance bookings), accommodation on site. Restaurant ⊙ every day for breakfast & lunch, morning & afternoon coffee & teas; à la carte menu until 18.00 & 20.30 on Fri & Sat.

The farmland around Holmbridge is traditionally home to sheep, but look up at the vertiginous slopes above the settlement and you will see fields of vines. Holmfirth Vineyard isn't an obvious location for wine growing: the sun rarely shines here and the slope isn't south facing. The Pennine winds can whip up an unwelcoming force across the northwest-facing hillside, prompting visitors to zip up their coats. You'd be forgiven for wondering why the owners, Ian and Becky Scheveling, thought it was a good idea to plant a seven-acre vineyard here. 'Someone asked me what's been a good year,' the vineyard manager and tour guide laughed when I visited. 'I told him, we haven't had one yet.' In truth the weather doesn't matter too much. The grapes used are hybrids, produced to withstand northern climes. Across the valley, the criss-cross of dry stone wall stretches up to the moors. The vineyard seems incongruous in this landscape, but it works. Inside, Luke offers a couple of rosés and a red to sample after explaining how the wine is produced. The wine is light and fruity – and slips down the throat surprisingly easily. It transpires that the Schevelings' vision for a winery on the edge of the Peak District wasn't such a daft idea after all.

Following in the tracks of the Tour de France

If you plan to trace the Peak District section of the 2014 Tour de France, you will need a car or a bike, as no public transport passes through the greater part of the TDF route. If you're up for cycling it, be warned, it's a route that challenges the fittest and most experienced cyclists – the organisers of the 2014 Tour de France sussed out the hilliest and most twisty routes in the Peak District. The most famous section is probably the stretch through **Holmbridge**, **Holme** and on up to **Holme Moss Transmitting Station** (a killer, particularly on a windy day)

Dovestone & Yeoman Hey reservoirs

OS Explorer map OL1; start: Dovestone Reservoir car park, ♀ SE013034; 3 miles around Dovestone & Yeoman Hey; easy waterside walking (but moderately difficult if heading on to the hills). No refreshments, so bring a picnic.

Dovestone and Yeoman Hey reservoirs sit in the middle of this dramatic landscape, the waterside managed by the RSPB, which has planted mixed woodland on its edges to encourage birdlife. I made my way around the two reservoirs on a mad March day with the wind, rain and sleet driving in, the kind of day that blows the cobwebs away. There's an easy-access path around Dovestone (wheelchair users will need to purchase a radar key from Disability Rights UK to access the path). Despite the bleak weather, the wild beauty of this rugged landscape drew me on to Yeoman Hey Reservoir.

From the car park, head past the sailing club buildings and on towards the **Life for a Life Plantation**. Here there's a forest of mixed woodland, the trees planted in memory of the deceased and marked with memorial plaques. The epitaphs under the trees (Scots pines, oaks, rowans and silver birches) make for poignant reading. But it's also an uplifting experience – the trees bring new life and a softness to this inhospitable landscape of rugged beauty. While this may be a 'forest of the dead', the name 'Life for a Life' given by the charity that runs the scheme, is fitting.

Further round the reservoir the fenced off nature area of **Ashway Gap** is a good place to pause for a picnic. Ashway Gap House once stood here, a Gothic mansion with fine views over to **Alderman's Hill**. All that remains of its grandeur is the set of steps flanked by stone pillars, but there's a picnic area and a trail to follow with some interesting willow sculptures. At the northern end of **Dovestone Moss**, above the site of Ashway Gap House, a plaque commemorates the owner's brother, James Platt, MP for Oldham, who was 'killed here by an accidental discharge of his own gun' in 1857. John Platt, understandably, abandoned the house after the incident, leaving Ashway Gap to the ravens. At the end of the eastern shore, you can continue on round Dovestone along the easy-access path across the dam wall, or head straight on to the narrow Yeoman Hey path, where fewer people venture. For a bigger challenge, and even fewer people, strike out from the southern end of Dovestone Reservoir for the remote **Chew Reservoir**, one of the highest reservoirs in Britain, and on to **Dish Stone** and **Dovestone Moss** before dropping down to **Greenfield Brook** and **Greenfield Reservoir**. This is great climbing country, taking in **Rob's and Wimberry Rocks** and **Charnel** and **Duck Stones**.

A bus serves Dovestone from Greenfield in the summer season, but it's less than a mile's walk from the village of Greenfield (served by trains and buses) to Dovestone Reservoir.

before dropping down to the A628. From there, the route bears right along the A616, then heads off down country lanes past **Langsett**, **Ogton reservoirs** and **Bradfield** and on into **Sheffield**. It seems a shame that the competitors had to keep their heads down to focus on spinning the wheels, for the views are second to none. For hobby cyclists willing to give it a whirl, you can take the route a tad slower, stopping to read the (fast fading) messages and distance markers sprayed on the roads – or for a pint in a wayside pub. Alternatively you can pause for breath at the top of a hill and drink in the vistas. The roads continue to stretch out across moorland before dropping away to the valley below, the country lanes meandering through woodland and over narrow bridges.

The Isle of Skye road

The only other main road that cuts across the top end of the Peak District National Park from Holmfirth is known locally as The Isle of Skye Road – an altogether more romantic name than the functional A635. The high-level road to Greenfield that snakes through an area of wilderness is actually named after a public house that once stood at Wessenden Head (demolished after a fire engulfed it). The pub apart, it's a fitting name for this skyline road, one of the most spectacular in the national park. It's a travesty that it isn't on any bus route – but what a fabulous route for the energetic cyclist. For the less energetic, the only real option is the car, but take it slowly, stopping frequently along the way to admire the views, or even better, wander out on to the moors. As the road drops down from Wessenden Head towards Greenfield, you really could be on the Scottish isle or in the Highlands rather than the heart of England. And although the hills don't even make it to 2,000 feet, their rugged, near vertical sides give the illusion of a hostile mountainous region.

5 SADDLEWORTH & UPPERMILL

Even though **Greenfield** sits at the foot of the popular Dovestone Reservoir on the western fringe of the Peak District National Park, it's nearby **Uppermill** that best serves visitors to the area. Start your tour of this attractive ribbon town at **Saddleworth Museum** on the High Street (✐ 01457 874093 ✐ www.saddleworthmuseum.co.uk). It houses a collection of local memorabilia, photographs, household, agricultural and industrial items, extending from prehistoric times to industrialisation and the growth of the textile mills. A surprisingly comprehensive and well-presented collection for a small town museum, it also has a handful of classic bicycles (including a Penny Farthing) along with a few old-timer vehicles. The museum includes a one-roomed art gallery and shop-cum-information centre.

Further along High Street, the pavements are lined with small independent shops as well as trendy and traditional cafés, restaurants and pubs. From Wade Row, a little park leads to the towpath on **Huddersfield Canal**. The leafy northbound path takes you past narrowboats and a gaggle of geese (if they're in the vicinity) to a lofty viaduct that dwarfs the canal bridge below it. This is the point where the railway line, the **River Tame** and the Huddersfield Canal meet.

Beyond the lock, you'll find **Brownhill Countryside Centre**, housing a stylish café (with waterside seating for warm, sunny days) and an **Interpretative Centre** upstairs, plus a servicing point for bicycles. Across the Dobcross New Road Bridge from the Countryside Centre is a quiet nature garden with a small woodland, meadow and pond along with a bird hide. Returning along the towpath to Saddleworth Museum, you get lovely views of the Peak District uplands.

On the canal itself you can cycle the towpath from **Greenfield** to **Diggle** or take an hour-long trip from just behind the Saddleworth Museum on the **Pennine Moonraker** (✆ 07711 180496 ✐ www.saddleworth-canal-cruises.co.uk ☉ w/ends & school holidays) which navigates a couple of the locks; on some Saturdays a two-hour Standedge boat trip runs from Diggle to Marsden (see page 25).

RUSHCARTS & MORRIS MEN

The August festival has its roots in an ancient tradition in which parishioners replaced the worn-out rushes that covered church floors with fresh reeds. At one time, every village church had its own rushcart, but nowadays there is just one to symbolise the parish tradition. It's a bizarre sight; the cart stacked high with reeds (cut from the lower slopes of Pule Hill) and decorated with heather and a banner. One of the morris men sits atop the approximately 13-foot-high stack with a copper kettle full of ale as the rushcart is paraded through the parish of Saddleworth. How he manages not to fall off in his drunken merriment is a mystery. Morris dancers come from far and wide to take part in the spectacle. On the Sunday the cart is taken to St Chad's Church above Uppermill, where the rushes are taken off and mixed with fragrant herbs and flowers before being spread out in the aisles.

Apart from the canal and moorland walks around Saddleworth, the communities play host to numerous festivals, both classy and eccentric. There's a strong music tradition in the valley with the **Diggle Blues Festival** running in June and Uppermill's **Saddleworth Folk Weekend** in July, while a band contest takes place in various village locations around Whit Friday. The community in Saddleworth has art and craft events aplenty, including the **Saddleworth Festival of the Arts** that takes place in June and the successfully revived **Rushcart Festival** (page 35).

Winding forward in time, the **Yanks are back in Saddleworth**, also an August festival, wallows in wartime nostalgia – from tea dances and wartime suppers to tanks, classic cars and period dress. The festival began on the back of the 1979 American movie, *Yanks*, much of the film shot in and around Uppermill and Dobcross. 'Sadly,' said the assistant at the information centre, 'we have yet to persuade Richard Gere to join us.'

¶¶ FOOD & DRINK

For such a little place, Saddleworth is buzzing with eateries, from traditional tea rooms and pub restaurants to tapas bars. Try **Kitty's** (56 High St, Uppermill OL3 6HA ✆ 01457 870555) for its chic décor, lovely riverside location and friendly service (the paninis are particularly good) or the **Limekiln Café** on the canal at Brownhill Countryside Centre (Wool Rd, Dobcross OL3 5PB ✆ 01457 871051). The food is organic, locally sourced and they use fair-trade products – and they serve a decent cup of coffee.

HADFIELD TO EDALE

Along the western peripheries of the Dark Peak, old mill towns and ancient market settlements sit tucked beneath the moors. Behind them, the highest swathes of Peak District moorland, Kinder and Bleaklow, provide some of the best rambling in the national park, usually approached from Glossop and Hayfield. Few roads penetrate the isolated moorland into the heart of the Dark Peak. The most notorious is probably the high-level A57, reverently referred to as Snake Pass by locals, and often closed in snowy winters. Further south on the A6 at Chapel, two further roads wind their way eastwards to Edale, a heart-lifting valley of soft green pasture lined with rugged ridges and soaring moorland. This quiet, isolated dale is the starting point for the Pennine Way, the long-distance trail that winds its way all along the spine of England to the Scottish borders.

6 HADFIELD

'Welcome to Royston Vasey', reads the sign in the television series *The League of Gentlemen*, followed by the ominous words 'You'll never leave!' Hadfield, an unassuming town that slopes down to Bottoms Reservoir (south of Dovestone and Saddleworth), is the real-life location for the fictional village, made famous in the dark, brooding and somewhat surreal comedy of the late nineties and early noughties. An information board by the car park on **Station Road** explains that Hadfield was chosen for *The League of Gentlemen* because it had 'a certain kind of architecture.' It's an ambiguous statement, leaving me to wonder what kind of architecture the programme makers had in mind exactly. In truth, Hadfield is an old-fashioned mill town with one long main street (**Station Road**) of gritstone terraced houses and a range of little shops and cafés. But the town's setting is anything but ordinary, at the bottom of Longdendale Valley, from where five reservoirs rise up through the valley above the town, flanked on either side by high moorland.

Longdendale Trail

✻ OS Explorer map OL1; start point, Platt St, Hadfield, ♥ SK024961; 12 miles there & back; moderately easy with a few sticky patches in wet weather.

The Longdendale Trail forms part of the **Trans Pennine Trail** that runs from Liverpool to Hull. This section follows the line of the dismantled railway from Hadfield to **Woodhead Tunnel** (closed off). It's superb for walkers, cyclists and horseriders. For ramblers, there are various access points along the trail leading up on to the moorland or down to the reservoirs, making for interesting circular walks. For cyclists, other than braving the B6105, there's no alternative but to return along the trail. **Torhead** car park has an information point, toilets and occasional mobile snack van. It's best to pack a lunch and enjoy the vistas from one of the trailside benches. The dismantled railway track is fairly level and makes for an easy cycle, particularly if the ground is dry and it's a still day. I cycled the trail on a cold January day when the sandy gravel path was sticky and filled with muddy puddles, and an icy wind funnelled through the dale. Come on a sunny, windless day when the reservoirs sparkle blue in the sunlight and the moors rise up in shades of greens and browns. With the five reservoirs spreading out along the valley floor – **Bottoms**, **Valehouse**, **Rhodeswood**, **Torside** and **Woodhead** – Longdendale is one of the most scenic dismantled railway trails in the Peak District.

While the A628 linking Manchester and Sheffield across the Pennines is choc-a-bloc with lorries, vans and cars, there's a quiet, secluded trail heading up the other side of the valley: the **Longdendale Trail**. Apart from *The League of Gentlemen* factor, this is Hadfield's main draw. And with the railway station close to the beginning of the trail (on **Platt Street**), it's easily accessed from Manchester and further afield – and you can take your own bike on the train.

7 GLOSSOP

🏠 **Wind in the Willows Country House Hotel** (page 240)

South of Hadfield, Glossop lies outside the national park but is almost entirely encircled by it, a basin caught in the Dark Peak. The town is an excellent base for trekking the Bleaklow and Kinder massifs, the highest moorland hills in the Peak District National Park, and for off-road cycling along the Sett Valley, Longdendale Trail and for a circle of the Derwent Valley reservoirs at the other end of Snake Pass.

It's fair to say that Glossop is a sprawling and gritty mill town surrounded by dramatic beauty. As in so many fringe Peak District towns, some of its mills have been converted into shops and apartments, while others have disappeared from the townscape. The centre of the town gathers around **Norfolk Square**, named after the Howard family – the Dukes of Norfolk who built the elegant buildings here. Across the road the grand marble-arched **Market Arcade** leads to the **Market Hall**, a reminder of the more prosperous Victorian era. With indoor and outdoor markets on Thursday, Friday and Saturday and a whole range of independent stores, Glossop is a great place to come shopping for anyone wanting to get away from the monotony of many high streets.

🍴 FOOD & DRINK

It's encouraging to see the range of fresh, local produce in Glossop's shops. On the High Street, **Praze Fine Food** (✆ 01457 860916) sells delicatessen food, while **J W Mettrick and Sons** (✆ 01457 852239) has top quality meats on offer. Next door **Sowerbutts** (✆ 01457 852520) is known for its fresh fruit and vegetables. For bread and pies call in at **The Peak of Health** on Norfolk Square (✆ 01457 865678). Apart from the regular market selling speciality bread and meats, the **Local Produce Market** (Glossop Market Ground, off Market St ☺ second Sat of the month) sells pies, cakes and preserves from local producers. **Laura's Coffee Lounge** (6 Henry St, SK13 8BW ✆ 07863546887) is a friendly, stylish coffee shop with decent lunches that's surprisingly inexpensive.

The Globe (144 High St West, SK13 8HJ ✆ 01457 852417; ☾ evenings only during the week) is a traditional Glossop pub with its own microbrewery, serving good vegetarian and vegan food. Check out the vegan ice cream with flavours such as amaretto, walnut, coconut and maple. There are also board games and regular live music to keep you entertained.

SHOPPING

Apart from the quality independent food stores, Glossop sells everything from clocks, books and antique furniture to vintage clothing, soft furnishings, crafts, art and jewellery. It's not difficult to while away a pleasant few hours browsing the specialist stores of this old mill town.

Bleaklow

Above Glossop, Bleaklow is one of the biggest expanses of moorland in the Dark Peak, and although mostly under 2,000 feet, it's a challenging place to walk as there are few paths and little in the way of defining features. Make sure you have experience of moorland walking and know how to use an OS map if you want to explore the moors. Otherwise join a guided walk (keep an eye on the Peak Park and National Trust websites; both organisations regularly arrange walks here). Either way, you will need to be well kitted out with waterproofs and sturdy footwear. You can approach Bleaklow from Old Glossop (the original village that lies on the outskirts of the present-day town) by bus, Doctor's Gate and the old Roman road that leads on to the moor.

"Bleaklow is one of the biggest expanses of moorland in the Dark Peak, and it's a challenging place to walk."

If you plan to approach Bleaklow from **Old Glossop**, it's a long haul up to the summit. You can start your exploration much higher up from the **Snake Pass**, where the **Pennine Way** intersects it. Be aware that there's no bus route along this road. **Bleak Head**, reached by the Pennine Way, along with **Bleaklow Stones** and **Higher Shelf Stones,** is over 2,000 feet. Close to the last of these is the US Boeing RB-29A **Superfortress Crash Site**. Despite the fact that the accident happened almost 70 years ago, the site is still strewn with fuselage, left as a memorial to the 13 crew who died on a routine flight between Lincolnshire and Cheshire in 1948. A remembrance service still takes place here annually, the rows of blood-red poppies and little wooden crosses in among the black peat a moving sight. Across the water-eroded channels, the wreckage

IAN HOWELLS, MOUNTAIN GUIDE

'A mountain hare,' Ian points to the animal scarpering up the slope, its plump body covered in a thick white coat with just a hint of summer fawn coming through. The long brown-tipped ears twitch, sensing danger from the humans below.

'Bleaklow's one of the best places in the country to see mountain hare,' says Ian, an accredited Mountain Leader offering private guiding in the Peak District. Going out on the hills with him adds to the richness of the moorland experience, I'm discovering. 'Through the British Mountaineering Council qualification, I can give people a bit more information about the area,' he tells me.

Ian stops to point out match head lichen with their fiery red tips and to show me the delicate pointed star moss. He points out a red grouse with its stubby wings, flapping comically – 'like a clockwork bird,' he laughs.

I ask Ian if there's really a need for a mountain guide in the relatively low-lying Peak District. 'The Dark Peak is an ever-changing environment. If you go to places like Bleaklow or Kinder – big, exposed plateaus – and the fog is coming down, you need good navigational skills.'

I see what he means: all around us wet snowflakes drift down, a scattering of cotton wool balls catching the heather. Beyond there's an eerie landscape of bog, and blackened peat gathers round *hags* – clumps of higher ground. We continue on past *groughs* – water-eroded channels. They look like pathways through the moors but soon disappear into nothingness – blind alleys. 'When there are no features, like you have on Kinder and Bleaklow, it's even harder to navigate,' Ian adds. We cut across the featureless moorland to reach our destination: the US Superfortress Crash Site hidden in the peat groughs. I wonder if I would have found it without Ian. Assured navigational skills apart, it's Ian's ability to communicate his passion for the Peak that makes him such a good guide.

You can find out more about Ian's guided walks at ⊘ www.comewalkwithmeuk.co.uk. See ad, page 55.

of the plane – an engine here, a pair of rusted wheels there; bits of undercarriage and mangled metal – stretch across the moorland like confetti. When the fog smokes through the wreckage, it's particularly eerie. It's thought that there are at least another half dozen crash sites on Bleaklow.

8 HAYFIELD & KINDER SCOUT

⋏ Hayfield Camping & Caravan Club (page 241)

The spread-out village of Hayfield is unceremoniously sliced in two by the busy A624 which runs between Chapel and Glossop. The Sett Valley

Trail begins from the newer side of the village, attracting cyclists and horseriders, while the older part, sitting below the Kinder massif, draws walkers from far and wide. There is a handful of little shops, pubs and tea rooms in the centre of the village, but most people head straight up the narrow Kinder Road and on to the much loved Kinder massif.

Although merely half the height of Britain's highest peak, Ben Nevis, Kinder Scout at 2,000 feet still feels like a proper mountain, with a muscle-aching, lung-busting ascent up on to the ridge. There are several approaches on to Kinder, but the traditional route, following in the footsteps of the famous mass trespass of 1932 (see page 15) is from Hayfield. If you are arriving by bus, follow the signs from the town car park to Kinder along **Valley Road** and **Kinder Road** to the Caravan Club site at **Bowden Bridge**.

"Kinder Scout feels like a proper mountain, with a muscle-aching, lung-busting ascent up to the ridge."

Most recently, I set off for Kinder on a breezy March day, accompanied by the rattle of woodpecker and a stampede of wizened leaves – the latter hinting at the high winds on top. If you choose to climb up to Kinder, pick a still, dry day if you can, when you don't have to battle the elements.

From Kinder Road, a cobbled path leads into open countryside above Kinder Reservoir. A track continues to **William Clough** and up on to the plateau, where it meets the Pennine Way. Kinder Downfall, the Peak's highest waterfall, is a good place to pause. Here, the River Kinder tumbles 100 feet over the precipice. The ridge continues to curve around the top of this natural amphitheatre. Most walkers drop down to Hayfield along the rocky track at **Coldwell Clough** before enjoying the easy, final stretch alongside the nascent River Sett down to Bowden Bridge. For those who complete this strenuous tramp, they can justly reward themselves in one of the village hostelries with a pint of the best.

⫙ FOOD & DRINK

There are a couple of inns in the village, offering the usual pub grub. **Rosie's Tea and Coffee Room** (41 Kinder Rd, SK22 2HS ⌀ 01663 745597) combines art and cakes and ticks all the boxes for a good breakfast, snack or lunch. Catering for outdoor enthusiasts, the helpful staff will even refill your flask with hot drinks.

The Roundhouse (café, bistro & restaurant at Steeple End Fold, SK22 2JD ⌀ 01663 742527) is conveniently next to the Sett Valley Trail and is a handy watering hole for cyclists and walkers, but is also great for a more formal evening meal.

9 CHAPEL-EN-LE-FRITH

🏠 **Rushup Hall B&B & self-catering cottages** (page 240)

Despite its vaguely suave French name, Chapel is a down-to-earth Peak District town south of Hayfield. Chapel-en-le-Frith means 'chapel in the forest', the 'forest' being any hunting ground, not just woodland. It was established by the Normans in the 12th century as part of the Forest in

Sett Valley Trail from Hayfield to New Mills

❋ OS Explorer map OL1; start: Hayfield car park, ♥ SK035869; 5 miles there & back; easy except for the short, sharp climb back out of New Mills; refreshments at Hayfield, Birch Vale & New Mills

First the clip-clop of packhorses, followed by the chuff-chuff of trains; then silence. The industry that lined this valley is all but gone now, as are the trains that carried raw materials and finished goods to and from New Mills. The railway closed in 1970, enabling nature to take hold again, and reopened as a walking, cycling and horseriding trail in 1979. The Sett Valley Trail, with its heart-lifting backdrop of hill and water, makes for a fine walk or horseride – and a short but very sweet cycle ride.

The trail starts from the car park at Hayfield, next to the bus shelter and information centre (the latter only open during the week at peak holiday times). At the start of the trail, there's an ancient copse, Bluebell Wood, with an easy access route round the nature reserve – not to be missed if you come in spring. I most recently cycled the trail on a bitterly cold winter's day, the crunch of ice under the wheel and the hills all around me covered in snow: it's a great trail to cycle, whatever the time of year. Further along, above **Birch Vale Reservoir**, there's an audio post relating the history of the valley, along with the singing of school children and the words of a local poet. Behind the audio post, the hillside is reflected in the reservoir, with **Pike Lantern** rising behind like a misshapen conical hat. From here the trail heads downhill to **Birch Vale**, crossing Station Road before continuing on to New Mills. It dissects the road again at **High Hill Road** on the edge of **Thornsett**, and again at **Watford Bridge Road**, before heading down into the suburbs of New Mills. Follow the signs for the town, past the leisure centre and under the road. Soon you will see the spectacular New Mills ravine. Head up into town for a well-earned lunch or coffee break (page 170). If you've come by bike, chain it up at the top of the ravine and continue on foot into **Torr Riverside Park** with its wonderful **Millennium Walkway**.

Retracing your steps, it's a gentle uphill climb back to Hayfield (once you leave the centre of New Mills behind) with great views of the High Peak unfolding, including glimpses of the Kinder Plateau.

the High Peak. Nowadays the town is often referred to as the 'Capital of the Peak District', a bit of a misnomer for this small town populated by less than 10,000 people. The most interesting part of town sits around Market Place and the cobbled Market Square with its ancient cross and wooden stocks. At the end of Market Place is the **Church of St Thomas Becket**. The church may be locked, but the graveyard has historical interest, containing the graves of soldiers who marched south from Scotland to support Charles I in 1648. Defeated at Preston, they were marched on to Chapel and imprisoned in the church, where they endured such dreadful conditions that 40 of them died. Another interesting corner is down the raised cobbled streets of Church Brow and Terrace Road, lined with town houses and terraced cottages. Above the town lies the village of **Combs** and **Combs Reservoir,** and beyond that the gritstone edge of **Combs Moss** and **Eccles Pike**, offering 360° views.

FOOD & DRINK

The Royal Oak (Market St, SK23 0HH ℘ 01298 938372), dating back to the 18th century, was once home to the local Justice of the Peace, as well as being the post and coaching house. The friendly staff serve up generous portions of decent pub grub. The trendier **Rems Café Bar and Restaurant** (29 Market St, SK23 0HP ℘ 01298 816577) offers bar food and a tapas menu, along with a nice secluded beer garden out the back. If you're after the ingredients for a picnic, **In a Pickle** (31 Market St, SK23 0HS ℘ 01298 816555) is your place. This is a friendly coffee shop and deli where you can also buy reasonably priced food to eat in or take away.
The No Car Café (Rushop Hall, Rushup Lane, Rushup SK23 0QT ℘ 01298 816218 or 07957 829828) epitomises the 'Slow' philosophy with its 'no car' clause, welcoming walkers, horseriders and cyclists. After a chilly day out on the hills, the converted barn with its blazing wood burner is a welcome sight. The owners serve homemade snacks, breakfasts and lunchtime dishes, all made on the premises.

10 THE CHESTNUT CENTRE

Castleton Rd, Chapel-en- le-Frith SK23 0QS ℘ 01298 814099 ℘ www.chestnutcentre.co.uk
℘ open all year except Christmas Day, Boxing Day & weekdays in Jan
In the UK otters are slowly making a recovery after being on the brink of extinction, but seeing these elusive, secretive creatures in their natural habitat requires a large dose of luck and patience. The Chestnut Centre just outside Chapel-en-le-Frith provides the opportunity to see these adorable creatures at close quarters. Even then, sightings are

A walk along Rushup Edge to Windy Knoll & the No Car Café

❊ OS Explorer map OL1; start: lay-by next to Rushup Lane on the Chapel to Castleton Rd,
♥ SK091824; 6 miles; moderate, with some gradual inclines; refreshments at the No Car Café only.

Rushup Edge is less visited than the ever popular Mam Tor and Great Ridge, lying to the east of it. It's a superb walk away from the crowds. On an early spring day, the only company I had along the ridge was a lark, trying its voice out after its winter lull. While the views are initially hidden in the stony trough, they begin to open out at the eastern end of the ridge. And what views! From the pastoral valley of Edale far below, to the line of The Great Ridge, dipping and rising in front of you, it feels as if you're walking on the roof of the Peak District. At the end of the ridge, the walk heads southward, dipping into the highest parts of the White Peak at **Windy Knoll**, then west past the imposing (and now disused) **Eldon Hill Quarry**. After a short route-march west along a main road, Rushup Lane, with its No Car Café, climbs northwards and back to the Sheffield Road lay-by where the walk began. There's an infrequent Chapel to Castleton bus service (school days) that stops here. Alternatively, you can walk up to Windy Knoll from Castleton (pages 94–5).

The walk starts three miles northeast of Chapel-en-le-Frith on the Sheffield Road. Next to the road lay-by, and opposite Rushup Lane, the Pennine Bridleway heads out over the moors.

1 Ignoring the Pennine Bridleway, follow the path that initially runs adjacent to the Sheffield Road. Climb steadily through a channel of rough stones.

2 Where the path divides, ignore the left turning (for Chapel Gate) and keep right, following the 'Castleton and Hope via Mam Tor and Hollins Cross' arrow on the green metal signpost.

At the top of the hill, the views start to open out, the eye drawn along the line of the Great Ridge. Look out for **Lord's Seat** on the left (just a cairn on a mound). It gives you a bird's-eye view of Edale with the Kinder Massif behind and the landslips that ripple down to the valley floor.

3 Approaching the saddle between Rushup and Mam Tor, take the right-hand path down to a gate leading on to Edale Road. Follow the road left for a very short distance, cross it and take the steps downhill, signposted for the Dale and Peak Forest. A short grassy pathway drops down to the Sheffield Road.

4 Cross it and go through the gate on to **Windy Knoll** (National Trust land), heading up the track until you come out at a third road (Winnats Road). Cross it and go through the gate leading to Rowter Farm (with a camping and caravan site), but instead of taking the farm road, head diagonally right along the grassy footpath through meadows, eventually following a dry stone wall over stiles to a rough stone track.

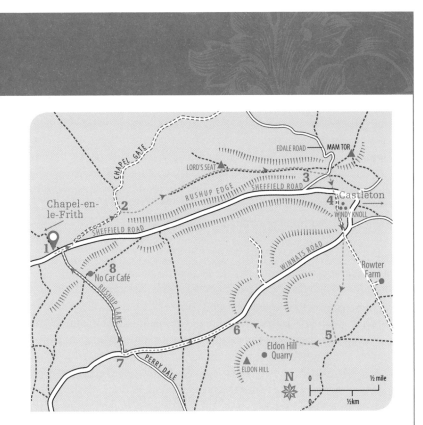

5 Turn right and follow the stony farm track past Eldon Hill Quarry until it meets Winnats Road again.

6 Bear left here on to the main road and follow it downhill past the pond on your left, walking along the verge to avoid traffic. (There is the option here to head through the new plantation past the lake and over farmland to Perry Dale opposite Rushup Lane, but be warned that the way is not well signed and doesn't follow the route outlined on the OS map).

7 Where the main road drops more steeply downward, take the right turn on to Rushup Lane (signposted Pennine Bridleway and South Head). Follow the narrow country lane upwards.

8 You'll find the No Car Café located on your right near the top of the hill. Stop for a well-earned break before walking the last short section of Rushup Lane to the Sheffield Road and back to the lay-by.

not guaranteed. While the North American river and giant otters didn't make an appearance on the last day I arrived, the Asian short-clawed otters and Eurasian otters were out and about, swimming, sniffing the ground and feeding.

Apart from the herd of fallow and sika deer in the parkland, there's an impressive variety of aloof owls, as well as foxes, badgers, pine martens, polecats and Scottish wildcats. While it would be preferable to see these creatures in their natural habitat, this is the next best thing. As it is, the Chestnut Centre carries out sterling conservation work, along with its breeding and education programmes. Although the centre seems to be aimed primarily at young children, this is a lovely place for anyone to visit. There's a café and shop on site, but take a picnic if it's a sunny day and bask in this tranquil setting below the moors.

11 EDALE & MAM TOR

🏠 **Losehill Hotel and Spa** (page 240), **The Cheshire Cheese Inn** (page 240), **Oaker Farm Holiday Cottages** (page 241), ⛺ **Upper Booth Campsite** (page 241)

Whenever I hear the name Edale, I think 'Eden'. The dale is a little piece of paradise – a green and quiet idyll surrounded by some of the best-loved hills in the Peak District, yet easily accessed by train with a station at Edale village. Before striding out into the countryside or on to the hills, stop off at the **Peak Park Moorland Centre**, packed with leaflets and suggestions for Edale and wider Peak District activities. This gives a chance to find out about the history and prehistory of Edale and the Peak Park, to learn how man and nature have shaped the landscape and to listen to audio recordings of people who have lived and worked in the area, from the gamekeeper to the farmer.

"Edale is a little piece of paradise – a green and quiet idyll surrounded by some of the best-loved hills in the Peak District."

For such a rural location, Edale plays host to a surprising number of annual events, both delightful and eccentric. Watch out for the **Edale Folk Festival** that usually takes place in May; the low-key **Edale Country Day** in June, showcasing animals and traditional rural crafts; the August **Edale Spoonfest**, centred round spoon carving (truly) and the equally crazy September **Great Kinder Beer Barrel Challenge**, when strong types and madmen haul a 72-pint beer barrel up Kinder, a challenging climb at the best of times.

🍴 FOOD & DRINK

Coopers Café (Corner Cottage, Grindsbrook Booth S33 7ZD ✆ 01433 670401) offers quality food in a lovely setting close to the Pennine Way.

For something special, head for **Losehill House Hotel and Spa** (Edale Rd, S33 6RF ✆ 01433 621219). The hotel has been awarded the Peak District Environmental Quality Mark. The locally sourced food is well cooked and beautifully presented in this elegant hotel tucked away in the Edale Valley. You will pay accordingly.

Penny Pot Café (Station Approach ✆ 01433 670293) is a pretty little stone building with a wood-clad interior, wood burner and soft sofas, plus outside seating. This National Trust café, selling no-nonsense food, is just the ticket after a hard day's walking or cycling in the hills.

The Cheshire Cheese (Edale Valley, S33 6ZF ✆ 01433 620381) was on the old salt-carrying route and the old cheese hooks are still in place. While travellers were known to pay in cheese, cash or card is the norm nowadays, and – rather than packhorse journeymen – the pub mainly caters to sightseers, cyclists and walkers rather than packhorse journeymen, who enjoy terrific food served up in cosy and characterful surroundings. Meanwhile, **The Old Nags Head** (Grindsbrook Booth S33 7ZD ✆ 01433 670291) is a popular pub in this beautiful valley (a welcome end point for the Kinder Beer Barrel Challengers), serving generous portions of good-value food.

Walking in Edale

Some of the most stunningly beautiful walking in the national park can be accessed from Edale: **The Kinder Massif** from **Jacob's Ladder** on the north side and the **Great Ridge Walk**, taking in **Hollins Cross** and **Lose Hill** on the other side. If you walk the Great Ridge to Mam Tor, you can drop down to Castleton (page 94) and continue your journey by bus and train.

For an interesting and informed commentary, you can ramble from **Edale Station** to **The Nabb** accompanied by the Edale audio walk guide, in the words of Sally Goldsmith, a writer and singer (download from Moors for the Future at ✆ www.moorsforthefuture.org.uk).

THE HOPE VALLEY LINE FOLK TRAIN

Once a month on a Tuesday night, the folk train (✆ www.hvhptp.org.uk) departs from Sheffield at 19.14, calling at all stations to Edale. The chosen band plays to its (sometimes surprised) train audience before disembarking at the Rambler Inn for more musical merriment, returning to Sheffield on the 21.29. What a fun way to take in a bit of ragtime, trad, roots, bluegrass, jazz or swing as you chug your way into the Peak Park.

The walk covers six miles and takes in some steep inclines. The **National Trust**, which owns and manages much of Edale, and the **Peak Park National Park Authority** organise walks and events in the dale throughout the year too. Check the ⌀ www.peakdistrict.gov.uk and ⌀ www.nationaltrust.org.uk for details. Look out for the **Hope Valley Community Rail Partnership** station to station free guided walks – and Folk Trains (information at ⌀ www.hvhptp.org.uk; page 47). Most famously, Edale is the start of the 270-mile Pennine Way, perhaps the best-known of Britain's National Trails, which traces the spine of the Pennines to Kirk Yetholm, over the Scottish Border.

Mam Tor – The Shivering Mountain

There's a car park just below Mam Tor with a nearby bus stop (but beware the service is limited). If you choose to walk from Castleton where there's a more regular bus service, there are two interesting approaches: through meadows and up the 'broken road' (an abandoned section of the A625) to the base of the mountain, or through the valley behind Peveril Castle. Linking the two makes for an interest-filled circular walk.

From the pass between Rushup Edge and Mam Tor, there's a short but steep stone stairway to the summit. It's worth the trudge for the views alone. You can retrace your steps to the car park or continue on along the Great Ridge, one of the most scenic walks in the Dark Peak.

"Legend has it that 'mother hill' gave birth to a series of mini-hills that gather round her feet."

Legend has it that Mam Tor, or 'mother hill,' gave birth to a series of mini-hills that now gather round her feet, a sweet and charming explanation for the peak's name. For a more scientific explanation, you need to understand Mam Tor's geology. The mini-hills, found on the southeastern face of the hill, are formed by landslides that have occurred because of the mountain's unstable geological make-up: the lower layers of shale underlying the sandstone are prone to slip, particularly after heavy rain. The 1,696-foot hill is also aptly nicknamed 'The Shivering Mountain'.

From the top, pause a while to watch the hang gliders and paragliders taking off from the ridge and enjoy the panoramic views of Castleton, Edale (curtained by the Dark Peak moorland), the Great Ridge that rises and dips a rocky runway eastward, and Rushup Edge to the west (page 44).

THE DARK PEAK MOORLAND WATERS

The numerous reservoirs west of Sheffield and Stocksbridge provide much of the drinking water required for these conurbations. But more than this, they provide a green and watery idyll for city dwellers and visitors alike. While the Derwent Valley reservoirs, surrounded by high moorland, receive visitors from far and wide, the smaller bodies of water on the eastern periphery, along with the picturesque Bradfield villages, have their own bucolic charm, and fewer people. They are all well worth a visit.

12 FAIRHOLMES & THE DERWENT VALLEY RESERVOIRS

A **shuttle bus** runs from Fairholmes as far as King's Tree on w/ends & bank holidays in the season when cars are banned beyond the visitor centre

🏠 **Ladybower Inn** (page 240), ⛺ **Swallowholme Camping & Caravan Park** (page 241)
Of all the many reservoirs that puddle the Dark Peak, those in the Derwent Valley are probably the best known – and as a result this is one of the busiest areas of the Dark Peak. **Ladybower, Derwent** and **Howden** are set in a magnificent landscape of sheltered woodland dales and contrasting wild moorland. Most visitors head straight for Fairholmes where an information centre has bike hire (☺ every day in summer & on w/ends out of season) and a kiosk selling a range of snacks and drinks. Come out of season, if you can, or early in the day – but try and come in clear, sunny weather to enjoy the intense blues of the water set against the vivid greens of the pines.

Fairholmes Visitor Centre also has CCTV footage of nesting birds, and there are opportunities to spot goshawks and sparrowhawks, as well as buzzards, merlins, peregrine falcons or red grouse on the paths above the reservoirs. From the centre, a range of walks fan out to match every level of fitness from gentle lakeside strolls to challenging moorland rambles. The centre provides maps and guides, and from the car park three colour-coded walks range from 40 minutes to three hours. Some of the most interesting moorland walks take in the pointed **Win Hill** (above Ladybower) and the dramatic rocky crags of **Alport Castles** (above Derwent).

During the construction of Derwent and Howden reservoirs in the early 20th century, a **model village** was built to house the workers and

The Derwent Valley reservoirs

OS Explorer map OL1; start: Fairholmes Visitor Centre, ♀ SK172893; 18 miles, but the route can be shortened by leaving out the section south of Fairholmes; refreshments at Fairholmes & Ladybower Inn; cycle hire: Fairholmes car park, Derwent Water S33 0AQ ☎ 01433 651261

One of the highlights of the Upper Derwent Valley is the mostly traffic-free cycle trail that circles all three reservoirs. While more undulating than the dismantled railway trails, it's still flat enough not to bust a gut. From Fairholmes, cycle up the access road on the west side of Derwent and Howden reservoirs before crossing the bridge just south of **Slippery Stones**. From here the cycling becomes a bit more challenging as it climbs up on to the moorland on a rough track. The path now heads down towards the reservoir again, this time on the east side. Eventually it meets **Derwent Lane**, continuing alongside Ladybower Reservoir. Turn right to cross **Ashopton Viaduct**, and right again on to the road that leads back to Fairholmes.

their families. Birchinlee (aka Tin Town), a temporary village, had it all: a railway station, hospital, school, pub, post office, shops, village hall and even a public bath house. And all made of metal. At the height of the construction work, there were almost 3,000 people residing in Tin Town, but on the completion of the dams, the workers and their families were dispatched and the village dismantled, corrugated sheet by corrugated sheet. One of the buildings survives – reconstructed on **Edale Road** in **Hope** for anyone who'd like to see what the original buildings looked like. At the actual site of Birchinlee on the western side of Derwent Reservoir, there's little trace of the village, but a stone wall plaque (complete with a picture of the village) marks the site of Tin Town. It can be reached by the footpath that follows the line of the dismantled railway. Look out too for the **Memorial to Tip** at Derwent Reservoir viewpoint near the dam. This beyond-the-call-of-duty sheepdog stayed by the dead body of his master for 15 weeks up on the moors until he was discovered.

For fans of **wild swimming**, check out **Slippery Stones** on the River Derwent above **Howden Reservoir**. It can get busy though, despite its isolated moorland location, and you will need to arrive early or late in the day if you seek any sense of solitude. There's a frothy pool, 10 to 12 feet deep, containing fresh water tinged brown from the peat – a bit like swimming in fizzy coke, as one wild swimming enthusiast observed. The packhorse bridge rebuilt at **Slippery Stones** is all that remains of

Derwent village, drowned in the building of the reservoir. In periods of drought, when the water levels drop significantly, the reservoir reveals the remains of the village; it was last seen in 2003.

The dam walls at Howden, Derwent and Ladybower are all impressive structures. You can walk across the dam wall at Ladybower and Derwent at weekends.

Derwent Valley Museum & the Dambusters

☺ Sun & bank holidays throughout the year, but best to phone the visitor centre at Fairholmes beforehand for opening times as the private collection is managed by the sole owner.

By the dam wall at Fairholmes, the Derwent Valley Museum – aka the Dambusters Museum – tells the story of the reservoirs' construction and the lost villages of Ashopton, Derwent and Tin Town, along with displays of old photographs. Its main focus, however, is the Dambusters' mission, with a life-sized replica of the bouncing bomb and a short film about the daredevils' exploits. Watch out for Dambuster flypasts on special anniversaries.

The **Dambusters**, aka 617 Squadron, RAF, came into existence in March 1943. Their mission was to bomb major hydroelectric dams in the Ruhr Valley, Germany's industrial heartland, with the aim of seriously interrupting power and water supplies to the Ruhr cities and crippling the steel industries that supplied ammunitions and tanks. When the squadron was put together that March, the men didn't have a working bomb or an aircraft fit for function. Neither did they have experience of low-level flying, nor the technical know-how to enable them to calculate the exact height required to drop the bombs. And there were still more problems to overcome: locating the dams, particularly under darkness; dropping the bombs with precision on a relatively small target; and creating a bomb that could do sufficient damage to the solid structures of the dam walls. Last of all, the bombs would have to breach the base of the structure to have a significant impact, so it would take precision and accuracy for *Operation Chastise* – the Dambuster raids – to succeed. Enter engineer and inventor Dr Barnes Wallis, who came up with the solutions.

"The Dambusters, aka 617 Squadron, RAF, came into existence in March 1943. Their mission was to bomb major hydroelectric dams in the Ruhr Valley."

The Dambusters would release a specially designed barrel-shaped bomb from a low enough height at the right speed so that the bombs would skip and bounce across the water before rolling down the dam face towards the base.

For six weeks the squadron practised on the Derwent Dam, infuriating the locals as they roared through the valley. The valley inhabitants held the Dambusters accountable for all sorts of misfortune, from damaged roof tiles to low egg and milk yield. As far as they were concerned, the pilots were out on the razz, wasting precious wartime fuel.

Retrospective knowledge is a great thing. Today, the local population see the Dambuster practice raids in a rather different light. The men are regarded as heroes who undertook difficult and risky operations that eventually breached two German dams and partially damaged another. At Derwent Water a plaque commemorates the 617 Squadron.

¶¶ FOOD & DRINK

Ladybower Inn (nr Bamford on the A57; S33 0AX ✆ 01433 651241) is a traditional pub with a prime position close to Ladybower Reservoir. In nearby Bamford, the **Anglers Rest** (Main Rd, S33 0DY ✆ 01433 659317), bought and saved by the local community, is now a delightful café-cum-post office-cum-pub.

13 BRADFIELD VILLAGES & RESERVOIRS

East of the Derwent Valley reservoirs, you'll find a much quieter corner of the Peak Park with four more reservoirs: Damflask, Agden, Dale Dyke and Strines, surrounded by the pretty stone villages of High Bradfield and Low Bradfield. The settlements are a great starting (or mid) point for some gentle waterside walking.

High Bradfield

It's worth the steep climb up from Low Bradfield. The quaint, elbow-shaped cobbled Jane Street has a fine Grade I listed church, **St Nicholas,** on the corner. It surely has one of the choicest graveyard views in the country, the church grounds dropping away to the valley below, the land then sweeping up the other side to pasture and moorland. As you walk along the path to the church, notice the ancient gravestones, some dating back to the 1600s. The church also has a memorial to the Dale Dyke Disaster of 1864 along with headstones commemorating some of the disaster's victims.

THE DALE DYKE DISASTER & THE LOST VILLAGE OF DAMFLASK

At midnight on 11 March 1864 Dale Dyke burst, the waters taking a corn mill, paper mill, wire mill, the Barrel Inn and most of the village of Damflask with them, before sweeping down Loxley Valley where almost 250 people lost their lives. It all began when a young labourer discovered a crack in the dam. He immediately warned the villagers of Damflask most of whom took heed, vacating their homes and moving to higher ground. One of the chancers, gung-ho 'Sheffield Harry' laughed and said he didn't care; he wouldn't get out of bed for anything. A short time later the water rushed through the village. Not surprisingly, Harry had a change of heart. But it was too late: he was found half a mile away from his home the next morning with just one sock on. The village is gone and in its place is a reservoir of the same name, Damflask Reservoir.

Behind the church, **Bailey Hill** is considered to be one of the best preserved and most dramatic motte-and-baileys in Yorkshire, while the 19th-century **Watch Tower** overlooking the graveyard at the bottom of Jane Lane is a particularly interesting building, constructed to deter grave robbers. Along the cobbled street from St Nicholas' Church is an attractive row of terraced houses, which were once the Bradfield Parish Workhouse providing shelter to the poor and dispossessed in the 18th and 19th centuries.

Low Bradfield

Low Bradfield is quite different in character from its lofty sister village at High Bradfield. Set in a pastoral valley, the village is centred round Smithy Bridge, a waterside picnic area, and the Ibbotson Memorial Field with its cricket pitch, bowling green and tennis courts. Much of the original village was washed away in the Dale Dyke dam breach of 1864. And even though the village today is topped and toed by two reservoirs, Damflask and Agden, the villagers have little to fear: engineering and safety standards have come a long way since the 19th century. Its position between the reservoirs serves walkers well, along with a surprising number of facilities for a small village, from the post office and village shop to the butchers, delicatessen and restaurant, the last three housed in **The Schoolrooms**.

Damflask Reservoir is a flat and accessible four-mile route with an easy-access path (no bicycles allowed), while **Agden Reservoir** has a

Langsett Reservoir – a circuit

OS Explorer map OL1; start Langsett car park, SE210004; 3 miles; moderately easy with a gradual climb up on to the moors

North of the Bradfield villages, a circuit of Langsett comes recommended, combining waterside walking, woodland and wide open moorland (with superb views back to the reservoir). The abandoned farm at **North America** on the edge of the moor was used for target practice during World War II, the shell pocks still evident in the ruined walls. An interpretative board by the picnic area in the car park tells the story of wartime training, while others outline the history of the reservoir and the natural history of the surrounding area. **Refreshments** are available in Langsett only, either at Bank View Café or the Waggon and Horses pub.

For a combined three-reservoir walk of **Underbank**, **Midhope** and **Langsett**, see the *Walkers are Welcome* website for Stocksbridge (www.stocksbridge-walkers.org.uk).

slightly shorter circuit of about two and a half miles, but with more ascents and a few country lane sections. Both walks take in woodland and waterside stretches. Nearby, **Dale Dyke** is another gentle meadow, woodland and waterside walk of about two and a half miles. A circuit of Strines Reservoir isn't possible, but the Dale Dyke walk passes by the northern and eastern end of Strines. Check out the excellent *Walkers are Welcome* website at www.bradfield-walkers.org.uk for more details.

FOOD & DRINK

Old Horns Inn (High Bradfield S6 6LG 0114 285 1207) serves standard pub fare, but is worth seeking out for its exceptional location near the church and overlooking the valley. There's an outdoor terrace and beer garden to make the best of the views over Bradfield Moors.

In the lower village, **The Plough Inn** (New Rd, Low Bradfield S6 6HW 0114 285 1280) is a traditional pub serving traditional British food and is excellent value for money. **The School Rooms** on Mill Lee Road, also in Low Bradfield (S6 6LB 0114 285 1920) has a farm shop and deli with a café upstairs in the eaves. Real ale enthusiasts should hunt out **Bradfield Brewery** (S6 6LG 0114 285 1118) at Watt House Farm, selling a range of cask ales from the farm shop. **The Nags Head** (S6 6SJ 0114 2851202), the brewery's first pub, lies close by on Stacey Bank and guarantees a fine selection of real ales to accompany good-value, honest pub grub. Check out the pork baguette and pies.

14 REDMIRES RESERVOIRS

Sheffield's inhabitants are truly blessed to have such a stunning moorland landscape in their backyard, including the Redmires reservoirs, just seven miles from the centre of Sheffield and even less if you live on the right side of town.

For an easy three-mile stroll follow **Redmires Road** (♀ SK264858) from the middle reservoir to the end. Climb the stile on your left and continue to skirt the three reservoirs over moorland before heading back to your starting point on the road through Redmires Plantation. As you follow the path through the heather, the reservoirs below laced with wading birds, it's hard to believe the busy city is just a stone's throw away.

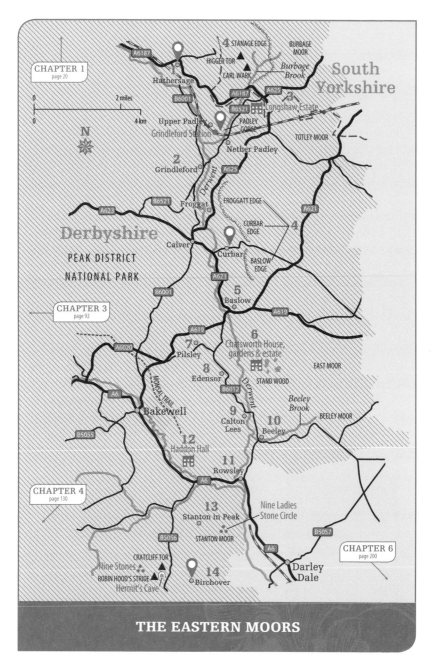

THE EASTERN MOORS

CHAPTER 1
page 20

4 STANAGE EDGE

BURBAGE
MOOR

HIGGER TOR

*Burbage
Brook*

**South
Yorkshire**

CARL WARK

Hathersage

A6187

B6001

A6187   A625

3

B6521   Longshaw Estate

Upper Padley

PADLEY
GORGE

TOTLEY MOOR

Grindleford Station

Nether Padley

2
Grindleford

A625

Derwent

FROGGATT EDGE

A623   B6521

Froggatt

A621

CURBAR
EDGE

4

Derbyshire

Calver

Curbar

BASLOW
EDGE

PEAK DISTRICT

NATIONAL PARK

A623

B6001

5
Baslow

A619

CHAPTER 3
page 92

A619

6

A6020

7
Pilsley

Chatsworth House,
gardens & estate

EAST MOOR

8
Edensor

STAND WOOD

A6

B6012

Derwent

Bakewell

*Beeley
Brook*

B5055

9
Calton
Lees

10
Beeley

BEELEY MOOR

12
Haddon Hall

11
Rowsley

A6

CHAPTER 4
page 130

13
Stanton in Peak

Nine Ladies
Stone Circle

B5056

STANTON MOOR

B5057

A6

CHAPTER 6
page 200

CRATCLIFF TOR

Nine Stones

14

ROBIN HOOD'S STRIDE

Birchover

Darley
Dale

Hermit's Cave

N

0   2 miles

0   4 km

2
THE EASTERN MOORS

Stately homes and handsome halls such as Chatsworth House and Haddon Hall are scattered along the Eastern Moors, tucked into valleys and flanked by woodland, or backed by great escarpments and moorland wilderness. The aristocracy, spending millions of pounds down the centuries, demanded a backdrop worthy of their pile. The Eastern Moors certainly fit the bill. The surrounding countryside makes for an extensive outdoor playground, with hunting on the uplands and fishing on the Derwent. Chatsworth provides free access to much of the woodland and parkland around the estate, with parking at the house and at Calton Lees for ramblers and picnickers. Beyond the stately home, the moors are criss-crossed with old packhorse trails, and going even further back, there are traces of an Iron Age road, the Portway, that linked ancient forts from Mam Tor to Harthill Moor. But the biggest draw for those who love the outdoors are the dramatic edges that stretch for miles with far-reaching views – or the tors with their weathered and strangely formed rock piles – in places such as Froggatt Edge and Carl Wark.

WALKING & CYCLING

Walkers are spoilt for choice on the Eastern Moors. Apart from the edges and tors that make up some of the best ridge walking in the Peak District, there are moorlands and waterside routes along the River Derwent. For long-distance walkers, the Limestone Way also dips briefly into the area.

There's relatively flat cycling through the Derwent Valley, but the main highway can be a bit of a squeeze in places – and busy with traffic. As with everywhere else in the park, there are plenty of quiet country lanes with excellent views that will give you a good work-out on the uphills. This is superb cycling country for mountain bikers too, particularly along Stanage Edge.

THE UPPER DERWENT VALLEY: HATHERSAGE TO BASLOW

The moors, edges and valleys that lie between Hathersage and Baslow are filled with myths and history. From the Charlotte Brontë and Robin Hood links at Hathersage to the Padley Martyrs outside Grindleford, this is an area rich in local colour. But most people miss out on this fascinating heritage and head straight for the edges that stretch from Baslow to Hathersage, drawn to the thrill of walking, scrambling, climbing and mountain biking on the escarpments, with their dizzying drops and bird's-eye views. Running along their length are wind-sculpted boulders, often piled Jenga-style. These edges have their own story to tell, littered with abandoned millstones that are a reminder of a long-lost industry.

1 HATHERSAGE

Sladen House (page 241), **YHA Hathersage** (page 241)

With the Hope and Edale valleys nearby and the edges of Stanage and Burbage, Higger Tor and Carl Wark all within a couple of hours' walk, it's easy to see Hathersage's appeal for outdoor enthusiasts – borne out by the outdoor shops that line the main street. And after a sweaty summer's day on the hills, there's no better place to head for a cooling dip than **Hathersage Outdoor Swimming Pool** (Oddfellows Rd, S32 1DU ℘ 01433 650843 ℘ www.hathersageswimmingpool.co.uk), which has been voted Britain's Best Lido by *The Times*, with good reason. Apart from the 30-metre pool, there's a café, bandstand, bowling green and a pleasant lawned area. They certainly go the extra mile here, with a sunrise swim for the summer solstice and a monthly night swim with live music in season. The pool is heated from March to the end of September – and remains open (unheated) on Saturday and Sunday throughout October and on a Saturday in November for hardy souls.

Hathersage started its life very differently as the sleepy hamlet of *Hereseige*, just a scattering of farmsteads on the knoll to the northeast

---

i TOURIST INFORMATION

Information Point, **Hathersage** Outside, Main Rd, S32 1BB
Information Point, **Baslow** Wheatsheaf Hotel, DE45 1SR

of the present-day centre. The rural character of the village disappeared with the onslaught of industrialisation. Soon mills, factories and workers' cottages sprang up among the farms, most gone now. At **Eastwood cottages**, factory lodgers paid 4d (2p) to sleep between shifts – often sharing the beds in shifts too. This part of Hathersage has a very different feel to it and is worth a detour, especially to have a look at the delightful **St Michael's Church**.

Church of St Michael

The Parish Church of St Michael and All Angels has one of the loveliest ecclesiastical positions in the Peak District, set in the hillside with views across to the Hope Valley and Stanage Edge. Before heading inside, check out the gargoyles, their rounded heads resting on top of the metal drains like dots punctuating a row of 'i's. They're a comical sight, all twisted mouths, grimaces, bulging eyes and stumpy noses. From the tower, even stranger creatures reach down menacingly. What tends to steal the show, however, is the grave of the legendary Little John, of Robin Hood fame. You'll find it signed near the entrance of the church.

We think of the forests around Nottingham as Robin Hood's stamping ground, but it would seem that the bandit and his disciples were kicking around the Peak District as well. Little John, Robin Hood's sidekick (though hardly little at over seven feet tall) was said to have been born in Hathersage. The plot of **Little John's Grave** and the local historical detail sound convincing, but there's no evidence that Little John actually existed beyond the

"The gargoyles are a comical sight, all twisted mouths, grimaces, bulging eyes and stumpy noses."

vivid imagination of the myth-makers. At best, the real-life John Little is woven into tales of bravado and adventure. On the site of the grave, there's a modern headstone marking a 14-foot plot which states: 'Here lies Little John the friend and lieutenant of Robin Hood'. He died in a cottage (now destroyed) to the west of the churchyard. Legend has it that Little John returned to Hathersage to live out his days after burying Robin Hood. It's said he dug his own grave under the old yew tree in the graveyard near the preaching cross, and requested that his cap, bow, and arrows be hung in the church (sadly not there). The story goes that Captain John Shuttleworth had the grave opened in 1798, whereupon a 32-inch thigh-bone was uncovered. Believe what you will.

Walking in the footsteps of Charlotte Brontë
❋ OS Explorer map OL1; start: George Hotel, Hathersage, ♥ SK229815; 6 miles; fairly easy, with a long but moderate climb on to Stanage Edge; refreshments in Hathersage only

This literary walk takes in the landscape and landmarks that inspired Charlotte Brontë's epic novel, *Jane Eyre*. It starts at the **George Hotel**, where Charlotte first set foot in **Hathersage**. It follows the path up on to **Stanage Edge**, a wild and dramatic landscape of moorland and distorted rock, befitting the novel's Gothic setting. It takes in Robert Eyre's imposing home, **North Lees Hall**, Thornfield Hall in the novel. It was at Thornfield that Jane's love interest, Mr Rochester, secreted away his demented wife. Inside **St Michael's Church**, you'll see the Eyre memorials, while the **Old Vicarage** next door to the church is where Charlotte spent several weeks in 1845.

1 Before setting off, nip into the **George Hotel** at the bottom end of the village. Charlotte alighted from her coach at The George after a long and arduous journey from Haworth in Yorkshire. From here she continued on foot to the vicarage. Hathersage is thought to be the village of Morton in *Jane Eyre*. Continue up the main street from The George, taking the cobbled lane behind the NatWest bank. At the end of Besom Lane turn left on to Baulk Lane. Ignore the sign 'To the church' for now and continue up the valley.

2 At **Cowclose Farm** a path diverges left, skirting the grounds of the farm before dropping down to **Brookfield Manor**. Go past it and continue upwards, following the tumbling **Hood Brook**.

3 Crossing **Birley Lane**, take the adjacent stile to continue up the valley. A series of gates leads you through woodland and meadow. Follow the sign for Dennis Knoll. Eventually you will come to a bridge in the middle of the field. Cross it and head for the building in front of you, following the path between two fences.

4 Turn left at the gap, following the finger sign for Dennis Knoll, and go through the gate to **Green's House**. Just past the yard, there's a public footpath signed on the right. Go through the gate and continue uphill, following the line of the dry stone wall. Just before the corner of a coniferous plantation, go through another gate, now following the line of trees to the road.

5 Here, at **Long Causeway**, turn left and walk along the road for a short distance until you come to **Dennis Knoll** car park. Take the rough stone track beside it and continue up towards Stanage Edge. The track curves right and up on to the edge.

6 Take the first access sign (a wooden post) off the track on the right towards the rock-strewn edge, keeping your eye open for the well-defined stone slab path leading down off the edge through huge boulders and sagging rock columns.

7 The path continues on into a gentler terrain of woodland, where it meets Long Causeway again. Cross the road and head down through the valley past the side of the toilet block. Soon you'll catch a glimpse of **North Lees Hall**. Turn left and continue downhill past North Lees.

8 The end of **North Lees road** meets Birley Lane (again). Almost opposite the junction you'll see a public footpath sign with a track leading to a farm lane. Follow the lane downhill towards Cowclose Farm, taking a signed footpath over the meadow behind the buildings (this time on the other side of the farm). Continue across meadows, following the fence and line of trees.

9 The path dips down to a slab stone bridge. Cross it and head up the steps, turning

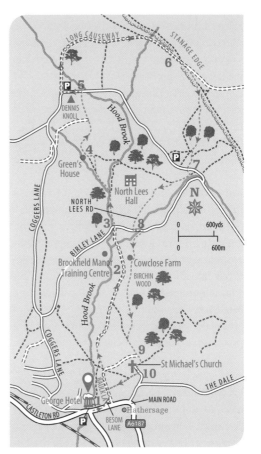

right into **St Michael's Church**. Drop in to see the Eyre memorials. As you pass the vicarage by the car park, you'll see where Charlotte stayed with her friend Ellen Nussey, sister of the vicar.

10 Go through the churchyard and head down the long section of gravestones (page 59), through a kissing gate and back down to Baulk Lane. Turn left back towards Hathersage's Main Street.

St Michael's has links to another historical figure: writer Charlotte Brontë of *Jane Eyre* fame. She stayed at the vicarage next door. Inside the church, you'll find memorials to the Eyre family dating back to the 15th century, the prominent Hathersage family who inspired Brontë's novel. Brass figures of Robert Eyre and his wife, Joan of Padley, are laid into the chest tomb beneath a grand stone arch in the sanctuary.

David Mellor Cutlery Factory & Design Museum

The Round Building, Hathersage S32 1BA ✆ 01433 650220 ⌕ www.davidmellordesign. com/visitorCentre ⊙ free guided tours of the Cutlery Factory Sat & Sun at 15.00; Country Shop, Design Museum & café open daily

In the woods just outside Hathersage (on the road to Grindleford) you'll find a set of traffic lights, a contemporary bus shelter, a modern square postbox, a stylish waste bin along with benches and bollards, all part of the David Mellor Design Museum. The row of urban street furniture with its clean, functional lines is a strange sight in this rural location, but a common one in Britain's towns and cities. Mellor, a designer from Sheffield, relocated his cutlery factory to the **Round Building** in 1990, an award-winning piece of architecture that was built on the circular foundation of the old Hathersage Gas Works. Adjacent to the factory, a more conventional building houses the **Country Shop** (selling stylish contemporary kitchenware), a café and the **David Mellor Design Museum**. The cabinet displays take you through Mellor's designs across the decades, a craftsman driven by his desire to create affordable, practical and beautiful objects.

The rocky crags of Higger Tor & Carl Wark

East of Hathersage, Higger Tor and Carl Wark rise out of the moorland like tabletops scattered with the crumbs of fallen rocks. The closest approach is from **Surprise View** car park, where the 272 Sheffield to Castleton service stops on the A6187. The **Padley Gorge Trail** also links the pathways that lead up to the tors, taking in the distinctive crinkle-creased Mother Cap, an isolated rocky pillar.

I've clambered over the tors on a late summer's day when the moorland has been brushed with a wash of purple heather and I've walked across them on a *dreich* winter's day when visibility has been restricted to the few feet in front of me. Despite missing out on the expansive views over the Peak District, there's something to be said for those mizzling days with nothing to distract you from the contorted rock masses looming out of the mist. While my over-active imagination sees an ogre's pile – flights of stairs, basins of water, tallboys and king-sized beds of rock with pillows of stone – my geologist husband sees gritstones laid down in the delta of a Mississippi-scale river; eroded blocks preserving cross-bedding, shaped and reshaped by the freeze-thaw conditions of permafrost and eroded further by the harsh, icy winds of the tundra at the end of the last Ice Age.

While Higger Tor has been shaped by the forces of nature, Carl Wark has in part been created by man. A hillfort was built on this site, possibly during the Iron Age 2,500 years ago, and refortified after the Romans left; its walls of gritstone boulders to the north and south forming a natural defence. To secure the fort, an earth rampart was erected and faced with a stone wall. Standing on Carl Wark on a particularly dirty winter's day, I found it hard to imagine how man lived in this bleak landscape.

¶¶ FOOD & DRINK

Millstone Country Inn (Sheffield Rd, S32 1DA ✆ 01433 650258) is a traditional pub just outside Hathersage with fantastic views over the Hope Valley. It serves good, unfussy food and a selection of six traditional cask ales.

Down in the village of Hathersage, **Cintras Tearoom, licensed restaurant and gardens** (Main Rd, S32 1BB ✆ 01433 651825) is a cosy café with friendly service. The ingredients are locally sourced and there's pleasant outside seating. On the other side of the main street, **Outside** (Main Rd, S32 1BB ✆ 01433 651936), containing every possible item needed for walking and climbing, has an upstairs café with food portions to match the outdoor enthusiast's appetite. In a similar manner, they serve no-nonsense, pint-sized mugs of tea or coffee. The food's hardly haute cuisine, but it's cheap, tasty and filling.

2 GRINDLEFORD

🏠 **The Maynard** (page 241)

Grindleford, a small and sleepy but beautifully placed settlement snuggled into the upper Derwent Valley a couple of miles southeast of Hathersage, is often bypassed as people rush on through to Hathersage and Longshaw Estate or to Chatsworth in the other direction. Having taught in the village school, I've seen the cycle of seasons here: greens turning gold and then red, followed by the silvers of mist and ground hoar in winter: a great spot at any time of year. Browse in the bespoke furniture store and the **Derwent Art Gallery**, or strike out into the surrounding countryside. The centrepiece of the village is the arched bridge that crosses the Derwent – a place to listen to the babble of the Derwent and drink in the views of the woodland below Froggatt Edge.

With Grindleford Station being at **Padley**, the village is one of the few Peak District settlements to boast its own railway. Arriving by train from Sheffield is a bit like stepping through the wardrobe into Narnia, for one minute you're in Totley on the edge of Sheffield, and the next in the Peak District National Park, ejected from city fringe to country by means of a long dark tunnel, almost four miles in length. From the station, there's a wealth of trails to explore along the Derwent River or up Padley Gorge to Longshaw Estate and the Peak District edges.

FOOD & DRINK

You can stop for a bite to eat at the elegant **Maynard** (✆ 01433 630321) or the **Sir William Hotel** (✆ 01433 630303) but for a more alternative experience, drop into **St Helen's Church** by the river. St Helen's is not only a building providing spiritual nourishment these days, it's also where locals come to pick up a few supplies or have a coffee and cake, along with walkers and cyclists. The **Church Vestry** is home to the **Grindleford Community Shop** (✆ 07519 797570 ♂ www.grindlefordvillageshop.co.uk ☉ 09.00–18.00 Mon–Sat & 12.00–16.30 Sun) and is run by an enthusiastic set of villagers, delighted to have a local food store again after the closure of the village shop some years back. They do an excellent line in take-away curries (supplied by a woman who once worked for an overland company) and freshly home-baked bread. The community seems to have thought of everything: there's even a bicycle service point – a box of tools and spare cycle parts. In the churchyard, a table and set of chairs are set up for dry days. The shop is closed when services, weddings and funerals are taking place.

Nether & Upper Padley

At Padley the road dips down to the railway station and the old station house, an attractive stone and clapboard building, now **Grindleford Café**. Next to the station, a bridge heads over the railway line, where the express trains thunder into Totley Tunnel. From the station at Upper Padley, a short walk leads to the ruins of Padley Hall along an unmade road.

All that remains of the hall is **The Gatehouse** with **Padley Chapel** (consecrated in 1933 in honour of the Padley Martyrs) on the upper floor (☉ Mar–Sep 14.00–16.00 Sun & Wed; contact the diocese for guided group tours ♂ www.hallam-diocese.com/visiting-padley-chapel).

The Catholic Fitzherbert family were used to living in fear at Padley Hall – their house had been raided more than once. With the execution of Mary, Queen of Scots in 1587 and the threat of a Catholic Spanish invasion in 1588, anti-Catholic feeling was running high in England. Padley Hall had become a place of refuge for Catholic men of the cloth, despite the considerable risk – harbouring priests had become an act of high treason. On 12 July 1588 two priests, Nicholas Garlick and Robert Ludlum, were discovered hiding in the walls of the manor house. The unfortunate men were taken to Derby, were they were hung, drawn and quartered (along with Catholic supporter Richard Sympson) and their butchered body parts displayed on poles at St Mary's Bridge as a gruesome warning to the nation. Meanwhile Sir Thomas Fitzherbert had been incarcerated in the Tower of London, where he died a few years later. After the raid, Padley Hall was confiscated by the Crown. An annual pilgrimage takes place every July from Grindleford Station to Padley Chapel to commemorate the Padley Martyrs and the bravery of practising Catholics under Elizabeth I.

Padley Gorge & Burbage Brook

Padley Gorge is an enchanted place of ancient woodland: oak and birch sprinkled with alder on the sides of the gorge. I've come here in winter when the ancient oaks are naked, their gnarled forms and bony fingers reaching for darkened skies. I've written poetry and drawn the oaks with charcoal: there's no better way to stop and really see the world you're living in. If the idea of sketching or writing poetry is more likely to cause stress than relaxation, just sit down on one of the moss-covered stones and lose yourself in these ethereal surroundings. The main paths are high above the gorge, but it's worth climbing down to the narrow, stone-strewn paths to the brook to watch the water tumble through the ravine, swirling in whirlpools of curved rock.

Further up on the moors, Burbage Brook has an entirely different feel. It's a popular place in summer, partly due to its close proximity to Sheffield, partly due to its exceptional views. If you visit in the school holidays or on a warm weekend, it looks more like Brighton Beach than a moorland wilderness. The grassy banks of the brook are packed with sunbathers, picnickers, families playing ball games and children paddling in the river. Come early in the morning or at the end of the day, if you can.

3 LONGSHAW ESTATE

Longshaw Estate ✆ 01433 637904; National Trust

The best way to approach the National Trust Longshaw Estate is from Grindleford railway station via Padley Gorge. For those who prefer a shorter stroll, park in the lay-by next to the Information Barn at the edge of the estate on the B6521 (there's a bus service on this road as well). Take time to drop into the **information barn** to look at the interpretive boards giving an excellent insight into local history, geology, flora and fauna along with the history of Longshaw Estate and the work of the National Trust who manage the land around it. As you walk in the direction of the house, there are spectacular views across the moorland to the 'tabletop' hills of Carl Wark and Higger Tor. This wild and open countryside has a Brontë-esque feel to it, contrasting the tamed Longshaw parkland with its Scots pines, rhododendron-lined path and duck pond.

Longshaw Pond, created sometime around 1827, is the domain of swans and mallards and other waterfowl. Further along, **Longshaw Lodge** was built as a bolthole for the Duke of Rutland and his shooting companions – George V and one of the Dukes of Wellington among their numbers. In World War I, Longshaw became a recuperation hospital for injured soldiers. While there's no stately home to view (the lodge is made up of private apartments nowadays), this is a wonderful place to come and reconnect with nature. The National Trust does some sterling work on the estate: the **Moorland Discovery Centre** caters for schools and families, offering a range of fun and educational activities and seasonal events, while the Trust offers free guided walks on a weekly basis. The kitchen garden behind the NT centre supplies the **café** during its short growing session in the uplands. Tasty, organic food aside, the outside seating makes for some of the best 'chews with a view' in the Peak District, weather permitting.

"There are spectacular views across the moorland to the 'tabletop' hills of Carl Wark and Higger Tor."

🍴 FOOD & DRINK

Grindleford Station Café Station Approach, Upper Padley S32 2JA ✆ 01433 631011. This 'Greasy Joe' café is a big hit with hungry walkers and climbers. It serves pint-sized cups of tea and filling, no-nonsense food in a rough-and-ready dining room (alongside a couple of 'no-nonsense' notices left as an affectionate legacy to the last, now deceased owner with a reputation of Fawlty Towers proportions).

Longshaw Tearooms National Trust Longshaw Estate S11 7TZ ✆ 01433 637904. Ingredients sourced from the kitchen garden behind – where possible during its short growing season. Lunches, snacks and drinks can be eaten inside or on the tables and millstones on the lawn – with some of the best views in the Peak District.

A walk through Padley Gorge to Longshaw Estate

✳ OS Explorer maps OL24 & OL1; start: Grindleford railway station, ♥ SK251788; 3 miles; moderate climb through Padley Gorge

This is one of the choicest ravine and moorland walks in the Peak District. It's a place to return to through the seasons: in autumn when the ground is carpeted in oak leaves; in winter mists when the mossed stones and twisted oaks take on a haunted, primeval appearance; and after the spring rains when the brook spills and spirals its way down through the gorge. Refreshments at Grindleford Station Café and Longshaw Estate Café.

From **Grindleford railway station**, walk across the railway bridge. Just past the clapboard house on the left, go through the gap in the stone wall on the right at the National Trust sign. (Ignore the sign pointing you further along the lane for Longshaw Estate.) Follow the track upward through the gorge, with **Burbage Brook** on your left. Take the higher wide path leading straight up the gorge to continue the walk.

Keep on following the track as it veers left, with the stone wall and the road next to it on your right. Ignore the gate leading out on to the road. Climb over the little hummock and ford the stream. Eventually you will come out of Padley Woods on to open ground with striking views over to **Carl Wark** and **Higger Tor**. There's a bridge crossing Burbage Brook, but instead of crossing the brook, take the steps leading up and on to the B6521.

Cross the road to the information barn and continue along the path signed for Longshaw Estate, passing a lake on your left.

At the end of the track go left through the gate and continue on to **Longshaw House** with an opportunity to stop for a drink and a snack. Follow the Longshaw driveway to the end and cross the main road again. Climb the stile beside the white gate and take the wide path straight downhill. Near the bottom of the hill, the track diverges. Veer left with the track as it curves round to follow the course of the brook.

Keeping Burbage Brook on your left, walk downhill over the moorland and back through **Padley Gorge**. Reaching a gate, go through it and continue downwards. At the end of the lane turn left and continue past the mill, over the bridge and back to the starting point at Grindleford station.

4 BASLOW, CURBAR, FROGGATT & STANAGE EDGES

From the rocky crags at Robin Hood's Stride and Cratcliff Tor to the edges of Baslow, Curbar, Froggatt and Stanage, the landscape on the Eastern Moors is full of drama and beauty. Great slabs of rock drop to the valley below, while behind them the moorland plateaus stretch to the skyline. The escarpments, tors and crags are an adventure playground for walkers, boulderers and climbers alike. With climbing routes such as the Black Hawk Traverse and the Flying Buttress on Stanage Edge, Insanity on Curbar Edge or Suicide Wall at Cratcliff Tor, the challenging nature of these climbs is left in no doubt. Famous 20th-century climbers such as Don Whillans and Joe Brown cut their teeth on the Peak District edges before going on to conquer the big boys in the Alps and Himalayas.

For the less adventurous, the edges are great for scrambling and simply walking along the top.

Starting with **Birchen Edge**, the escarpment is adorned with the pencil-thin **Nelson's Monument**, honouring Lord Nelson. Nearby, three boulders have been carved with the names of Nelson's ships: *Victory*, *Defiance* and *Royal Sovereign*. Climbers, in keeping with the nautical theme, have gone on to christen their conquered routes with seafaring names such as Crow's Nest, Sail Buttress and Trafalgar Crack. Baslow Edge and Curbar Edge can be accessed from **Curbar Gap**. Both are worth exploring. **Baslow Edge** has glorious views over to Chatsworth Estate and the Derwent Valley and takes in the **Wellington Monument**, commemorating Wellington's victory at the Battle of Waterloo (echoing Nelson's Monument over on Birchen), and the Eagle Stone. This exposed gritstone standing in splendid isolation on the moors has come about as the result of weathering. It takes its name either after Aigle, a Celtic god who was rather fond of hurling rocks around the countryside, or from Egglestone, meaning 'witches' stone'. Legend has it that the local women wouldn't entertain marriage until their suitor demonstrated his prowess by climbing the stone, appeasing the witches. It's also claimed that the witches' stone turns around when the cock crows. This idea could be linked to the rock's usage in prehistoric times for astronomical alignments.

"Climbers, in keeping with the nautical theme, have gone on to christen their conquered routes with seafaring names such as Crow's Nest, Sail Buttress and Trafalgar Crack."

Heading northwards from Curbar Gap, **Curbar, Froggatt, Burbage** and **Stanage Edge** make for magnificent walking with views across to Stony Middleton, Eyam, Grindleford and Hathersage, while the rocks themselves are a pleasure to walk through with their wonderfully sculpted formations, sprinkled in places with abandoned millstones.

FOOD & DRINK

Chequers Inn Froggatt Edge S32 3ZL ℘01433 630231 ☙www.chequers-froggatt.com. This pub in a lovely location serves up a variety of real ales and a range of fresh meat, game and fish dishes. Not the cheapest option in the area, but the food is cooked to a high standard.

Grouse Inn On the B6054 at Froggatt Edge S11 7TZ ℘01433 630423. Offers a varied menu in a stunning location.

Derbyshire Craft Centre and Eating House Calver S32 3XA ℘01433 631583 ☙www. theeatinghousecalver.co.uk. Offers quality food next to the craft shop, which is piled high with delightful gift ideas – partners who don't care for shopping can linger with a newspaper and a second cuppa.

5 BASLOW

It would seem all roads lead to Baslow: the ribbons of highways curling through the moors from Chesterfield and Sheffield, and from the direction of Manchester, knot together at two large roundabouts that bookend the village. It's not just the meeting of roads that make Baslow such a busy place. The village is dotted with upmarket pubs and eateries, and designer and souvenir shops, while the Chatsworth Estate lies on its doorstep. Come to Baslow out of season, as I did most recently on a damp, melancholy autumn day, and you'll have the village mainly to yourself.

Baslow is divided into three areas: Bridge End, Nether End and Over End. **Bridge End**, the oldest part of the village, is a good starting point for an exploration of the village. Cross the **Old Bridge** from **Bubnell Lane**, with its little stone watchman's booth and impossibly low doorway. Here the villagers took it in turn to man the bridge, collect toll charges and fine anyone breaking its weight restrictions (usually with lead and millstones). The toll house, not much bigger than a sentry box, is grandly known as **Mary Brady's House**. Mary, who slept rough there, must surely be one of the few beggars to have had the honour of a building named after her.

A walk along Curbar Edge & the River Derwent

❃ OS Explorer map OL24; start: The Bridge Inn, ♥ SK246744; 4 miles; moderately easy; refreshments: Derbyshire Craft Centre at Calver & the Chequers Inn at Froggatt (page 69)

This walk takes in sustained views along the entire length of Curbar Edge, while showcasing the great platforms of rock and layers of weathered crags. From here a woodland path drops down to the River Derwent and the contrasting pastoral valley of wetland and meadow. The walk starts from the **Bridge Inn at Calver**. There's a small amount of parking around the Bridge, where there are also bus stops. The route takes in a steep climb up the road to Curbar village; after that it's nearly all off-road walking. The edge path and river section are level and easy going.

1 Take the road opposite The Bridge Inn and follow the right fork up **Curbar Hill**, signposted for the village. It's a steep climb up the road and on through Curbar, where Curbar Hill becomes Bar Road.

2 Just past the speed limit signs indicating the end of the village, go through the gap on the right that leads directly up through fields, cutting out the switchback on the road. The path veers left along a dry stone wall to meet the road further up. There's a track running along the grassy verge by the side of the road on the right, so you don't have to walk on the road.

3 Ignore the path heading right leading to Baslow Edge. Instead drop down to the road, cross it and take the path adjacent, leading up on to Curbar Edge.

The path along **Curbar Edge** is well defined and sits slightly back from the edge. Take time to wander over to the rocky edges to really appreciate the craggy formations.

4 Once the path drops down, look out for a small signpost on the left (about 1.2 miles from Curbar Gap). It leads off along the base of flat slabs. Keep your eyes peeled for a path on the left leading steeply downhill through the trees, just a short way along the base of the rock face. As it's not signposted, it's easy to miss. If the path starts to rise sharply upwards again, you've gone too far.

5 Head down the path, watching your step on the steep uneven ground. It will widen and flatten as you continue on. Soon you will reach the A625 with the **Chequers Inn** on your right – a good place to stop for a pint or lunch.

6 Take the path directly opposite the exit on to the main road. Head down it until you reach a second, more minor road – **Froggatt Lane**. Turn right and follow the road downhill until you reach the pretty humpbacked **Froggatt Bridge**.

7 Cross the bridge and climb the stile on your left at the other side (signposted New Bridge and Calver). Follow the track through pine trees with the River Derwent on your left. The dappled reflections on the water on a sunny day are lovely. Look out for brook lamprey at **Calver Marshes** (an elusive eel-like fish best seen in spawning time between March and June).

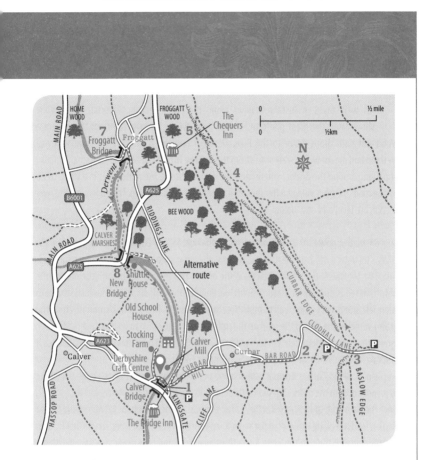

8 Cross the road at New Bridge and continue on along the gravel track past the **Shuttle House** (used to house the sluice machinery), still keeping the river on your left, and on past the weir. Cross the meadows, passing by the caravan park at **Stocking Farm**. Notice the attractive barn-like building on your right. It was actually the **old school house**, built in 1817. Head down the lane past the imposing **Calver Mill**, an old cotton mill that's been converted to apartments. The lane comes out next to **The Derbyshire Craft Centre**.

    Note: An easier 2.5-mile walk sticks with the river valley. Instead of heading up Curbar Hill, take the left junction on to Dukes Drive. Go through the gate on the left where the stone wall runs out. The riverside path goes all the way to Froggatt Bridge. Cross it and follow the river back to Calver, with the river on the other side now.

At the other end of the village, you'll find **Nether End**, with its lovely old stone buildings, shops and hotel set around **Goose Green**. From here you can enter **Chatsworth Park** via the 17th-century packhorse bridge, past a row of pretty thatched cottages and on through the kissing gates. Inside the parkland, look back at the rather impressive **Golden Gates**, dating back to the first Duke. The walk to Chatsworth House via the park is a wonderful way to approach the stately home, particularly when the autumn trees are a riot of colour, or in winter (post-Christmas) when the ground's covered in frost or snow.

St Anne's Church

Next to the Old Bridge, the church boasts three oddities. The first is the **sanctuary knocker** on the main entrance door. It was used by fugitives seeking safe haven from the law. As long as the fugitives stayed within the confines of the church, law enforcers couldn't touch them, while at the same time, the church bell was rung to warn the good people of Baslow of a potential criminal in their midst. The second curio is the **dog whip** that sits in a glass case just inside the church door. The whip, with its three-foot-long prong, was used by the official church whipper to bring the congregation's dogs to order during the service – and other strays away from the door. Whippers were also employed in local churches to keep disorderly humans in check – and to wake up any snorers (the job of the wonderfully named 'sluggard waker'). It's believed Baslow possesses the only intact church whip today. The last *objet de curiosité* is found outside on the east tower. The **clock face** doesn't have the usual 1 to 12 numerals. Instead the letters and numbers spell out 'VICTORIA1897', particularly confusing when the clock hands land on the numbers. This was a gift from an esteemed local doctor, Dr Wrench, in commemoration of Queen Victoria's Diamond Jubilee.

FOOD & DRINK

Baslow is foodie heaven with plenty of choice, whatever your budget or taste. **Charlie's Bistro** (✆ 01246 582619 🔗 www.charliesbaslow.com) is a tastefully furbished bistro and restaurant opposite St Anne's Church. The breakfasts here are particularly popular. **Fischers, Baslow Hall** (✆ 01246 583259 🔗 www.fischers-baslowhall.co.uk) was owned by various influential Baslow families over the decades, including eccentric electrical engineer and inventor, Sebastian Ziani de Ferranti. The restaurant is situated in the elegant Edwardian house surrounded by attractive grounds and serves exquisite food with prices to match.

THE CHATSWORTH ESTATE & VILLAGES

Moving south along the Derwent Valley to Chatsworth estate, the Peak District softens to gently sloping woodland and meadow, flanked by escarpment and moorland. Below Chatsworth House, the River Derwent winds its way through parkland dotted with mature trees and sprinkled with herds of deer and flocks of sheep. Beyond the house, it's worth exploring the hinterland of woodland, an extended pleasure garden as well as the acres of open parkland and the villages (all wood painted in the trademark 'Chatsworth blue') that lie just south of the stately home – and all with free access for walkers. There's a wide range of one-off and annual events taking place at Chatsworth over the year, from talks to exhibitions, concerts and food fairs. Check the website for more details.

6 CHATSWORTH HOUSE, GARDENS & ESTATE

Off the B6012, DE45 1PP ✐ 01246 565300 ✐ www.chatsworth.org ◔ Apr–Dec; house: 11.00–17.30; garden: 11.00 (10.30 in the summer)–18.00. Check website for seasonal variations.

⚓ Chatsworth Park Caravan Club Site (page 241)

Hundreds and thousands beat their way to Chatsworth's door on a daily basis. The sheer volume of visitors can be overwhelming, but don't be put off by this, for Chatsworth is hugely worthwhile. Pick your time carefully: the garden empties at the end of the day, and is quiet first thing in the morning. Experience the seasonally planted landscape on a bright autumn or spring day, rather than in the summer holidays or in the pre-Christmas period if you can.

A potted history of Chatsworth

The history of Chatsworth really begins with Bess of Hardwick. Four times wed, she extended her wealth and influence with every marriage, until she was the second most powerful woman in England after the Queen. Bess persuaded her second husband, Sir William Cavendish, to purchase Chatsworth Manor in 1549 for the princely sum of £600. Thereafter her son William – the notoriously quick-tempered fourth Earl (later becoming the first Duke) of Devonshire – greatly altered the house. Starting with the south front, he quickly developed a taste for home improvement, going on to rebuild the east, west and north fronts–

completing the project just before his death in 1707. In the 1760s, his great grandson, the equally industrious fourth Duke called on the skills of 'Capability' Brown to replace the formal gardens with a more natural and romantic look. It was the fifth Duke who married the feisty Lady Georgiana Spencer, the beautiful socialite with a penchant for politics and gambling, and subjected her to a *ménage a trois* with her friend, Lady Elizabeth Foster – as portrayed in the film *The Duchess*.

In the 19th century, the sixth Duke, the 'Bachelor Duke', redeveloped much of the garden with Joseph Paxton to include features that are admired by visitors today, including the rockery and Canal Pond along with the Emperor Fountain. Fast forward to the end of World War II. After years of wartime neglect, the house was finally reopened to visitors in 1949. A year later, Edward Cavendish, the tenth Duke was dead and the ensuing death duties threatened the Cavendish estates. Hardwick Hall had to be relinquished and although Chatsworth House was saved, valuable works of art and rare books from the house had to be handed over in lieu of cash. The eleventh Duke, Andrew Cavendish, succeeded his father, his elder brother killed in action during the war. Andrew married into the notorious family of Mitford sisters that included a devotee of Hitler, the wife of fascist Mosley, and an active communist. Andrew's wife Deborah, more conventional, married respectably, but was no pushover, playing a crucial role in developing Chatsworth House as a successful tourist attraction. On the death of his father Andrew in 2004, Peregrine Cavendish became the twelfth and current Duke of Devonshire.

"Chatsworth House is a grand and opulent treasure trove of design, art and sculpture."

Chatsworth House

What the Peak District lacks in terms of museums is made up for in Chatsworth House. The stately home is a grand and opulent treasure trove of design, art and sculpture. From porcelain, silver and textiles, to Neoclassical sculptures, furniture, drawings, *objets d'art* and other curios from around the world, Chatsworth is the V&A of the Midlands. The house has more than 120 rooms, although only 30 or so of them are open to the public. Nonetheless, with more than half a mile of corridors, state rooms, halls and galleries, along with a private chapel, it's enough to satisfy the most demanding of visitors. The highlights include the

Painted Hall with its intricate floor-to-ceiling depictions of Julius Caesar and the superbly convincing *trompe l'œil* of a violin and bow hanging from a door in the State Music Room. Meanwhile the **State Rooms** have remained virtually unaltered from the 17th century. George II slept in the **State Bedroom**, while the **Queen of Scots Chambers** in the east wing are where the ill-fated queen lived in captivity. From the cosy and womb-like library, containing over 17,000 books, to the sumptuous **Great Dining Room** lined in red silk; the **Oak Room** with its dark panelling and carved heads (taken from a German monastery), to the luxuriously adorned marble **Chapel,** there's much to feast your eyes upon. The most impressive pieces are found in the **Sculpture Gallery**, where two lions guard the entrance to **The Orangery** and the shop.

Chatsworth Garden

The garden makes an impression right from the start with its Conservatory Wall and greenhouses filled with camellias, roses and exotic fruits. Don't miss the nearby Alice-in-Wonderland-like Topiary Garden, complete with table and chairs, a sofa and staircase, or *Revelation* by Angela Conner, a water-powered kinetic sculpture of exquisite beauty and ingenious engineering (sadly plagued with technical problems and not always in working order). A path along the whimsical blob-like Forms of Growth leads to the Kitchen Garden, impressive in scale and diversity. From the top corner, a woodland path follows the walled perimeter of the garden. Few wander here, yet it's a charming and quiet hinterland of miniature stone bridges and babbling streams set in managed woodland. Deviate off the path down to the Temple at the top of The Cascade, another water installation of impressive design and engineering – only this one dates back to the turn of the 18th century.

In the far perimeter of the garden, the Arboretum and Pinetum contain an impressive collection of conifers including the giant redwood – and my favourite, the Brewer's weeping spruce, a curtain of fine pine needles sometimes bejewelled with dew or rain droplets. Close by, the Grotto has wonderful views over to the Grotto Pond, a riot of colour in autumn. A path leads from here down through The Ravine to the Angela Conner Grove and more sculptures, where you'll recognise some well-known British faces. The nearby Maze was once the site of Joseph Paxton's Great Conservatory. Too large to heat in times of wartime austerity, it was dismantled. The stone wall foundation now contains the maze,

KEEPING UP WITH THE JONESES: A VISIT FROM THE TSAR

When in 1844 Tsar Nicolas I announced a planned visit to England, the sixth Duke of Devonshire, Chatsworth engineers and garden designers went into a frenzy of activity. Labourers worked through the night by the light of flares to create a structure that would surely impress. In a case of 'keeping up with the Joneses', the Duke, all too aware of the Tsar's great fountain at Peterhof Summer Palace in St Petersburg, decided to build an even bigger and better version at his own Chatsworth House. Sir Joseph Paxton, the great gardener and designer of his day (and later to become designer of the Crystal Palace for the Great Exhibition of 1851), was roped in to lead the project. Building a fountain of this dimension was never going to be an easy task. It would require practical and creative design skills, along with engineering and mathematical knowhow... and a bit of money. Undeterred, Paxton set to work, ordering the moors above Chatsworth Estate to be drained and 100,000 cubic yards of earth to be removed in order to create a body of water large enough to feed the fountain. The aptly named 'Emperor Lake' contained 11 million gallons of water which was then piped through 15-inch cast-iron pipes for 130 yards to the site of the fountain. At its maximum, the fountain could expend 330 gallons of water per minute and rise to the heady heights of 296 feet. The project was a triumphant success, but alas the Tsar neglected to visit Chatsworth, and never saw the magnificent fountain built in his honour.

but the Coal Hole that once took coal underground in small wagons to the conservatory boilers still exists – a dimly lit tunnel to duck through. It emerges at Paxton's Rockery. Don't miss the Willow Tree Fountain behind slabs of rock, squirting out water from its metal branches. It has all the whimsy of the more modern installations, but the original willow tree dated back to 1695. From the rockery, steps lead down to The Strid, a pretty ornamental pond filled with carp. Further down, the Ring Pond is surrounded by mischievous lop-sided topiary bushes, while the equally whimsical Serpentine Hedge snakes off to one side. You can leave the Ring Pond here and follow the main path alongside the Canal Pond, with its Emperor Fountain.

Throughout the garden there's a mix of permanent and temporary statues and installations, some classical in style, others contemporary, edgy and challenging. From the Canal Pond and the Emperor Fountain, the path leads past the South Lawns and Seahorse Fountain, and on between the house and Capability Brown's expansive Salisbury Lawns back to Flora's temple and the Stables. Every time I visit Chatsworth,

I fall in love with this exciting garden all over again, not least because its creators are constantly redefining the grand and stately space with a sense of adventure and fun.

¶¶ FOOD & DRINK

There are numerous eateries at Chatsworth, from the **Cavendish Restaurant** to the **Carriage House Restaurant** at the stables with its lovely courtyard. There are also 'food to go' kiosks, but I'd recommend seeking out one of the Chatsworth village tea rooms or pubs (page 83) away from the hordes. Alternatively, bring a picnic for fine alfresco dining in a quiet corner of the garden.

Stand Wood

🏠 **The Hunting Tower** (page 241), **Swiss Cottage** (page 241)

For those who baulk at the price of the entrance ticket for Chatsworth, there is a wonderful alternative in Stand Wood, far from the madding crowd high above the house and gardens. It's accessed from the approach to Chatsworth Farm and Adventure Playground at the top of Chatsworth car park, and along the estate service road. Bar the parking costs at Chatsworth House, it doesn't cost a penny. Walking in these woods is a bit like wandering through the pages of a Grimm story, with its romantic Hunting Tower and fairy-tale Swiss Cottage, both perched above woodland gardens and hidden glens. And in all of this, you'll have a bird's-eye view of Chatsworth far below. On the service road, follow the sign on the left pointing up to **The Dell.** Here **The Aqueduct** thrusts out of the canopy of vegetation. Water is carried along the conduit before plunging over the 80-foot drop. In hard winters the water freezes, forming sculpted icicles that trail off the end. Higher up, a bridge crosses the top of the aqueduct. From here the eye is led along the aqueduct's conduit, down the line of the Cascades far below in the gardens and through the gap in the woodlands to the hills on the other side of the valley. Nothing is accidental. From the aqueduct, a zigzagging

"There is a surprise around every corner in this dense woodland of ash and birch, cherry and chestnut, spruce and sycamore."

staircase leads to a second, smaller waterfall, **Sowtor Stone**, and links the higher and lower pathway extending along the steep hillside. There is a surprise around every corner in this dense woodland of ash and birch, cherry and chestnut, spruce and sycamore as well as rowan, holly and yew. The planting is no happy coincidence either, for although this part of Chatsworth is outside the walled perimeter of the present day garden, this area was designed and planted out by Paxton as part of the extended Chatsworth pleasure gardens.

To the west of the Dell and the aqueduct, the **Hunting Tower** (available as a holiday let) was built around 1582 for Bess of Hardwick – and is by far the best surviving Tudor building at Chatsworth. Sitting on an escarpment 400 feet above the house, it provided hunters with extensive views over the estate and deer park, and was probably used to host grand banquets. It's an impressive building with its curved turrets and diamond leaded windows, each of the four turrets topped with a lighthouse-styled tower and a lead dome.

On the eastern perimeter of the estate are four lakes, including the **Emperor and Swiss lakes**, created to provide water for Chatsworth Garden's various water features. Although the Emperor Lake was created for practical reasons, this tranquil spot, caught between clearing and woodland, is great for a picnic or a lakeside amble. Drink in the views across the still waters, where the occasional grey heron stands sentry on the shoreline. Further along the service road, **Swiss Cottage** (also available as a holiday let) sits in splendid isolation flanked by woodland on the shores of Swiss Lake.

Beeley Moor & Beeley Brook

On the eastern edge of Stand Wood, at a signed crossroads, a fingerpost points in four directions: to Park Farm, the lakes, Chatsworth House and to Beeley and Hob Hurst's House. The last isn't actually a house, but a mound with a ditch on Bunker's Hill, a Bronze Age burial site. Hob Hurst refers to a mythical character, an elf or giant, who was thought to inhabit the mound and its surrounds. On the other side of a stepped wall, the old packhorse route heads out across the open expanse of Beeley Moor. At the other end, a path heads down through a delightful woodland ravine to a farm lane and on into Beeley village.

Through Chatsworth's parkland

From Beeley a tree-lined meadow leads to the humpbacked Calton Lees **Bridge** on the B6012. The kissing-gate on the other side of the bridge follows a grassy pathway beside the River Derwent to Chatsworth House. The solid but roofless Chatsworth Mill stands beside the water, partially destroyed by fire. On the other side of the river, there's a good chance of spotting deer; and if not here, elsewhere on the estate. Picnic tables encourage a spot of alfresco dining and a dip in the river when the weather's good. When Chatsworth House finally comes back into view, it's a commanding sight in the valley flanked by woodland and hill.

THE CHATSWORTH VILLAGES

From Baslow to Rowsley, the Chatsworth estate road (the B6012) winds its way through parkland. Off to the sides of the road, there are three delightful estate villages developed to house the estate workers and their families: Pilsley, Edensor and Beeley along with the hamlet of Calton Lees. While only a few of the grace-and-favour cottages remain, the villages retain their quintessential estate character with their tell-tale Chatsworth Blue woodwork and rustic elegance. It's a shame so many visitors speed straight past the villages in their haste to reach Chatsworth House, for it's worth stopping off at these traditional, stone-built settlements – not only for their history and architectural interest, but also for their delightful tea rooms, restaurants and pubs.

The best way to take in the villages is to walk from one to the other, starting with Beeley. Cross the tree-lined flood plain on the other side of the B6012 from the village, over Calton Lees Bridge at the end and up the lane past the garden centre, turning right to cross New Place Wood and down to Edensor over the parkland. From Edensor head up the village road that becomes a churned up track. Turn right into Handley Lane and right again on to the B6048, leading to Pilsley. From Pilsley follow the B6012 to the triangular junction leading to Chatsworth. Head across the parkland to the River Derwent and follow the riverside path back to Calton Lees and Beeley.

7 Pilsley

Of all the Chatsworth settlements, Pilsley feels the most lived in – less 'chocolate-box' perfect than Beeley and Edensor and a little rougher round the edges. Northwest of Chatsworth, Pilsley has a strong community vibe, the only Chatsworth village in possession of a shop, post office *and* school. While most visitors head straight for the commendable Chatsworth Farm Shop and Restaurant on the other side of the B6048, it really is worth taking an amble around this village. It lacks the unfettered architectural indulgence of the Edensor buildings, but there are still echoes of the Italianate village in the detail of some cottages. Once you've taken in the picture-book school house and terraced houses and cottages that line the village greens, High Street and dead-end lanes, you can check out the Richard Whittlestone Wildlife Gallery selling original wildlife paintings along with limited edition prints and cards. For those who'd like to replicate the timeless classical elegance of the aristocracy and their country houses, **Penrose Interiors** is the place to shop. Once you've visited the art gallery and home interiors shop, you can head for the **Devonshire Arms**, always a good option when the farm shop café is filled with coach parties.

8 Edensor

🏠 **Gardener's Cottage** (page 241)

I've visited Edensor (pronounced En'sor) in snow, when it looked like a Bruegel painting with its great spire soaring into a blue sky, and rustic villas huddled round the foot of the church as if in prayer. All that's missing are the peasants skating on a lake and the hunters on the snow-covered hill. The closest estate village to Chatsworth, half a mile to the west, isn't actually inspired by Flemish architecture, but by the Italianate school – combined with Norman, Gothic and Jacobean influences. It was designed by the sixth Duke's head gardener Joseph Paxton and his architectural assistant John Robertson, then later by George Henry Stokes.

MOVE THE VILLAGE – IT'S RUINING MY VIEW

A hill or village, it didn't matter – the Dukes of Devonshire simply had them removed if they interrupted their view.

In the 18th century, when Edensor was clearly visible from Chatsworth House, the fourth Duke decided it was time for a relocation of the village. However, he died before the remodelled Edensor was complete and it was left to the fifth Duke to carry on with the task. In the end, it was the sixth Duke who roped in Paxton and Robertson to create a brand new village on the present day site.

All that remains of the original Edensor is a single house built into a hollow of the hillside on the other side of the B6012. It's said that when its tenant refused to leave, the Duke caved in (knowing the house couldn't be seen from Chatsworth). Others believe that there never was a stand-off: the Duke left Park Cottage standing in compassion for his tenant suffering from typhoid at the time. Either way, Park Cottage (now called Gardener's Cottage and available as a holiday let) is a curious sight, sitting in splendid isolation and enclosed by its garden wall.

Robertson arrived at Chatsworth with a portfolio of architectural styles. The Duke, too distracted or indecisive, flicked through the catalogue and simply chose one of each design. This would explain the mishmash of styles at Edensor, enough to make the purist shudder in distaste. Edensor, it could be argued, is the Portmeirion of Derbyshire with its self-conscious rendition of Italianate architecture – a sort of Victorian theme park. But for most who visit Edensor nowadays, it's impossible not to fall in love with the model village. From the walled village enclosure to the tree-lined avenues surrounding a triangular green, from the great church on the hillside to the lanes of romantic cottages, this is a place to seek out the individual details on each building – corbels, cornices, copulas; pedimented windows and doors; hipped roofs, balustrades and signorial towers.

It fell to the seventh Duke to complete Edensor with a new church. The then existing church, with its square tower and mismatched windows, no longer made the grade. George Gilbert Scott was called upon to design something more visionary and the eminent Victorian architect met the challenge in spades, building a church which incorporated parts of the old church in 1870. **St Peter's Church** makes a big statement in a small village. Its soaring spire rises dramatically out of the countryside, the kind of steeple usually associated with large towns and cities, while steps rise steeply to the north doorway, dividing into a double stairway. Inside there's a magnificent timber roof like the hull of a great ship turned upside down, but it's the grandiose monument in the **Cavendish Chapel** that I found most interesting. It commemorates Bess of Hardwick's two sons, William (the first Earl of Devonshire) and Henry Cavendish. The wealth and position of the two brothers is unquestionable, with the Earl's coronet and robes on one side and his ceremonial armour on the other. Then you look to the effigies laid out on the black Ashford marble with the bones of Henry next to the shroud of his brother William – the skeleton contrasting the pomp and circumstance of robe, crown and armoury. Death is a great leveller.

Most of the great Dukes and their families are buried here at St Peter's, as is Sir Joseph Paxton – engineer, Crystal Palace designer and Chatsworth landscape gardener extraordinaire. Paxton's tombstone is found at the centre of the old graveyard in long grass. Higher up are the Dukes' gravestones, surprisingly modest and largely unadorned. Another famous individual was buried here, at least by association:

Kathleen Cavendish. She was the sister of John F Kennedy and wife of Billy Hartington, the eldest son of the tenth Duke of Devonshire. Hers is a tragic story. Having married Billy in 1944, he left her just five weeks later in May to take part in the allied invasion of Europe. By September he was dead, killed in action. Four years later, Kathleen herself was dead, killed in a plane crash, just 28 years of age. She'd given herself up to misfortune – and a small plane caught in the eye of a storm. A flat tablet of stone sits at the foot of Kathleen's headstone – a record of John F Kennedy's visit to his sister's grave on 29 June, 1963. As I stood in the spot where John F had once stood, I looked up to see a small bi-plane overhead circling the pale autumn sky. It was a poignant moment.

9 Calton Lees

🏠 **Russian Cottage** (page 241)

South of Edensor, the hamlet of Calton Lees is made up of a scattering of houses and farm dwellings, along with Calton Lees Garden Centre and café. From here, you can ramble up the quiet valley lane towards the Russian Cottage (available as a holiday let) and on into the hills and valley between Bakewell and Chatsworth.

10 Beeley

Southeast from Calton Lees, Beeley is a leafy idyll set within a landscape of moorland, coniferous woodland and tree-lined meadow, its stillness only interrupted by the clucking of hens and the babble of Beeley Brook. The names of the village lanes and cottages echo their bucolic surroundings: Church, Pig and School Lane, Brookside and Chapel Hill; Pear Tree, Orchard and Brookside cottage, the Nook, and the Old Smithy. Most of the dwellings are privately owned now, Chatsworth Blue giving way to creams and whites in the cottage woodwork. But Beeley will always have the Chatsworth signature stamped on the architecture of its buildings, such as the Swiss-style, Y-shaped cottages opposite the Devonshire Arms, with their steeply pitched roofs and latticed windows. Known as the **Paxton Cottages**, they were actually designed by George Henry Stokes (who'd married Paxton's daughter). The stroll over to Chatsworth from the village is delightful, as is the climb up to Beeley Moor via Beeley Brook (page 78) – or you can just stroll round the village, stopping by the **Devonshire Arms** or the **Old Smithy**.

FOOD & DRINK

Chatsworth Farm Shop and Restaurant On the other side of the B6048 from Pilsley, Chatsworth Estate DE45 1UF ✆ 01246 583392 ⌂ www.chatsworth.org/farmshop. The farm shop is a gastronomic paradise for foodies, with its quality butchery, bakery, creamery, greengrocers and delicatessen. Some 60% of the quality produce is produced or prepared on the Chatsworth Estate – and much of the rest is sourced from Derbyshire farms and food producers. The popular café behind, with wonderful views over to Edensor and Chatsworth Estate, serves seasonal, locally produced dishes in line with the farm shop.

Edensor Tea Cottage DE45 1PH ✆ 01246 582315 ⌂ www.edensorteacottage.co.uk. This is a charming, rustic licensed café in Edensor. Snacks and lunches are served, but it's the cakes that are truly irresistible.

Devonshire Arms, **Pilsley** (DE45 1UL ✆ 01246 583258 ⌂ www.devonshirepilsley.co.uk) **& Beeley** (DE4 2NR ✆ 01629 733259). Both are rustic but contemporary Chatsworth inns, and both under shared management and serving good quality food – much of it locally sourced. The pubs pride themselves on their hand-pulled, locally brewed ales. I love the bartering service both pubs offer – free beer in exchange for home-grown vegetables. Both inns also offer tastefully furnished rooms. Be prepared to pay Chatsworth prices.

The Old Smithy tearoom and shop Chapel Hill, Beeley DE4 2ND ✆ 01629 258927 ☺ closed Mon. Who can resist a hearty Angler's, Apprentice's and Blacksmith's breakfast, or the healthier Fruits of the Forest breakfast? I can vouch for the lunches too in this tastefully restored building. While there you can pick up a few food items, locally sourced, from their shop.

ROWSLEY TO BIRCHOVER

Prehistoric rock art, Bronze Age stone circles, a medieval manor house and a Victorian mill are just some of the historical landmarks that lie between Rowsley and Birchover. This is an exciting and diverse landscape of immense historical interest that moves between inky woodland to colour-washed moorland, interspersed with curiously shaped and isolated outcrops.

11 ROWSLEY

🏠 **Congreave Farm B&B** (page 241), **The Peacock at Rowsley** (page 241)

At Rowsley the River Wye and River Derwent kiss before continuing their journey together southward. Rowsley has been in the domain of Haddon Hall since feudal times, passing through the Vernon and Manners families as reflected in the elegant town houses and backstreet artisan cottages, along with the 17th-century **Peacock Inn**, now a luxury boutique hotel.

The village forms a Y-shape around the confluence of the Wye and Derwent Rivers. **Little Rowsley**, straddling the Chatsworth Road, shooting off to the left. It's in this part of Rowsley that Chatsworth Estate made its mark, not Haddon Hall. Here Paxton built an Italianate railway station, but came unstuck when the Duke of Devonshire decided he didn't want a railway running through his grounds in the Derwent Valley after all. Fortunately, the other Duke associated with Rowsley, the Duke of Rutland, came to the rescue by agreeing to have the railway rerouted through his estate along the Wye Valley. The upshot of this was that Paxton's elegant station was left stranded in the wrong valley. Nowadays the railway building makes a pleasing centre point (and a curious one for those who don't know the history of the building) in **Peak Village**, a retail outlet centre.

Caudwell's Mill

Rowsley DE4 2EB ✐ 01629 734374 ✆ www.caudwellsmill.co.uk ☉ shop: 09.00–17.00; mill: 10.00–17.00

On the other side of A6 from Peak Village, you'll find Caudwell's Mill with its working museum, designer studios and workshops, craft shop and café. There has been a mill at Caudwell since medieval times, but the mill standing today was built by a Victorian named John Caudwell in 1874. The mill continues to operate, selling quality flour to visitors and local businesses. The museum, a series of interconnecting rooms, corridors and floors stacked with unfamiliar machinery and objects, can be overwhelming. It takes a little perseverance to untangle the belts and pulleys from the Archimedean screws and elevators, along with the sifters, graders, rollers and purifiers, in order to come to grips with the entire process of flour-making from grist to powder. Around the mill, cobbled pathways are lined with little workshops and studios, from the **jewellery gallery, glass studio** and **mill forge** to a carpentry business designing furniture from recycled wood. A wooden shed opposite the mill that once stored sacks of grain is now a **craft shop** crammed to the rafters with tempting wares. **Caudwell's Mill café**, a lovely wooden building (its timber taken from an old Scottish mill), sits on the bank of the River Wye with the wooded crest of Peak Tor above it, like a scene from a naïve painting. Ducks and swans invariably float by, and if you're lucky, you just might see a kingfisher skimming the water.

12 HADDON HALL

Bakewell ℐ 01629 812855 ◊ www.haddonhall.co.uk ☉ Apr–Christmas

Lady Jane Grey, The Princess Bride, Jane Eyre, The Princess and the Pauper, Elizabeth, Pride and Prejudice and *The Other Boleyn Girl*: they've all been filmed at Haddon Hall. The stately home – one of the finest examples of a mostly unaltered medieval manor house in the country, is found on the A6 between Bakewell and Rowsley. On the day I arrived, just a couple of weeks before Christmas, I could see why it's a favoured location for period dramas and films. With the medieval hall's dramatic hilltop position, the little humpbacked bridge and the River Wye tripping its way eastward, it's a hopelessly romantic setting. At the gated entrance above, I could see Lord and Lady Edward Manners, her ankle-length skirt billowing in the wind. Admittedly, the owners of Haddon Hall are not usually at hand to 'greet' visitors – I'd just arrived on the day of a photo shoot.

Inside, steps lead up to a stone-flagged courtyard. Gill, friend and Haddon Hall guide, took me into the chapel, a fusty corner-building of quiet beauty and sanctuary. The focal point of the chapel is the effigy to the nine-year-old Lord Haddon, lovingly sculpted by his mourning mother, Violet, Duchess of Rutland. The boy, pale and unblemished in smooth alabaster, looks as if he's just fallen asleep. All around him, the rough white-washed walls are covered in 14th-century faded patterns and paintings, including three skeletons on one wall, grinning manically.

Across the courtyard, the fire in **The Great Hall** is blazing and the Christmas tree is decorated. This is a particularly lovely time to visit Haddon Hall, which doesn't have the large-scale commercialisation of Chatsworth. There's a fine **Minstrel's Gallery** to one side of the room. Gill tells me Shakespeare's father performed here. There's also a manacle and lock in the room, once used to shackle any guest who didn't down their tipple fast enough, the remains of the drink

"The focal point of the chapel is the effigy to the nine-year-old Lord Haddon, lovingly sculpted by his mourning mother."

poured down their sleeve, so the story goes. The dining room behind the Great Hall is still used from time to time to entertain the owners' guests, presumably without the use of the manacle. Opposite the Great Hall, the **Tudor kitchens** are laid out as they would have been in times of yore.

A GUIDE'S STORY OF HADDON HALL

Gill Shimwell is an actor, storyteller and writer, as well as guide at Haddon Hall. She talks about her relationship with the manor house and the people who visit it.

I love Haddon Hall because the family that put the stones down in the 1200s are still the same family here today. The family moved out in the 1700s for 200 years to go and live at Belvoir Castle, leaving the house as if they'd just walked out the door. Anything they weren't interested in was considered old junk and left to gain worms and dust at Haddon, but now it is considered a great collection of early Tudor furniture. There's something wonderful about pushing back those great doors – the original doors George Vernon put in. Everything's quite hefty; chains rattle, and there are times when a gale blows through. You stand there, welcoming people, packing in a little bit of humour, answering questions, giving information and in they go.

I also love meeting the people who are old enough to have memories of their own childhood in an old farmhouse, or as a carpenter or blacksmith, and they identify with Haddon Hall because it doesn't have the grandeur of a later stately house. Then there are the extra things that go on: the Tudor groups and musicians, who come and cook, make things, play instruments or do a dance. I especially love it after a special event when everyone's gone home. It's nearly midnight, all's quiet, the fires are dying down, and it's just us clearing up. It's like being backstage before the sets are painted and the fire buckets are put in place – there's that feeling of the real thing. It's certainly an anchorage for me.

When guiding, some of the visitors are hot on architecture, dates or kings, but I like the stories. I love the way everything weaves together: the writing, storytelling, theatre; the imagination. When you look at the history of the Peak District, the mining communities or cottage lives, you find stories which are significant, moving and frightening. And you begin to understand why the made-up stories are so powerful – dealing with the unseen parts of life, when life was dark and houses were dimly lit and you wanted to be safe as you walked home. The Peak District, like Haddon Hall, is a place full of atmosphere.

Upstairs, the **Long Gallery** panelled in Haddon oak stretches out along the side of the house with views to the Elizabethan gardens below. The ladies of the house paced up and down the gallery (the 'gym' of the day), not caring to expose their pale skin to the outside sunlight. Further on are two more rooms adorned in tapestries rich in detail. From this corner of the house, steps lead down to the formal gardens, planned by renowned garden designer, Arne Maynard, and best viewed in summer when the roses and clematis are in bloom.

13 STANTON IN PEAK

Stanton in Peak, viewed from the A6 south of Rowsley and Haddon Hall, is a scene of particular rural loveliness, set among rolling estate parkland. This genteel village centred round **Stanton Hall** is home to the Thornhill family and possesses some of the finest 17th- and 18th-century homes in the Peak District, some initialled WPT (after William Paul Thornhill). Of these, the elegant **Holly House** is particularly interesting, with some of its sashed windows filled in to reduce the hefty window tax of 1697. Visit **Stanton in Peak Open Gardens** (page 11) if possible, to appreciate the tucked-away alleyways and colourful cottage gardens. Finish off with a pint of the best in the old-fashioned pub, **The Flying Childers**, so-called after an all-conquering 18th-century racehorse owned by the Duke of Devonshire.

14 BIRCHOVER

⋏ Barn Farm Campsite (page 241)

Birchover makes a good striking out point for Stanton Moor and the Nine Ladies Stone Circle, or to the craggy rocks of Cratcliff Tor and Robin Hood's Stride. But it's worth pausing for a while in this attractive village – a linear development flanked by birches on a ridge (as its name suggests). Take time to wander down the side lane beside the Druid's Inn to Rowtor and Jesus Chapel, built by Thomas Eyre.

The mysterious world of Rowtor Rocks

Few know of this magical place hidden behind **Druid's Inn** at the western edge of Birchover. From the lane beside the pub, a public footpath sign unceremoniously points to a muddy track of weeds. You will have to push your way upwards in summer and duck the brambles and nettles. It's worth the effort though: on turning a corner, there's a jumble of caves, tunnels and precariously stacked slabs of stone. Among the rocks are carved-out staircases, scooped-out rooms and alcoves, as well as chiselled-out benches and chairs. Some of the rocks are engraved with mysterious swirls and symbols.

The hewn steps, rooms and chairs were carved by an 18th-century vicar, Thomas Eyre. He saw Rowtor Rocks as his very own playground; a place to be creative and contemplative too. From one of the chairs he'd carved from the rock, he'd view the hills and dales spread out below him, drawing inspiration for his sermons.

Rambling through Birchover & Stanton Moor

❊ OS Explorer map OL24; start: Druid Inn, ♥ SK236622; 2 miles; fairly easy, with one short sharp climb up on to the ridge & mostly level walking on Stanton Moor

The magnificent circular walk on Stanton Moor via Birchover is filled with points of interest along the way. The highlight, of course, is the Nine Ladies Standing Stones, while the Earl Grey Tower makes for an interesting detour. It's also worth hunting out the strangely formed cairns, or glacial erratics, dotted round the edge: the Duke of York (with a 'Y 1826' and a crown etched on to the surface), Cat Stone, Duchess of Sutherland, Gorse Stone, Heart Stone and Andle Stone. If you're feeling agile, you can attempt the Cork Stone with footholds and metal grips in place to aid the climber. Refreshments available at Birchover.

A path directly opposite the **Druid Inn** leads steeply upwards on to the ridge behind the village. It's a slow upward slog to the Stone Works car park exit. A left turn out of the car park and on to the main road leads past the stone works and quarry to a public footpath sign on the right, pointing the way to Stanton Moor. The curious Cork Stone is found at the top of the path. Another left turn and a well-trodden path crosses the moor past abandoned quarries before dropping through birch trees. Keeping right, the walker comes out into a clearing wherein stands the **Nine Ladies Stone Circle**.

At the information board beside the stone circle, an adjacent path slopes downwards towards the edge of Stanton Moor. Sitting on the edge of the ridge is a squat, angular stone tower,

The etched symbols, however, are prehistoric rock art. There are five of them in all, appearing faintly in the weathered gritstone. It's difficult to know what the symbols represent: The zigzag line – a snake? The wing-like curve – a bird? A series of touching curves – the petals of a flower? There are cup marks and rings, and the clearly defined shape of a cross. Rowtor feels like a scene from *Lord of the Rings*.

The Nine Ladies Stone Circle

Just a short walk from the top of Birchover village, you'll find the Nine Ladies on Stanton Moor, an impressive sight on the hillside, shrouded in mystery and mythology. The Nine Ladies refers to nine stones, but a tenth stone was actually uncovered in 1976.

One of the stories surrounding the ancient site will make you think carefully about dancing on the Sabbath: the nine ladies, along with

Earl Grey Tower. The tower was built by the Thornhill family of Stanton Hall. Rising out of Stanton Moor Plantation, it's an incongruous sight in this area of wilderness. The tower was constructed in 1832 to commemorate one of the most important bills ever passed in British history – giving every man the right to vote. It was Charles Grey, the second Earl Grey and Prime Minister of the time, who pushed through the reform bill with the help of public pressure despite stiff parliamentary opposition, particularly in the House of Lords.

Not far from the Earl Grey Tower is **Stanton Moor Edge**, purchased by the National Trust to protect it from further quarrying. Make time to climb the stile into the National Trust land. The views are extensive and it's fun to scrabble among the rocks, hunting out the strangely shaped erratics and the inscribed stones. **Gorse Stone** is an elevated platform that was used by the Druids to address their people, while the **Duchess of Sunderland Stone** is inscribed with a coronet and 'HS 1830.' Back near the Earl Grey Tower, you'll find the **Cat Stone** with the inscription 'EIN 1831.' Like many of the other rocks, including the Cork Screw, it has steps cut into the sides of the soft rock.

From Stanton Moor Edge, the path heads downhill to the road. After a short section of uphill climbing, a signposted left turn points the way to **Barn Farm**. The chances are that you'll see a couple of peacocks on the farmhouse roof, or a handful of alpacas grazing in a field as you skirt the farm. From the end of the farm lane, it's a short walk back down into Birchover.

their fiddler, were turned to stone on Stanton Moor for ignoring the fourth Commandment – *Remember the Sabbath Day*. It's a nice explanation for the nine small, upright stones set in a circle with its additional 'king stone' (the fiddler) some 40 yards further back. The stone circle is actually an ancient burial site, created in prehistoric times, around 4,000 years ago. Here rituals and ceremonies marked the daily routines of life and work, the changing seasons and the circular nature of human life: fertility, birth and death. Indeed, dancing was probably part and parcel of those ancient rituals. It remains a popular site with modern-day pagans who come here to celebrate the summer solstice. They continue the tradition of ancient worship with their offerings of crystals, flowers and food. The small stone circle may not have the scale or majesty of Stonehenge, but it still conveys a sense of mystery and beauty in this lonely spot surrounded by moor and birch.

¶¶ FOOD & DRINK

The Druid Inn (Main St, DE4 2BL ✆ 01629 653836) is a stylish pub serving locally sourced food. Further along the village, the **Red Lion** (Main St, DE4 2BN ✆ 01629 650363) is run by Sardinian-born Matteo and his English wife. Sardinian evenings are on offer along with weekly Sunday night music sessions (it's a joy to hear Matteo play the Sardinian pipes). Despite its Italian ownership, the establishment remains the quintessential British pub of oak beams and roaring fires in winter. Plans are afoot to extend the business to include a dairy, with the micro-brewery (producing Bircher Best) already up and running. Check out Matteo's delicious Birchover Blue cheese (available to buy on occasion).

Cratcliff Tor & the Hermit's Cave

Cratcliff Tor and its surroundings have a haunting beauty. From the scattered rocks and tumble-tower tors to the medieval hermitage and the prehistoric enclosures connected by the ancient Portway, you can feel the hand of history here.

You'll find Cratcliff Tor just off the B5056, west of Birchover (♀ SK229619). The 172 bus service between Bakewell and Matlock halts right at the bottom of the lane leading up to the tor. Ask for the Dudwood Farm stop. There's also a lay-by with parking for a handful of cars nearby. The lane, signposted the Limestone Way, heads uphill towards Cratcliff Tor and Robin Hood's Stride. The farm track veers right to Cratcliff Cottage, but the Limestone Way continues straight up over the grass.

The Cratcliff Tor path is found next to 'Hilary's seat' (a bench), where there's a sign for 'occupation path'. Through the gate, the path heads along the wooded escarpment before dropping slightly downhill to **Hermit's Cave**. The cave, more of an overhang really, is flanked by yews and enclosed with a black metal railing. Its wall is carved with a medieval carving of the crucifixion. Next to it, there's an alcove, for a candle perhaps, while the low-lying shelf of rock was probably the hermit's bed. Little is known about the hermit, apart from a couple of possible references to him found in the Haddon Hall kitchen documents of 1549. One records a payment to 'ye harmytt' for 10 rabbits, while the other refers to 'Ye Cratcliffe Hermitte', and lists a payment of fourpence made to him for guiding travellers safely to Haddon.

Above Hermit's Cave, a path leads to the top of the crags where you can stand on the wide, flat platforms of rock that drop vertically to the cottage below. Venture out on to them if you dare. The views are dizzying – as are the drops.

Robin Hood's Stride & Nine Stones

A little further up the Limestone Way, a stile on the left leads to Robin Hood's Stride. On a crisp, frosty morning, I could see why Robin Hood's Stride is also known locally as Mock Beggar Hall. Through the shifting mist, defused with winter sunlight, it looked like a rambling castle or a fortification, with its pillars of rock and great walls of gritstone. In explanation of its better-known name, Robin Hood's Stride, the story goes that the bandit strode between the two pillars of rock, positioned almost ten feet apart at either end of the rocky outcrop – making Robin Hood a man of very long legs, or great athletic agility. For us mere mortals, the scramble to the top of the tor is not too difficult – although the ridged tower, looking like an egg-slicer on top of the rocky outcrop, will be beyond the mettle of most.

Robin Hood's Stride is the place to reconnect with your inner child; where you can leap from stone to stone and squeeze between and under blocks of gritstone. And when you've run out of breath, you can choose your rock, sit back and watch the boulderers, or enjoy the solitude if you come at a quieter time. Back on the Limestone Way, head further up the rise towards fields where the **Nine Stones** can be seen, another ancient stone circle. The name is a bit of a misnomer as only four are visible. On the day I visited, the stones were particularly atmospheric (despite the bizarre positioning of the farmer's trailer in the centre of the circle) with views back to Robin Hood's Stride, appearing and disappearing in the mist.

"On the day I visited, the stones were particularly atmospheric with views back to Robin Hood's Stride, appearing and disappearing in the mist."

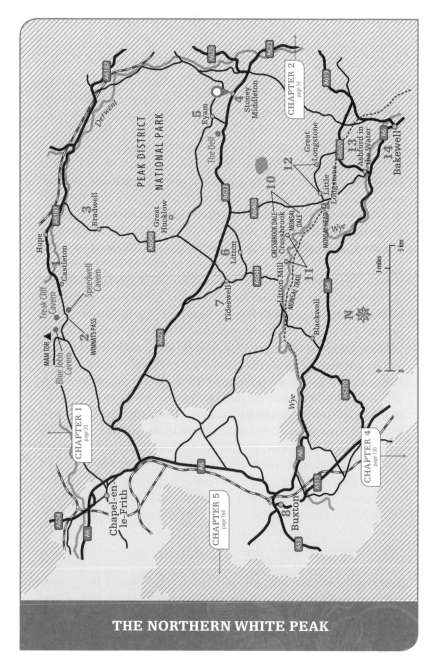

THE NORTHERN WHITE PEAK

CHAPTER 1
page 20

CHAPTER 2
page 56

CHAPTER 4
page 130

CHAPTER 5
page 164

PEAK DISTRICT
NATIONAL PARK

MAM TOR
Blue John Cavern
Treak Cliff Cavern
WINNATS PASS
Speedwell Cavern
Castleton
Hope
Bradwell
Great Hucklow
The Delf
Eyam
Stoney Middleton
Great Longstone
Little Longstone
MONSAL HEAD
MONSAL DALE
CRESSBROOK DALE
Cressbrook
Litton Mill
MONSAL TRAIL
Litton
Tideswell
Blackwell
Ashford in the Water
Bakewell
Buxton
Chapel-en-le-Frith

Derwent
Wye
Wye

A6187
A625
A623
A619
A6
A6020
A6187
A6049
A6
A623
A6465
A6440
A623
A53
A515
A6
A515
A6
A5270
A624
A6

N

3 miles
5 km
0
0

1
2
3
4
5
6
7
8
9
10
11
12
13
14

3

THE NORTHERN
WHITE PEAK

Limestone is smothered beneath gritstone on the Dark and White Peak boundary, and great caverns lie hidden beneath the rock near the town of **Castleton**, inviting exploration. From here gritstone gives way to the limestone plateaus that sweep south and eastward in this part of the northern White Peak, a landscape chequered with dry stone walls and criss-crossed with public rights of way and old packhorse trails. Between the uplands there are deep incisions, as if some giant had taken a knife and slashed the surface of the earth. These dales, flanked by walls of grassland and rocky escarpments, are largely uninhabited by humans, but are rich in wildlife. A few bear the stamp of man, lined with watermills and workers' cottages. Above the dales, attractive villages of stone buildings huddle together in the patchwork of fields, or isolated farmsteads sit caught in the dips of the undulating landscape. This area is encircled by roads and settlements that cut through the wider valleys or sit on the plateaus: **Bradwell** and **Great Hucklow** to the east; **Tideswell**, **Litton**, **Eyam** and **Stoney Middleton** straddling the A623. The isolated communities are brought together by the lively market town of **Bakewell** to the south and the elegant spa of **Buxton** to the west, linked by the A6. Connecting the towns and villages is a vast network of pathways offering walks of great diversity and beauty. The northern White Peak is a wonderful place to explore on foot.

WALKING & CYCLING

Some of the loveliest and quietest dales are to be found in this area: Cressbrook, Miller's, Chee, Tideswell and Monk's dales; Monsal and Deep dales and Lathkill, to name but a few. Combine them with quaint Peak villages such as Cressbrook, Litton, the Longstones and Tideswell for variety and interest. For cyclists (and horseriders), the Monsal Trail

i TOURIST INFORMATION

Castleton Buxton Rd, S33 8WP ✆ 01433 620679
Buxton Pavilion Gardens, St John's Rd, SK17 6KN ✆ 01298 25106
Bakewell The Old Market Hall, Bridge St, DE45 1DS ✆ 01629 816558

is within easy reach of Buxton and is one of the most picturesque cycle trails in the UK. For road cyclists, there are plenty of single-track roads, virtually empty of traffic. Simply consult the map and plot your route.

⸙ CYCLE HIRE

Blackwell Cycle Hire ⬙ www.peakblackwellcyclehire.com. Parking at Wyedale car park SK17 9TE (bus stop opposite at Topley Pike quarry entrance).
Hassop Station Cycle Hire DE45 1NW ✆ 01629 810588 ⬙ www.hassopstation.co.uk/cycle-hire ◔ all year

AROUND CASTLETON

It's with good reason that **Castleton** is called the Gem in the Peaks. From the ruins of **Peveril Castle**, standing sentry over the village, to the sweeping line of The Great Ridge connecting the foreboding wall of **Mam Tor** with Rushup Edge (page 44), this is a dramatic setting. Add to the mix a series of impressive show caves that lie on the edge of the town, a curiously abandoned 'broken road' and the drama of the **Winnats Pass** gorge (once a coral reef), and Castleton shouldn't be left off the visitor's itinerary.

To Slow right down though, slip off the Hope Valley Road on to the B6049 and explore **Bradwell** (of ice cream fame) with its hinterland of sleepy villages and winding country roads – including the skyline ridge route along Back Lane to the highest pub in Derbyshire.

1 CASTLETON

🏠 Rambler's Rest Guest House (page 242), **YHA Losehill Hall** (page 242)
Four exciting show caves surround Castleton village, two of which lie under **Treak Cliff Hill**. Here the semi-precious **Blue John** stone (only found in this one location worldwide) is still occasionally mined before being carted down to Castleton, where it's cut, crafted and polished, then sold in the town's jewellery and gem shops.

Before hitting the caves or shops, it's a good idea to head for the **visitor centre** in the village. Apart from the opportunity to arm yourself with information leaflets, there's a small museum that will give you a potted history of the area from the geological development of the landscape to the people who live and work in it: the miners, farmers and everyone else in between. The section focused on Castleton through the seasons showcases the village as a delightful year round destination. But if possible, visit the town on Garland Day (also known as Oak Apple, Shick-shack or Arbour day – take your pick). This ancient festival takes place at the end of May, when the Garlanded King leads a procession on horseback with his female escort through the village. Christmas in Castleton is also atmospheric, with carols in the caves and the village decked out in festive lights and decorations.

Peveril Castle

Market Place S33 8WQ ✆ 01433 620613 ⊖ Apr–Sep; English Heritage

With its crumbling stone and great arched windows, the atmospheric ruin of Peveril Castle is one of England's earliest Norman fortresses. The site was founded sometime after the Norman Conquest of 1066. The castle is named after William Peveril, the King's agent for the Royal Forest of the Peak – basically one big hunting playground created for the pleasure of the royal family. The castle was the administrative centre for the large estate and a base for visiting monarchs, although ironically they rarely if ever visited. The ruin of the stone **keep** that stands today was built by Henry II in 1176. Only a partial shell remains of the original, but there's enough to give the visitor a good idea of what the castle was like. Tucked away in one corner of the keep, there's a garderobe – a medieval toilet, a hole that drops away to ground far below it. Judging by the less than sweet aroma, modern-day visitors have been trying it out. History apart, it's well worth the effort of making the steep ascent to the castle for the extensive and rather lovely views over to Cavedale, Castleton, the Hope Valley, Mam Tor and the wider Dark Peak.

THE CASTLETON CAVERNS

The four show caves above Castleton are the biggest draw to the area (along with its outdoor pursuits). Each cave has its own individual character and all of them have their unique selling point: Blue John for its drama and scale; Treak Cliff for its beauty; Speedwell for its atmospheric boat trip; and Peak Cavern (The Devil's Arse) for its grand entrance and history. A combined ticket for Speedwell and The Devil's Arse will shave off some of the cost.

Blue John Cavern

Mam Tor S33 8WA ⌂ www.bluejohn-cavern.co.uk ✆ 01433 620638 ⊙ all year

The small unassuming shack on **Treak Cliff Hill** at the top of the 'broken road' (page 100) does little to herald what lies beneath: a great chasm of rock that descends over 200 feet into the belly of the Earth. Here the meltwater of the inter-glacial periods sliced through the limestone, leaving the imprint of swirling, cascading waters. Ripples spread out across the cavern walls, while curtains of flowstone spill to the cave floor. There are smooth sculpted curves where water once circled whirlpools, and in one place a great boulder is wedged in a fissure that was swept along by the force of the glacial waters. The rock formations may be impressive (although there are no stalactites of any significance), but it's the sprinkling of unique Blue John mineral (see page 94) that draws visitors to the cave with its striking bands of the blue-purple and yellow mineral. Nowadays, the Blue John miners continue to trudge their weary way through the cave system, tramping almost 250 steps downwards and back up again – day in, day out; year in, year out. Their job is mainly to transport visitors rather than Blue John these days, but a trolley, windlass and bellows left beside old workings are a reminder of the cave's original function. The steps follow the course of the dried-up riverbed through six natural chambers. It's in the **Variegated Cavern** towards the bottom that the full force of nature is evident, its water-sculpted walls and ceiling scalloped, fluted, grooved and etched. Below the **Viewing Platform**, the dried-up riverbed, strewn with boulders and rocks, plunges downwards through the **Great Hall** before disappearing into the darkness beyond. Ultimately, it's the sheer scale and power of nature that merits a visit to this cave, not the traces of Blue John.

Treak Cliff Cavern

Buxton Rd, S33 8WP ✆ 01433 620571 ⌂ www.bluejohnstone.com

Treak Cliff Cavern sits in the lower part of the same hillside, below the 'broken road', the only other cave of the four to contain the unique Blue John. It's a long hike up steep steps to the entrance of the site, a rough-and-ready building cobbled together with stone, wood, cement and galvanised corrugated iron. From here, a steep and featureless passageway leads to a series of spectacular and varied caves, making the arduous trudge worthwhile. The **Witch's Cave** has large deposits of the sought-after Blue John, including **The Pillar**, worth millions of pounds. As the cavern's *pièce de résistance*, it will never be removed – and if it were, the cave would collapse. Further along, **Aladdin's Cave** is an explosion of colour with its cascading sheets of flowstone: white calcite combined with orange-tinted iron, green copper and black lead. In **Fairyland**, stumpy stalagmites mushrooming from the floor contrast with the delicate stalactites that hang suspended from the ceiling like tapered candles on their ends. Further on in **Dream Cave**, you can give free rein to your imagination. Visitors see different things: a crucifix or elephant; a stork standing on one leg; the head of a curly sheep, trout or a dragon. In one place a stalagmite (nearly four feet in length) and a stalactite almost meet, with just over an inch between them. The phrase 'so near and yet so far' has never seemed so appropriate – for it will take hundreds and hundreds of years before the tiny gap closes and forms a column. The cave system finishes in the grandly named **Dome of St Paul's**, not unjustified, for in this cavernous space the almost luminous stalactites drape from the cave in glowing opulence.

Speedwell Cavern
Winnats Pass, S33 8WA ☎ 01433 623018 🖥 www.speedwellcavern.co.uk

'Now that the door is closed, you're doomed,' the guide said. This was his opening gambit, and set the tone for Speedwell's main selling point: an eerie boat-trip through a long, dark, flooded underground tunnel; a kind of stripped-back, watery version of a fairground ghost train. You'll find this atmospheric manmade cave at the bottom of scenic Winnats Pass.

Having negotiated the steps and climbed into the boat, our guide warned us, 'If you're claustrophobic, scared of the dark, scared of water – or all three, you're done for.' No-one bailed out and the boat departed, bumping its way along the tunnel, the roof inches from our head. The horizontal passageway was blasted by the Speedwell miners in their hunt for lead. It was, as it turned out, a wasted expenditure of energy: the miners worked the cave system for 21 years only to make a loss of £11,000 – a lot of money in the 18th century.

Crashing along the dimly lit tunnel, the guide described the abysmal working conditions for the men and small children who worked the mine. At **Halfway House**, we pulled into a lay-by to allow for another boat's passing. 'We set off 21 weeks ago with 12 people. Now we've got five,' the ghostly voice from the boat floated across to us. The young guides clearly enjoy the banter, and a chance to spice up their scripts with macabre jokes.

The natural Speedwell Cavern above you at the end of the adit is somewhat featureless – but with a height of around 200 feet, it has a cathedral-like presence. Below, a deep vertical shaft called the **Bottomless Pit** once dropped 500 feet – until it was filled in by the rock spoils dumped there by miners. As it turns out, the bottomless pit is a mere 36 feet deep these days.

Peak Cavern – The Devil's Arse

Castleton S33 8WS ℘ 01433 620285 ⚲ www.peakcavern.co.uk

I prefer the original name for Peak Cavern – the colourful Devil's Arse, but the public relations people of Queen Victoria's day clearly panicked when Her Majesty announced her intended visit, and swiftly changed the name to the more boring, albeit politer Peak Cavern.

The approach to Peak Cavern from Castleton's **Goosehill** along the cottage-lined gorge is delightful, but when you turn the corner to the massive cave entrance, it's quite a sight. The cave mouth is the largest in Britain at around 60 feet high and 100 feet wide. There may not be much in the way of stalactites and stalagmites, or impressive rock formations, but you can feel the hand of history here. A whole community of rope-makers lived just inside the entrance for approximately 400 years, manufacturing rope for the local mining industry. Nowadays, guides demonstrate how the ropes were made before leading visitors on through the cave, explaining the reason for the cavern's original name. It transpires that when the cave drains of water after flooding, it emits strange sounds rather like flatulence. Back in the day, folks believed the further you descended into the bowels of the earth, the closer you came to the underworld and the devil – in this case with serious digestion issues.

Given its grandiose scale, Peak Cavern is a popular set location for films and TV adaptations. A few props have been left lying around as mementos, including a Father Christmas looking the worse for wear and slowly morphing into the Grim Reaper. Best of all, though, is the

CHRIS MILLNER, NATIONAL TRUST RANGER

Driving up the winding road to the top of Winnats Pass, Chris Millner says to me 'I'm from Castleton so Winnats Pass and Mam Tor are close to my heart. Everything comes together here where the limestone meets the gritstone. Then there's the geology, archaeology and history written into this landscape: The Bronze Age hillfort at Mam Tor, the ancient Odin Mine here and Peveril Castle down in the valley.' Chris swings into one of the National Trust-owned farms at the head of the ravine and we stride out on to the hillside. It's a dramatic spot with the land falling away to the valley floor and Castleton in the far distance. 'I love the beauty of the Peak District landscape,' says Chris. 'But it's more than that to me as a ranger. I see the mosaic of landscapes and the processes that are taking place: the regeneration or decay of woodlands; an area of white moorland that was covered in heather a hundred years ago; the reseeding of flower meadows.' We drop down the side of Winnats Pass. Below, a matchbox car snakes up the ravine.

Chris shows me bands of Blue John on a rocky outcrop and the secured metal entrance to an old mine.

'I wouldn't do anything else,' Chris reflects. 'I love the creative and practical sides of the job: constructing a gate or stile; repairing paths; planting trees – helping nature along. It's great to chat to the ramblers too, curious about what we're doing. We try to increase their understanding of the National Trust and the wildlife; maybe they find out about a more unusual species of bird, such as the ring ouzel that nests in the crags here. Then there are the volunteers who want to give something back into the countryside, and once they start they find out just how enjoyable it is. They might help build a wall that will be here in two hundred years, or plant a tree that'll be here in three or four hundred.' As we head back up towards the farm, I hear a sweet piping sound. 'Meadow pipits,' Chris says as they fly across our vision in a jerky flight. I'm also gaining a more intimate knowledge of the Peak District.

long winding slide at the end of the cave, used in the TV adaptation of *The Chronicles of Narnia*. I was itching to wing my way down it. Sadly it's not an option open to visitors.

¶ FOOD & DRINK

1530 Cross St, S33 8WH ✎ 01433 621870. The 1530 refers to the age of the building in this British, Italian-influenced restaurant offering a value-for-money menu. Try the Devil's Arse pizza if you dare.

Rose Cottage Café Cross St, S33 8WH ✎ 0114 258 2705 ☺ open for breakfast, lunch or brunch. This is the place to go for a cream tea on a sunny day with its comfortable outdoor seating set in a delightful garden.

The Causeway Shop Back St, S33 8WE ✆ 01433 620343. All-day breakfasts (including gluten-free bread), freshly made sandwiches and cream teas are on offer, with a shop of enticing wares to ponder as you eat.

Ye Old Nag's Head Cross St, S33 8WH ✆ 01433 620248. A good choice of beers and decent food are served in this traditional pub with contemporary furnishings. Eat on a Saturday night and you can combine your meal with live music, or round off your evening on a Friday night by taking part in the quiz or bingo game.

2 WINNATS PASS

One of the most dramatic sections of road in the Peak District (and a particular favourite with athletic cyclists) Winnats Pass winds its way up through a deep ravine of scalloped hills and towering limestone pinnacles. The hillsides on either side of the road were once coral reefs – remnants of a time when Derbyshire lay under the ocean. In more recent history (1758), a pair of young elopers, Allan and Clara, making their way to the Peak Forest (the Gretna Green of the Peak District back then) were robbed and murdered by three miners here. It's said their spirits still haunt Winnats Pass, and if you listen carefully through the wind and the rain, you can hear their plaintive voices pleading for their lives. It's certainly a dark, brooding place when the weather closes in and the wind whistles down the gap. With the closure of the A625 below Mam Tor (page 46) Winnats Pass is the only westbound route out of Castleton.

THE ABANDONED MAM TOR ROAD

In 1819 the Sheffield Turnpike Company constructed the A625 between Sheffield and Chapel-en-le-Frith. A section of the road wound its way down the lower slopes of Mam Tor (page 48), traversing the path of the landslip in two places. It was a confident and determined choice of routing – or an arrogant and foolhardy one. For the next 160 years or so, a constant battle ensued between man and nature; the road repeatedly damaged, repaired, destroyed; reconstructed and destroyed again – with layers of tarmac and gravel extending to nearly seven feet in places. In 1977, when there was yet another landslide, the road had to be reduced to single-lane traffic. Finally in 1979, the engineers sensibly surrendered to Mam Tor: 'Mother Hill,' and indeed Mother Nature, was not to be messed with. Mam Tor Road was closed for good, the traffic rerouted to the more stable Winnats Pass. Today 'the broken road' is enjoyed by walkers, who marvel at the great drops and cracks in the tarmac. Head up through the meadows from Castleton to reach the doomed road.

3 BRADWELL & AROUND

⚲ Brosterfield Farm Cottages (page 242)

Bradwell is a name familiar to icecream lovers. Less known is the sprawling White Peak village that gave it its name, found on the cusp of the Dark Peak between Hope and Tideswell. Here Grandma Hannah, a lady of great determination and enterprise, created her butter-rich ice cream recipes by hand in her small kitchen without electricity (the ice brought in by train from Sheffield) before going on to sell the ice cream all over Derbyshire. Grandma Hannah is long gone, but the original Grandma Hannah's parlour kitchen still exists and continues to serve ice cream.

In truth, there is little other reason to come to Bradwell. It's a rambling village with a mish-mash of architectural styles, but it has a strong community with some of the friendliest people I've encountered in the region. Typical of the Peak District mining villages, it's crosscut with little lanes and jitties that lead out on to the hills.

Great Hucklow above Bradwell, once famous for its Playhouse, is now known for its gliding club, while east of Great Hucklow the **Barrel Inn** in **Bretton** lays claim to being Derbyshire's highest pub. To reach the inn from Great Hucklow, follow the narrow turnpike road, Back Lane, along Hucklow Edge. Here the land drops away on either side to reveal uplands of dry stone walls, the long, ruler-straight lines like an abstract Kandinsky of greys and greens. To really appreciate this scenic road, it's best walked or biked. The Barrel Inn, sitting on the White and Dark Peak boundary, has extensive views – across five counties on a clear day. Backtracking along Back Lane, this time take the lower road to **Foolow** with its chocolate-box setting centred round the village greens, perfectly rounded duck pond, bijou church and handsome stone houses.

"The Barrel Inn, sitting on the White and Dark Peak boundary, has extensive views – across five counties on a clear day."

The teensy-weensy **St Hugh's Church**, originally a smithy, was purchased by the local population in 1888 so that they wouldn't have to make the trudge to neighbouring Eyam. Inside, I found a kettle, biscuits, tea and coffee, along with a note inviting me to help myself in exchange for a small church donation. It seemed like a good deal to me: a cuppa in the tranquillity of this sweet little church.

🍴 FOOD & DRINK

The Bakehouse Netherside, Bradwell S33 9JL ✆ 01433 621254. Friendly, value-for-money establishment selling a range of sandwiches and lunchtime meals, cakes and hot drinks. There are a couple of tables inside, although most food is sold for take-away.

Grandma Hannah's Parlour Kitchen Bradwell's Dairy Ice Cream, Worthy Court, Bradwell S33 9LB ✆ 01433 621646 ⊙ May–Sep 14.00–17.00 daily, including bank holidays & at w/ ends between Easter & Spring Bank Holiday. See page 101.

Samuel Fox Country Inn Stretfield Rd, Bradwell S33 9JT ✆ 01433 621562. Excellent gourmet food with prices to match in this inn that pays homage to the inventor of the modern metal-ribbed umbrella. **Barrel Inn** Bretton S32 5QD ✆ 01433 630856. Fresh, nicely cooked local produce and well-kept beers are on offer in this cosy pub, with some of the finest views in Derbyshire.

Bulls Head Foolow S32 5QR ✆ 01433 630873. This friendly family-owned pub, set in one of Derbyshire's prettiest villages, serves quality food at reasonable prices. The Sunday roast is particularly good value.

STONEY MIDDLETON TO TIDESWELL

Fanning off from the A623, there's a wealth of Derbyshire villages rich in story and history, yet bypassed by many visitors intent on reaching honeypots such as Chatsworth House. What a shame: from the topsy-turvy village of **Stoney Middleton** with its rare and rather lovely octagonal church to the tragic plague village of **Eyam**, this is certainly a fascinating area.

Further west, **Tideswell** boasts a 'cathedral' of exquisitely detailed wooden carvings. Around these rural settlements, infrequently visited dales offer the Slow traveller tranquil walks and a chance to reconnect with nature.

4 STONEY MIDDLETON

From the A623, Stoney Middleton isn't very inviting – its roadside houses splattered by passing lorries and trapped in a deep cut of rocks and scruffy woodland. The scars of quarrying and industry further add to the bleakness of this valley, but don't let this put you off – for behind the narrow squeeze of the A623 is a delightful higgledy-piggledy settlement of individual houses. Above the restaurant of Little India there's an imposing rocky promontory called **Lover's Leap**.

Heading further east, the **Toll House** sits on the left next to **Grove Garden**, a tranquil public space of brook, bridge and bench – apart from the lorries that hurtle along the road next to it. The Toll House, no longer taking monies for the old turnpike road, sells fish and chips instead (reportedly some of the best in the county). From the Toll House, head up the hill towards **Bottom Cliff** and **The Fold**, lined with cottages that have been stuffed into the hillside. If you continue out on to the steep meadow, you will eventually reach Eyam – this is a great way to approach the plague village (page 104).

"St Martin's was built in 1415 by Joan Eyre of Padley in thanksgiving for the safe return of her husband from the Battle of Agincourt."

The Nook, towards the bottom of Stoney Middleton, leads past Brookside cottages to **St Martin's Church**. St Martin's (patron saint of cripples and soldiers) was built in 1415 by Joan Eyre of Padley in thanksgiving for the safe return of her husband from the Battle of Agincourt. While the original building, bar the tower, was destroyed by fire, St Martin's Church is an ecclesiastical rarity with its octagonal nave – the only one of its kind in Derbyshire. The area around **The Nook** has been a place of worship since Celtic times, the warm springs emerging here thought to have healing properties. Above The Nook, the lane twists right one more time, leading to a restored Roman-style **bath house** built in 1815, with its partitioned baths for men and women, changing rooms and fireplaces. The interior of the bath house can be viewed through the secured iron-wrought gates.

5 EYAM – THE PLAGUE VILLAGE

Both beautiful and heart-breaking – there's nowhere in the Peak District with such a tragic history as this lovely upland village. The plague occurred between 1665 and 1666, but continues to stamp its effects on the village today. While Eyam (pronounced Eem) wasn't the only place outside London to be affected by the Black Death, it's the way in which the villagers sacrificed their lives for the greater good that makes its story so profoundly moving. Cutting themselves off from the rest of the world, the villagers managed to isolate the deadly disease and stop it from spreading to the rest of the Peak District – even when their instinct was to run. All this was made possible under the steely leadership of the Reverend William Mompesson and his assistant, Thomas Stanley.

A walk from Stoney Middleton to Eyam

✻ OS Explorer map OL 24; start: Toll Bar Fish & Chip Shop, Stoney Middleton,
♀ SK229755; 3 miles; fairly easy with a short sharp climb out of Stoney Middleton

This circular walk takes in some fascinating points of local history: the Boundary Stone that isolated the plague village of Eyam; the graves of the victims; a Roman bathhouse and the locally unique octagonal Church of St Martin's.

Not only is the walk crammed with local interest, the second part in particular features excellent views over to Chatsworth, Froggatt, Curbar and Baslow Edge. There's limited parking at the starting point in Stoney Middleton, but there's a regular bus service passing through the village, stopping just below the Toll Bar Fish and Chip shop at Grove Garden. Pick up refreshments in Eyam (page 109) – making sure you leave time to explore the tragic plague village, either during the walk or at another time.

1 Immediately after the **Toll Bar Fish and Chip Shop** leave the main road and turn right into **The Bank** (a side road). Take the first left into **The Fold**. After a few yards, the road divides in two. Follow the left fork signposted 'Byway open to all traffic to Eyam 1'. This is **Cliff Bottom** leading to Mill Lane as indicated on the stone wall.

2 Climb the narrow road flanked by houses and on past the **Wesleyan Reform Chapel** on the right with its attractive stained-glass windows. It was the first building in Stoney Middleton to have electricity.

3 Just before the last houses on the lane, go through the wooden gate on the left and head up the well-defined grassy pathway that rises steeply through the meadow.

4 Part way up the hill, you will come to an information board and the **Boundary Stone**. Food was left for the plague victims here, who left money in the six drilled holes (soaked in vinegar to prevent the spread of the disease) in exchange. This was as far as Stoney Middleton and Eyam residents could stray on this hillside from their respective villages during the plague.

5 A second gate leads through to a narrow path enclosed by dry stone walls. Continuing straight on, go through two farm gates and downhill along the tarmac road of **Lydgate** into the village of Eyam. Notice the **Lydgate Graves** on the left, surrounded by a small stone enclosure – these are the graves of George Darby and his daughter who died exactly two months apart in 1666.

6 Lydgate meets Eyam's main street. You can stop to explore the village, pause for refreshments or continue on with your walk.

7 Turn right on to **The Causeway** and continue along the main street (the B6521). Take the left-hand side road on to **Riley Lane** just before the 'single track road with passing places' sign and follow the quiet leafy road.

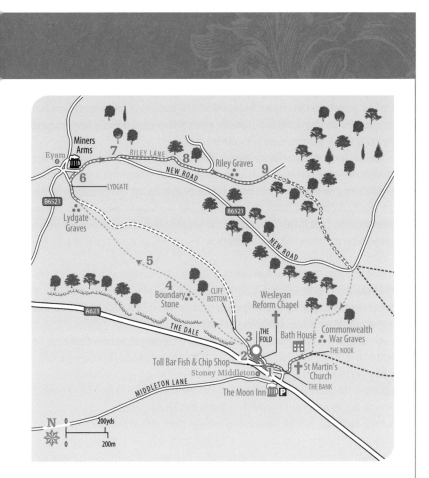

8 Where the road forks, keep right. Here leafy vegetation gives way to upland pasture. Soon you'll see a stone enclosure in a field on your left. Cross the field to the enclosure to visit the **Riley Graves** (page 109), where you will find the six graves and tomb of Mrs Hancock's children and husband – all plague victims.

9 Where the way divides again, take the right fork signed 'byway open to all traffic' and head down the rough churned-up track. It drops through woodland until it reaches the B6521 again. Cross the road and follow the stony track opposite downhill through more woods to Stoney Middleton, past the restored **Bath House**, and if you haven't done so already, drop into the unusual octagonal **St Martin's Church** (page 103).

Eyam Museum

Hawkhill Rd, S32 5QP ✆ 01433 631371 ☉ Mar–Nov Tue–Sun

To understand the enormity of the sacrifice made in Eyam, start your tour of the village at the museum opposite the main car park on Hawkhill Road. The information boards in this small museum give the visitor an understanding of what the villagers were up against: a poor understanding of pandemic diseases, the limits of medical knowledge at the time and the often misguided treatments.

What the museum lacks in exhibits is made up for in the carefully documented accounts of individuals and families – along with its wider impact on the village – all powerful and moving. While the informative medical section makes clear no-one knows with any certainty what type of plague struck Eyam, or even if the plague was brought to Eyam from London by means of flea-riddled cloth, there's no question about the devastation it caused in this small Derbyshire village.

Cucklet Church of the Delf

From the museum head downhill and turn left on to **Church Street**, right into New Close and left again into Dunlow Lane. Follow the sign for **Cucklet**. Mompesson held services out in the open meadow here in

ADVICE FOR THE AFFLICTED

Source: Eyam Museum

Medical advice came in all shapes and guises, sometimes contradictory, but freely given by the Plague Approved Physician, quacks and anyone else with an opinion. Here are a few examples:

- Avoid dancing, running, leaping about, lechery and baths
- Ward off evil by drinking heavily, and satisfying one's cravings and lusts in an endless round of merriment and pleasure
- Pluck, and place the tails of a pigeon on the sore (also a chicken or hen is very good)
- Take a live frog and lay the belly of it next to the wound

- Keep large and speckled spiders in the room
- Ring bells or discharge cannons, muskets and blunderbusses – to break up the stiff air
- Do not sleep in the daytime
- Snuff tobacco
- Bottle wind

the **Delf**, fearing the closed environment of the parish church would quicken the spread of the disease. An annual memorial service takes place here each August, with villagers acting out tableaux from the plague in costume.

It's thought this is also the place where a betrothed couple looked out for each other across the brook, having been separated by the quarantine. Emmott Sydall, who lived at

"The handsome Jacobean manor house is currently in the care of the National Trust."

Bagshaw House in Eyam, had fallen in love with the son of a flour miller, Rowland Torre, from the next village of Stoney Middleton. Emmott, worried Rowland would catch the plague, begged him to stay away, but the two agreed to look out for each other at Cucklet – from a distance. Even when Emmott no longer appeared, Rowland continued to walk up the hillside each day in hope. It was in vain: when the quarantine was finally lifted, Rowland was one of the first outsiders to enter Eyam. He was met by one of the villagers who told him, 'Ah, Rowland, thy Emmott's dead and buried in Cussy Dell.'

Eyam Hall & Craft Centre

Main St, S32 5QW ✆ 01433 639565 ◷ closed Mon (check National Trust website for winter times); National Trust

Returning to the main street, call in at the **information barn**, a good place to pause with its green area, picnic benches and village stocks before heading to the National Trust **Craft Centre** across the road attached to Eyam Hall.

The hall was built six years after the plague infestation by Thomas Wright for his son John and his wife, Elizabeth of Kniveton – not a bad wedding gift. The handsome Jacobean manor house has gone on to serve eleven generations of the Wright family, and is currently in the care of the National Trust. The family portraits of the Wright family still deck the **entrance hall**, along with a solemn Elizabeth as a child posing with her parents and sister. Bookending the fireplace are two (almost) unique pieces of furniture, bacon settles used for storing cured meat (with the only other known surviving settle on Lindisfarne). The **staircase** to the upper floor predates the house, while the rest of the rooms contain furniture accumulated over the centuries. Look out for the scratched scribblings and drawings on various windowpanes, a curious pastime in the Wright household; also the severed head on one of the Flemish wall-hangings in the ceiling-to-floor **Tapestry Room**. Many of them date to the 1500s. Before leaving, take time to wander through the secluded **Walled Gardens** with views across to St Lawrence's Church.

The Plague Cottages

Continue past **The Sheep Roasting Jack** (its rotating spit put into action during the August **Carnival Week**) and on to the **Plague Cottages**. The green plaques outside the pretty row of terraces bring home the devastating effects of the plague: all nine family members at **Rose Cottage** were taken, while Mary of **Plague Cottage** lost 13 relatives. It was here that the tailor George Viccars lived – the first victim to be taken by the plague in the Midlands (see box below). The blame for the plague at Eyam has rightly or wrongly remained with the poor tailor over the centuries.

Next door, Jane, the only survivor in the Hawksworth household, lost 25 family members in all. On the other side of the road, you'll find Emmott Syddall's home, where nine members of the family perished.

St Lawrence's Church

St Lawrence's Church sits next to the Plague Cottages and, in a church full of beautiful stained-glass windows, it's the modern **Plague Window** that captures my attention. It tells the story of the disease in a series of pictures: William Mompesson counselling his parishioners; family gathered round the sick bed; the parcel of cloth laid out on the table; Emmott and Rowland reaching out across the river. In the south aisle, a register lists the names of those who died in the plague. Before leaving

THE TAILOR & THE FLEAS

One summer's day in 1665 George Viccars, a tailor, took delivery of cloth sent up from London. Damp, it was laid out in front of the fire to dry. It would seem that Viccars had not just been delivered fabric, but some of London's wildlife – the cloth was infested with fleas that harboured the dreaded bubonic plague. Up until then, the Midlands of England had been unaffected by the plague, but within a week George Viccars was dead, and by the time the disease had taken its last victim in Eyam in 1666, just over a third of its population had survived, and all because of the tailor, his cloth and its fleas. At least that's the theory.

the church look up to see the faded **Nave Murals** of the Twelve Tribes of Israel that pre-date the plague, along with a skeleton.

Outside, you'll find the tomb of Catherine Mompesson, who insisted on staying with her husband, William, in the village. While William survived, Catherine was sadly taken by the plague. The August commemoration service departs from her grave before making its way to the Delf where her husband preached. There's also a monument to Thomas Stanley in the graveyard, the rector who assisted Mompesson in isolating the village.

¶¶ FOOD & DRINK

Eyam may be small, but visitors are spoiled for choice when it comes to cafés serving quality food – Stella's Kitchen, Village Green and Eyam Tearooms. There's even a small grocer's store – a rarity in villages these days. The centre of the settlement around **The Square** is a good place to stop for a break, with its village shop, tea rooms and pub.

Eyam Tearooms The Square, S32 5RB ✆ 01433 631274. The friendly owners bend over backwards to provide their customers with good service and decent home-cooked food. Dog friendly.

Miners Arms Water Lane, S32 5RG ✆ 01433 630853. This historical pub, predating the plague, serves quality food, locally sourced.

Village Green The Square, S32 5RB ✆ 01433 631293. The building encompasses a tea room, delicatessen and bakery, with some imaginative cake combinations: try the courgette and lime cake, or the whisky fruit cake. The owners cater for vegetarians and customers with gluten or lactose intolerance.

On the fringes of Eyam

If you are happy to walk a little further, demarcated boundary points are found on the edge of the village: the **Boundary Stone** southeast of Lydgate (page 104) and **Mompesson's Well** on Edge Road to the north. Food, medicine and money were left at both sites for plague victims.

High above the village to the east, you'll find the **Riley Graves** (belonging, not to a family of Rileys, but to the Hancock family) on Riley Lane in an exposed field surrounded by a small stone enclosure. The story behind the Riley Graves is particularly heart-breaking, not least because the Hancock family had been left unscathed in the first wave of the disease. At the beginning of summer 1666 they must have harboured hope of survival in their isolated farmhouse. But in the second wave that appeared with the warm weather, the dreaded illness arrived on their doorstep.

The first two children died on 3 August. As Mrs Hancock was trying to come to terms with her loss, the plague struck again, taking her husband and yet another two children. By 10 August – in the space of a week – Mrs Hancock had lost all six children in the household. It was left to her to drag the corpses one by one to a field near the house, dig the graves, and bury her loved ones.

As I read the worn inscriptions on the gravestones on a bright, windy day with the clouds scudding across the sky, it was hard to imagine how Mrs Hancock must have coped in the aftermath of the plague.

6 LITTON

The Wriggly Tin (page 242), **YHA Ravenstor** (page 242)

With numerous nature reserves protecting internationally important wildlife (including Cressbrook, Monk's, Chee, Miller's, Deep and Tideswell dales) all within spitting distance, Litton is the ideal walking base (or pit stop on a ramble). Be careful not to overindulge if you visit the popular Red Lion pub – the village stocks are just outside. This village straddles an elongated village green with its mix of humble cottages and grander 17th- and early 18th-century houses. Visit the village in spring when the verges are covered in daffodils if you can or at the end of June for the well dressing and Wakes (a religious holiday celebrated in parts of northern England) when Litton celebrates in good old-fashioned tradition with stalls, a fair, barbecue, a tug-of-war and a torch procession.

FOOD & DRINK

Litton Village Shop and Post Office ✆ 01298 872881. Post Office, tea room, shop, library of donated books, community hub and information point – it's all happening at Litton Village Shop. There's a table in one corner of the store, and a range of cakes displayed on the counter with more seating outside on the pretty village green.

Red Lion Church Lane, SK17 8QU ✆ 01298 871458. Atmospheric and cosy 18th-century pub incorporating a number of small rooms with low beams, thick stone walls, wooden panels and log fires. The pub has a reputation for good food, especially the roasts.

7 TIDESWELL

Merman Barn Bed & Breakfast (page 242)

After Bakewell, Tideswell is the largest settlement inside the national park, and at over 1,000 feet (just off the high-level A623), the village has expansive views out over the Peak District – and a lot of weather. I last visited on a winter's day with icy sleet driving across the streets, wrapped up and ready to explore this sprawling upland settlement more closely.

It's said an Anglo-Saxon called Tidi founded Tideswell over 1,300 years ago. Tideswell continues to be known affectionately as Tidza to this day, while the locals have earned themselves the equally 'charming' nickname of 'Sawyeds' – all because of one Tidzan bright spark. The story goes that the drunken man took it

"Tideswell has expansive views out over the Peak District – and a lot of weather."

upon himself to free a distressed cow he'd found with its head stuck in a field gate over towards Litton. After pondering for a while, the man came up with an inspired idea: he'd saw the cow's head off – a rather drastic solution. Whatever the truth of the tale, Tideswell retains its strong rural identity. It's grown and adapted over the centuries: lead mining is a thing of the past; the grammar schools are gone too, along with the silk and velvet mills, but the buildings remain along with the gritty character of the village. You can pick up a **Tideswell Trail** leaflet from various businesses around the village to guide you through its streets with its stories, characters and historical buildings.

St John the Baptist Church (the Cathedral in the Peak)

The Cathedral in the Peak is Tideswell's crowning glory. However, St John the Baptist is not really a cathedral, but it gets its elevated title because of its grand scale in this village location. Inside are alabaster effigies, grand tombs and fine brass plates, but it's the wooden carvings that make this church a joy to visit. From the screens, pulpit and lectern to the stalls and organ casing – the detail in the wooden carvings are superb. Many of them were created by local man Advent Hunstone, who portrayed the life of the church through his carvings: baptism, confirmation, ordination and visiting the sick, along with animals, birds, vegetation and buildings. There are 150 motifs or so, but my favourite is of the organist carved into the casing of the pipes. There are older, wonderfully detailed **Suffolk Carvings** in the choir stalls that were unveiled in September 1875 in the newly reopened chancel. These were created by a Mr Tooley of Bury St Edmunds and portray exquisite figurines, animals and mythical creatures (along with a delightful carving of a bird feeding her young in the nest). The oldest carvings in the church date back to medieval times.

¶¶ FOOD & DRINK

In 2009 **Taste Tideswell** came about after a successful bid to the Big Lottery Fund's Village SOS Programme. While the cookery school failed, the community kitchen garden still flourishes behind the church along with the annual Tideswell Food Festival in May. The village's businesses, cafés and restaurants continue to be committed to locally grown produce. See ⌨ www.tastetideswell.co.uk for details.

Peak District Parlour Chapman Hse, Queen St, SK17 8JT ✆ 01298 873100. The deli counter offers a range of cake and pastry options for take-away or eating in. Breakfast and lunch menu available.

Three Stags Heads Wardlow Mires SK17 8RW ✆ 0871 9511000. For a taste of authentic Derbyshire, look no further. Located east of Tideswell on the A623, this is a proper local pub, filled with characters, not least the owners, Geoff and Pat Fuller. Geoff, a potter, is a curmudgeonly character who could be a Viking with his long flowing white hair and drooping moustache. Known for his plain speaking, it's not uncommon for him to turn away people from the door with a cursory 'There's nothing for you here'. Don't ask for lager, as the sign warns, and don't get your mobile phone out. But if you do manage to 'pass go', this is a wonderful pub, barely changed since it came into existence in the 17th century. It's all dark walls and dog paintings, steaming windows and smoky fires; ceramic tankards, stuffed animals and whippet dogs (who seem to own the place) – along with decent ales. Try the Sunday late afternoon folk sessions for real atmosphere. Geoff also organises an art and food festival annually.

Tindalls Bakery and Delicatessen ✆ 01298 871351. Tideswell Pies, puddings and pastries to take away. Try the Tidza Pud for a twist on the Bakewell version. A long-established business, using some recipes that go back hundreds of years and include 'wakes cakes', 'fidgety pasties' and 'thar cakes'.

8 BUXTON

🏠 **The Old Hall Hotel** (page 242)

Buxton and the surrounding area have always remained outside of the park, largely because of their industrial value – on my map it sits in a long finger of grey surrounded by a swathe of green denoting the national park. Today, many of the lucrative limestone quarries are still active, with chunks of hillsides removed in the quest to satisfy man's insatiable demand for aggregates and cement. The working quarries have left unsightly holes in the White Peak, and the exposed rock faces stand as raw scars on the landscape. But between and beyond the quarries is an area of real beauty made up of deep dales, hillsides of thick vegetation, open moorland and the softer, greener rolling landscape of farmlands. In all of this sits the handsome part-Georgian, part-Victorian spa town of Buxton, the Bath of the Midlands.

AROUND THE OPERA HOUSE

An ideal place to start an exploration of Buxton is at the **Opera House** beside the Pavilion Gardens. Inside and out, it has the feel of an opulent Victorian theatre. The opera house is actually Edwardian, built in 1903 to the design of renowned theatre architect, Frank Matcham (who also designed the London Coliseum and Palladium). The highest opera house in Britain, it makes an impression from the start with its handsome stone exterior and twin leaded domes. The interior, from the white marble foyer to the detailed Baroque plasterwork by De Jong and exquisitely painted panels, was meticulously restored to its original glory in 1979, with further restoration across the new millennium. Join one of the Saturday coffee morning tours to find out more, or attend one of the shows and soak up the atmosphere. From comedy and music to ballet and theatre, there's something for everyone.

From Water Street below the Opera House, an electric vehicle in the style of an open-top Victorian tram named the **Wonder of the Peak** does hourly tours of the town in season, including Higher Buxton and Poole's Tavern. The converted milk float is the optimal 'Slow' experience with a top speed of 12 miles per hour.

From Water Street, head along **The Square** with the elegant **Old Hall Hotel**, home to Mary, Queen of Scots between 1576 and 1578, as the plaque testifies, while under house arrest. Directly behind Old Hall Hotel on **The Crescent** are the **Mineral Baths**, the site of the original Roman Baths that yielded a stash of Roman coins, pins, bracelets and rings during an archaeological dig in 1978. Further along on the right you'll find **St Anne's Well** with **The Slopes** (an area of green) behind. Anglo-Saxons believed the well to have healing properties. The water piped from a geothermal spring deep under the ground is the same water bottled and sold by Buxton Mineral Water Company, but here you can fill your bottles up for free.

Next to the well is the **Pump Room**, with plans for restoration, and across the road the magnificent **Buxton Crescent**, inspired by Bath's Royal Crescent. This beautiful, Grade I listed set piece was built for the fifth Duke of Devonshire in the 1780s, a fitting statement of grandeur for a man of position. Sadly the Crescent became structurally unsafe over time, and has lain empty since the 1990s. With a leaking roof, a great deal of the interior was badly damaged. The roof has now been made secure and plans are in place to restore the Crescent to its former glory, reopening as a luxury hotel and spa with a public arcade, hopefully before the end of this decade. Adjacent is **Cavendish Arcade**, the site of the original **Thermal Baths**. It still retains the character of the old baths with its embossed decorative tiles, and revamped stained-glass barrel roof. The arcade is made up of boutiques, vintage clothing stores and craft shops – a far cry from the main shopping thoroughfare off Terrace Road, which is filled with chain stores and thrift shops.

BUXTON MUSEUM & MARKET PLACE
Terrace Rd, SK17 6DA ✐ 01629 533540 ⊘ www.derbyshire.gov.uk/leisure/buxton_
museum ☺ Apr–Sep closed Mon & Sun, except bank holiday w/ends; free entry
Terrace Road leads to Buxton Museum and Art Gallery, built in 1880 and opened as the Peak Hydropathic Hotel. Little remains of the old hotel interior, but look out for the original Art Nouveau stained glass, designed by George Wragge. The Boyd Dawkins study encapsulates the Victorian passion for collecting, researching and cataloguing, packed to the gunnels with busts, paintings, books, scientific manuscripts, stuffed animals and other curios. Sir William Boyd Dawkins, along with Dr J W Jackson, were involved in significant excavation finds in Derbyshire. Upstairs, a warren of rooms and passageways takes you through the natural and industrial history of the Peak, from prehistoric animal remains to Roman, Bronze and Iron Age tools and ornaments.

Terrace Road comes out at **Higher Buxton** and the **Market Place** (with its open market every Saturday and Tuesday), surrounded by shops, pubs and restaurants. If nothing else, take time to visit **Scrivener's Books and Bookbinding** (✐ 01298 73100) – not so much a secondhand bookshop as an experience.'Be warned, if you go in there,' a passer-by said to me,'you won't come out for hours.' Shelves of books, ornaments and curios are crammed in over five floors, including the attic and cellar. In the latter, along with a kitchen range and stone sink, a makeshift display in one corner pays homage to the Higher Buxton archaeologist Micah Salt. There's no café on the premises, but there's a wall unit with kettle and cups for self-service drinks and soft seating around. Settle in and enjoy.

THE PAVILION GARDENS

Bath Road will take you to the Pavilion Gardens, a Victorian landscaped park created in 1871 at the bequest of the seventh Duke of Devonshire. The riverside setting across 23 acres, along with its miniature train, playgrounds, bandstand, lakes, bridges and rockeries, draws families, couples and everyone else in between. Next to the gardens is **The Pavilion** with its elegant domed **Octagon Hall**, its eight sides encased in glass and wood. The Octagon is in constant use for craft fairs, food festivals, fêtes and concerts, while the rest of The Pavilion houses two cafés and a coffee bar, a tourist information centre, gift boutique, art gallery and the **Arts Centre** (Buxton's second theatre, opened in 2010), alongside a swimming pool and fitness centre. Linking the Pavilion and Opera House is the long narrow **Winter Gardens** conservatory, another slice of Victoriana filled with palms and exotic plants. On the corner of St John's Road and Manchester Road is **St John's**, an unusual church built in a Neoclassical Tuscan style.

"The Octagon is in constant use for craft fairs, food festivals, fêtes and concerts."

From there, head up the hill to the **Devonshire Dome.** An impressive space, it laid claim to the largest unsupported dome in Europe at one time. The building began its life as the fifth Duke of Devonshire's stables in 1779, became a hospital and is currently part of the University of Derby. Apart from the restaurant and café, you can take advantage of a commercial spa offering beauty treatments, a hydrotherapy pool, sauna and steam rooms.

POOLE'S CAVERN & BUXTON COUNTRY PARK

Green Lane, SK17 9DH ✆ 01298 26978 🖳 www.poolescavern.co.uk

On the southern edge of the town, Poole's Cavern and Buxton Country Park are well worth a detour. The cavern is more accessible than the Castleton caves, although there are a couple of places with ten or so steps. The rest of the cave is well surfaced, flat and even, with handrails for support. Poole's main selling point isn't just its relative accessibility, but its long chambers lined with stalactites. Particularly impressive are the delicate 'straw' stalactites and the unusual stalagmites coloured rusty orange by the seeping of water through iron ore dumped on the site of Grin Low Woods above. The visitor centre next to the cave has some interesting exhibits along with a shop and café.

From the car park, steps snake their way up through woodland to **Solomon's Temple**, a rather overblown name for this squat, slightly skew-whiff two-storey Victorian folly. Solomon is not a biblical reference, but refers to Solomon Mycock, who had the building erected in the 1800s to keep the local unemployed busy. The 20-foot-high structure, alternatively named Grinlow Tower, sits on top of the 1,400-foot **Grin Low** hill with sweeping views across to Buxton and the surrounding countryside. The tower may not live up to its name in grandeur, but the outlook from the top, and the half-mile woodland walk leading to it, shouldn't disappoint.

▒▏ FOOD & DRINK

Old Hall Hotel The Square, SK17 6BD ✆ 01298 22841. Claiming to be the oldest hotel in England (and home to Mary, Queen of Scots for a time) the Old Hall serves good food in fine surroundings.

The Dome at Buxton 1 Devonshire Rd, University of Buxton, SK17 6RY ✆ 01298 28345. Don't be put off by the fact that guests are essentially guinea pigs for the catering students – the service and food, under the discreet, watchful eye of the tutors, are second to none.

The Duke 123 St Johns Rd, SK17 6UR ✆ 01298 78781. A notch above the average pub grub; quality food that's good value for money.

The Tea Chest George St, The Old Courthouse, SK17 6DH ✆ 01298 73514. If you are fussy about tea, this is the place to come: the timer that accompanies the loose tea infusion means you can have your tea to your preferred strength. Good for lunch and cakes.

EVENTS

There's a wide range of events taking place in the Opera House, Octagon and Arts Centre at the Pavilion Gardens year round, from the Artist and Designer Fair to the Garden Plants and Craft Show, alongside markets and bazaars. Check ⌂ www.visitbuxton.co.uk for further information.

December/January Pantomime at the Opera House.

March Buxton Festival of World Cinema.

April Buxton Brass Band Festival.

July Buxton Festival and Fringe Festival. Music, theatre, comedy and lectures; one of the best regional fringe festivals in the country.

August Buxton Family and Puppet Festival.

September Buxton Bandstand Marathon – a celebration of music and musicians.

October Octoberfest – a wide variety of cask beers on tap at the Buxton Beer Festival, plus the Real Ale Trail and live music.

MONSAL HEAD TO BAKEWELL

Take a right turn off the A623 at Wardlow Mires and continue on through Wardlow to Monsal Head. Here you'll find deep-cut dales and sheer limestone cliffs that drop down to the River Wye at Water-cum-Jolly. The Monsal Trail passes through here, a dismantled railway that takes in some impressive Victorian engineering. To the east and south of Monsal Head, the historical villages of the Longstones and Ashford-in-the-Water are steeped in ancient customs and local traditions. These rural settlements are served by the handsome market town of Bakewell, where key tribal groups converged in the Middle Ages, as All Saints Church testifies. For walkers and historians alike, there's much to see and do in the area.

9 MONSAL HEAD

🏠 **Monsal Head Hotel** (page 242)

As I stand at Monsal Head looking out at the steep-sided hills and the River Wye sweeping a curve through wide grassy meadows to an arched viaduct, the scene evokes the words of poet William Blake: 'England's mountains green' and 'pleasant pastures'. It's a view that epitomises the romantic ideal of England: a valley of verdant loveliness with a couple of 'dollhouses' and handkerchief plots squished in adjacent to a little clapper bridge. Beyond, Cresswell Mill sits at the head of the valley with Litton Mill out of sight. The mills also evoke Blake's words of 'secluded hills' and 'dark Satanic mills' – a smear on this tranquil landscape with their stories of child abuse and ill treatment in the 1800s, especially at Litton Mill. This iconic viewpoint, off the B6465 between Ashford in the Water and Wardlow, is a honeypot for visitors who gather here to take photographs or linger on a bench with an ice cream, often unaware of the dark history in the dales below. Apart from the ice cream van, there's a small souvenir shop and tea room, along with the Swiss-styled Monsal Head Hotel and adjoining Stables Bar. But come out of season, dawn or dusk to enjoy the views in solitude.

🍴 FOOD & DRINK

Monsal Head Hotel and Stable Bar DE45 1NL ✆ 01629 640250. The rustic Stable Bar has many original features – the sloping flag floor and horse stalls. Enjoy real ales or a bite to eat among the stone bull's head, the horse tack and the hay rack. Well-cooked food is served next door in the elegant restaurant for a more formal dining experience.

10 MONSAL & CRESSBROOK DALES

The little road dropping down from Monsal Head to the valley floor of Monsal Dale leads to **Cressbrook**, a village stuffed into the sides of the narrowing valley behind the mill on the edge of the flood plain. Sir Richard Arkwright, unfazed by the remoteness of the location of Cressbrook, built a small wooden cotton mill here around 1780. When it burned down a few years later, it was replaced with a more fireproof version and extended by William Newton between 1814 and 1815. In a state of near-dereliction, the handsome Georgian-style mill with its lovely bell tower was rescued in the 1990s, scrubbed down and converted into chic apartments, some of which are available as holiday lets. Today the large mill complex seems at odds with its rural setting and village of thimble-sized mining cottages and alpine-style terrace cottages built as part of Arkwright's model village. Just across the road a metal gate leads to a forgotten millpond and weir enclosed by a high wall. The only sign of life when I visited there was

NOCTURNAL WILDLIFE IN CRESSBROOK DALE

It was a warm summer's evening in June, the light of the day fading out. My son and I headed for Cressbrook Dale as the sun dropped low on the horizon, orange oozing through the sky like ink on blotting paper. On the elbow of the road above Cressbrook village we met up with fellow adventurers, joining us on a guided moonlight walk. Together we tumbled into charcoal woods, feeling a rush of air, before seeing the dark blurry shapes of bats. We stepped over a stile into the open-sided valley, the light fading fast now. Stretching out in front of us was a guiding strip of green fluorescent dots like lights on an airport runway: our first glow worms. We crossed a narrow wooden bridge and climbed the rise to a dewpond. Black beady eyes stared into our torchlight. We peered at the lumpy, misshapen creatures with their serrated backs, something between fish, frog and lizard: great crested newts. Knowing there was a badger sett across the valley, we settled down on the hillside. For a moment we thought we saw their silhouettes on the hillside; there, then gone. Returning back through the dale, the flickering lights of tea candles in jam jars guided us this time, not glow worms.

Occasional twilight walks such as this one are led by voluntary and conservation bodies including the Peak Park. Keep an eye on the events sections of Peak District websites such as ⊘ www.visitpeakdistrict.com. Otherwise choose a clear, moonlit night, pack a torch and head into one of the dales to get a different perspective of the Peak District. It's the best time to see the Park's wildlife.

a pair of swans, caught in the basin of steep-sided woodland. Continuing uphill along the road, you'll find the entrance to Cressbrook Dale, known for its wildlife, in particular its early blooming purple orchids – and part of the Derbyshire Dales National Nature Reserve that's managed by Natural England.

11 FROM CRESSBROOK TO LITTON MILL

Behind Cressbrook Mill a public footpath passes alongside Dale Terrace, originally called Apprentices Row as many of the child labourers were housed here. It was also known as Pancake Row, and although the reason for the name is unknown, I like to think the children were treated to pancakes and poetry by one of Cresswell's more benevolent managers, William Newton – the self-styled 'Minstrel of the Peak'. It's a fanciful idea, but it's certainly true to say the child apprentices at Cressbrook lived and worked in relatively favourable conditions under Newton. Stapled on to the end of this row of simple rendered white houses is a curious Gothic folly, a castle-like attachment of thick stone walls, battlements and towers, adorned with an arched door and windows. It's thought it may have been the apprentices' chapel. Around the corner, the limestone at Water-cum-Jolly drops straight to the level of the dammed river. As if sculpted by a potter, the stone is moulded and shaped by rain run-off in groves of pale blues and dusty pinks between the grey-white. The wide expanse of river, looking more like a lake at this point, was dammed for Cressbrook Mill, and although the waterwheel is long gone, the water still rushes over the weir, echoing the curve of the limestone buttress. When it isn't flooded, the path under it leads to Litton Mill. Squeezing at times beneath the white-washed buttresses of this limestone ravine, the riverside walk is one of pure delight, a kind of *Wind in the Willows* experience. Indeed, if you're lucky you may catch a glimpse of one of the water voles that inhabit the banks of the river, and if not a vole surely a moorhen, little grebe or dab chick – or at least the common mallard or swan. At Litton Mill the track takes you past a long complex of mill buildings packed into the deepest and darkest cut of Miller's Dale, so different in character from Cressbrook Mill with its wide open outlook across the flood plains. This place has a dark history, the mill known, above all, for its heartrending abuse of workhouse children, often brought from London on empty promises, and made to live and work in the most shocking of conditions.

Indeed it's been suggested that the isolated siting of Litton Mill was no accident, its workforce abused and exploited in the most appalling manner away from prying eyes. Life was so miserable here some children threw themselves to their death from the mill windows. Others died in horrendous factory floor accidents and were buried out of sight in unmarked graves up on the hills.

Despite its dark location and foreboding past, Litton Mill is a surprisingly charming village today, with its bohemian riverside cottages with mismatched windows and doors and elegant mill apartments. Look out for the wooden fingerpost after the last building on the left and opposite a long row of terraced houses. It leads to the Monsal Trail and will give you an alternative route back to Cressbrook.

The Monsal Trail

The 8-mile trail can be walked, but in my opinion it's best seen from the seat of a bicycle or the saddle of a horse. For walkers, I'd recommend combining sections of the trail with the dale below, taking in Cressbrook, Litton Mill and Blackwell Mill for variety and interest. If you choose to cycle the trail, bikes can be hired from either end (page 94).

When the plans for the railway were first proposed, artist, writer, poet and critic John Ruskin strongly opposed it, along with other conservationists. Despite their opposition, the track was laid and an impassioned Ruskin (not one to rein in the rhetoric or mince his words) said, 'There was a valley between Buxton and Bakewell, once upon a time, as divine as the Vale of Tempe ... You enterprised a railroad through the valley – you blasted its rocks away, heaped thousands of tonnes of shale into its lovely stream. The valley is gone and the Gods with it, and now, every fool in Buxton can be in Bakewell in half an hour, and every fool in Bakewell at Buxton; which you think is a lucrative process of exchange – you Fools everywhere.' After the railway's closure in the 1960s (how happy Ruskin would have been) four of the tunnels were closed off to the public, and the trail from Bakewell came to an abrupt halt at Headstone tunnel. Finally in 2011, the remaining tunnels were reopened, all with surfaced floors and lighting, to the delight of ramblers, cyclists and horseriders. Now, there are six tunnels

"When the plans for the railway were first proposed, artist, writer, poet and critic John Ruskin strongly opposed it."

along the length of the trail: **Headstone, Cressbrook, Litton, Chee Tor (1 & 2)** and **Rusher Cutting**. Cycling through the tunnels is great fun – dodging the drips (and walkers), while peering through the dimly lit tunnel to the daylight beyond. Travelling northwest from Bakewell, the landscape is initially gentle and pastoral, but becomes increasingly wild and dramatic towards Miller's Dale, its great limestone slabs and the River Wye squeezing through the ever-narrowing valley. The entire trail shows off Victorian engineering at its best – not just in the impressive cuttings and tunnels that slice through the limestone and burrow under the hills, but also the wonderful 300-foot-long Monsal viaduct with its five 50-foot span arches. Do stop at this point and take in the views of the Wye Valley as it sweeps around the hills in a spectacular horseshoe curve – it's one of the highlights of the trail.

⅔ FOOD & DRINK

Blackwell Mill Cycle Hire ⊖ closed over winter. Found at the end (or beginning) of the Monsal Trail and offers snacks and drinks, tuck shop-style.

The Brewstop Cressbrook ⊖ most w/ends. At the Brewstop in the **Old Apprentice House** the three Mabey children have been put to work selling snacks and drinks for walkers and climbers; their parents claim it will help them improve their maths and give them some pocket money. It seems appropriate in this building that once housed the Cressbrook Mill child apprentices. The rough stone-clad interior through a large archway has a cave-like feel and still houses an old horse trough, along with other bits of rusting kitchen equipment. The owners stock Fairtrade and locally sourced foodstuffs.

Hassop Station Café DE45 1NW ✆ 01629 815668. This beautifully restored railway station has terrace seating right on the Monsal Trail. Apart from tasty sandwiches, soups and other light bites using locally sourced food, the old station also has bike hire and a bookshop.

12 THE LONGSTONES

Just north of Bakewell are two of the most picturesque villages in the area, Great and Little Longstone, tucked into a quiet corner of the White Peak beneath Longstone Edge. The main street of **Great Longstone** is lined with stone and whitewashed cottages, with some elegant 18th-century houses at the upper end softened by greens and mature trees. Close by is the **Crispin Inn** – Crispin, the patron saint of shoemakers, references the cobbling industry that once flourished in the village, alongside stocking-making, courtesy of the Flemish weavers who settled here. It was the lead industry, however, that made the biggest contribution to the wealth and expansion of the village. Mining has long since ceased, but the village is still a thriving community, possessing a village shop, butcher's store and a second pub, the **White Lion**. Off Main Street, you'll find the **Church of St Giles**, beyond the lych gate, a Grade I listed building with a fine medieval oak roof of moulded beams, carved flowers and foliage. Visit Great Longstone on their **Open Gardens** weekend (page 11) to see the village up close and personal or during Well Dressing Week (page 11) for both Longstones in the summer. From Great Longstone, the road curves west to **Little Longstone**, a scaled-down version of its 'greater' neighbour; just a handful of cottages, a manor house, the **Pack Horse** inn and a diminutive chapel of charming simplicity. From here, it's just a short walk to Monsal Head.

13 ASHFORD IN THE WATER

The riverside idyll of Ashford in the Water could be a setting for a Thomas Hardy novel. Just a few miles out of Bakewell towards Buxton, the village is known for two idiosyncratic historical practices: the Sheepwash and Virgin Crants. The first is found at **Sheepwash Bridge**, an ancient packhorse bridge that crosses the River Wye. The ewes were enticed over to their lambs, placed in a pen on the other side of the river, then caught and sheared, with the added bonus of clean fleeces from the river crossing. Further down the main street, the **Holy Trinity Church** is known for its **Virgin Crants** (crowns). Following another ancient practice, funeral garlands (known as Maidens' Garlands) were hung from the roof of the church. Four of these Virgin Crants are still hanging up in the church today, the oldest dating back to 1747. Made from white paper and cut into rosettes, the garlands were fixed to a wooden frame that were carried before the coffin of a young virgin in the funeral procession before being hung up in the church.

⏮ FOOD & DRINK

Aisseford Tea Room Church St, DE45 1QB ✎ 01629 812773. This sweet, bijou tea room on the main street serves freshly baked cakes, sandwiches and other snacks for take-away or eating in. The little lean-to overlooking the lawn out back is great for rainy days, but the handkerchief-sized garden, with its wandering hens, is the best place to unwind, weather permitting. There's also a range of gifts and cards for sale, made by local craft artists.
Ashford Arms Church St, DE45 1QB ✎ 01629 812725. This popular village pub serves good food in lovely surroundings, with a relaxing beer garden.

14 BAKEWELL

⋏ Greenhills Holiday Park (page 242)

It's no wonder that Bakewell, with its riverside setting, handsome steepled church on the hillside and streets of honey buildings, throngs with visitors. But leave the main shopping thoroughfares behind and head up the hill to explore the little streets surrounding All Saints Church, or out of town along Brook Side towards Lumsford, and you will soon find an altogether quieter Bakewell.

All Saints Church

Spread out across the hillside and with its soaring spire, All Saints is an impressive sight. The history of the church in Bakewell goes back a long way, probably to the Romans who came to the Peak District to mine lead. Certainly, evidence of a medieval church is found in two small Saxon crosses located in the church grounds. The older of the two, by the south transept, is carved with swirling scrollwork, an engraved crucifixion, a horse and squirrel-like creatures.

The **south entrance** is stacked high with pieces of carved masonry: it's thought the stonework was used to demarcate ownership of land surrounding the town, where several tribal lands converged in Bakewell during the Middle Ages. There are sculpted creatures, typical of the Mercians; vine scrolls from the Anglican Northumbrians; Celtic interlay from the Norse Vikings and weave patterns from the Danish Vikings. Up in the rafters there are the heads of four grotesques, half-hidden in twigs and dried leaves and squeezed into a corner, looking as though they are having a giggle at the expense of passers-by. On the other side of the entrance, the symbols of occupations are engraved on the medieval stones: the shears of a wool merchant; an archer's bow and arrow; a priest's chalice and the keys of a bailiff perhaps. It's astonishing to see so much Saxon history casually crammed into this small church entrance.

Inside, **Vernon Chapel** contains memorials to Bakewell's most influential families, primarily the Vernons and Manners. The grand monument, commemorating George and Grace Manners (founder of the local Lady Manners School), leaves no doubt as to their importance. Among the other chest tombstones is a medieval knight (Sir Thomas Wendesley), kitted out in chain helmet and full armoury – his missing nose, hands and feet irreverently at odds with his stately composure.

Close by are the alabaster effigies of Sir George Vernon and his two wives, Margaret and Mawde, looking strangely twin-like in their almost identical attire, hair-dos and dainty features. Here you'll also find the **monument to Sir John Manners and Dorothy Vernon**, the subjects of a controversial union. When Dorothy Vernon of Haddon Hall fell in love with John Manners, the son of the first Earl of Rutland, all hell let loose, for the Manners were Protestant and the Vernons Catholic. Dorothy's father, Sir George, forbade the union, leaving Dorothy torn between her lover and her father. One night in 1563, Dorothy slipped away unnoticed through the crowds attending a ball given in her honour by her father. She ran down the steps into the garden and over the footbridge to the waiting carriage. Inside John Manners greeted his lover before whisking her off to be married. Luckily for Dorothy (unlike the unfortunate Juliet) she was soon reconciled with her father, and inherited his considerable estate a couple of years later when he passed away. No-one knows for sure how true this story of elopement is, but it has certainly been great fodder for speculation – and dramatisation in the form of books, plays and literature.

Exploring the rest of the church, don't miss the intricately carved 14th-century font, the beautiful Pre-Raphaelite stained-glass window designed by Henry Holiday, the heraldic shields, detailed wood carvings and the mosaic floor.

Bakewell Old House Museum

Cunningham Place, off North Church St, DE45 1DD ✆ 01629 813642 ⌖ www. oldhousemuseum.org.uk ◷ Apr–Oct

What a delightful little museum this is, with its eclectic collection of objects and memorabilia. It may have an old-fashioned, provincial feel to it, but this only adds to the charm. On visiting the museum, it was clear that it's precious to the army of local volunteers who run it. And no wonder for this historical building was nearly lost to the town and the wider world. Condemned and declared unsafe in the 1950s, it had a demolition order slapped on it. Bakewell and District Historical Society fought and won the battle to have the building preserved and protected, going on to establish the Old House Museum. When I arrived, the volunteers were sitting behind the desk, alternately knitting and jumping up to welcome visitors. The manager who showed me around was clearly proud of the museum and its achievements – and it's this enthusiasm,

THE BAKEWELL PUDDING

The Bakewell Pudding started off as a happy accident sometime in the 1800s at the White Horse (now the Rutland Arms Hotel). There are variations on the story, but my favourite is the account of Mrs Greaves, the landlady, who had left instructions for her cook to make a jam tart on the request of visiting noblemen. The hapless cook, instead of stirring the egg mixture and almond paste into the pastry, spread it on top of the jam. When cooked, the egg and almond paste set like egg custard. Luckily, everyone liked the new recipe and the Bakewell Pudding was added to the inn's menu.

Three separate businesses in Bakewell lay claim to the original Bakewell Pudding these days: the **Bakewell Tart Shop & Coffee House** sells three different types of Bakewell tart alongside the traditional Bakewell Pudding, while the purist **Bloomers** and the **Old Original Bakewell Pudding Shop** stick with the traditional recipe.

Nowadays there are many different forms of the English dessert, usually made with a flaky pastry base covered in jam and topped with an egg and almond paste filling. The modern, iced-top, commercially made adaptations are very different from the original pudding. While the current pudding bakers in Bakewell keep their recipes a closely guarded secret, Mrs Beeton was more than happy to share her version.

Mrs Beeton's Bakewell Pudding

Ingredients

450ml/¾ pint of breadcrumbs	55g/2oz of sugar
600ml/1 pint of milk	80g/3oz of butter
three eggs	25g/1oz of ground almonds; jam.

Preparation method

Butter a pie dish, add the breadcrumbs, covering them with a layer of strawberry or any other kind of jam. Mix the milk with the beaten eggs, the ground almonds, and the butter and sugar. Beat all the ingredients together, pour into the dish and bake for one hour at a moderate heat.

commitment and energy that have earned the pint-sized attraction the accolade of Derbyshire Museum of the Year. The house goes back to the time of Henry VII when it was built for Ralph Gell's steward, Robert Plant, responsible for collecting tithes from local farmers and Gell's tenants. It became a gentleman's residence in Elizabethan times, complete with servants' quarters, a large fireplace and a garderobe – the indoor toilet that was a rare luxury at the time. In 1777, Richard Arkwright, having arrived in town to build yet another mill, took over the house, dividing it into five cottages for his factory workers.

The museum artefacts reflect the activities that went on inside the house through the centuries. The first room displays items found under the floor, from buttons and marbles to the skeleton of a rat, while the adjoining rooms have a host of exhibits used for daily household chores. Upstairs the collections become even more random. There's a nod to the war years, a collection of fabrics, Kodak cameras and antique toys. Among the displays are a boy's shoe complete with metal sole and heel (nailed on to hinder the child's penchant for running away), and the foot and tooth of a circus elephant that went on the rampage in Bakewell before it was located and shot dead on Haddon Hill.

Bakewell Agricultural Business Centre (weekly cattle market)

Bakewell's Monday cattle market is well worth a visit even if you don't have a flock of sheep or a herd of cattle to sell. It takes place on the far side of the River Wye, in the Agricultural Business Centre, which stands

AUTUMN FORAGING WITH HARTINGTONS OF BAKEWELL

Hartingtons 🕾 01629 888586 👝 www.hartingtons.com

It's a grey, mizzling autumn day in Bakewell – not a promising start for a day scouring hedgerows and woodland for wild food; more a day for curling up under the duvet. But on arrival at Hartingtons, tucked under the eaves of a converted mill by the river, all negative thoughts are dispelled.

Chris Horne, director of the cookery school with partner Julie Ryalls, couldn't be more welcoming. Handing me a steaming cup of coffee, the couple share their passion for food: 'Artisan cookery certainly fits in with the Slow philosophy. It's about taking local produce and making something from scratch. It takes time, but the outcome is worth it.'

Hartingtons offer a host of courses, from bread and cheese making to beer brewing, but today I'm foraging with Chris and Rose Bax of *Taste the Wild* who also run courses on how to find your own food. This is the ultimate in Slow food: searching the countryside for your ingredients before cooking them.

We head up into the woods, squelching under damp russet leaves and soon spot our first fungus – jelly ears on an elder tree. 'Knowing your trees will help you identify mushrooms with more confidence,' Chris explains. Nearby, we find dead men's fingers, blackened digits rising from the earth; candle snuff, looking exactly like its name; deer mushrooms and pink spur, and at the other out in this town of mellow stone buildings, with its six futuristic looking brilliant-white domes. The building caused a flurry of controversy when it was erected in 1981. But no-one can question its success – it's one of the top livestock markets in the UK and a colourful reminder that the Peak District National Park is a living landscape serving those who work the land.

On a Monday morning it feels as if the Peak District's entire farming community has descended on Bakewell for market day. They come tumbling off the hills in their Land Rovers and silver trailers along with the occasional tractor. Farmers in tweed coats, Barbour jackets, peaked caps and wellington boots stride business-like around the centre, sometimes with a collie in tow. The sounds of lowing cattle and the bleating of sheep mingle with that of the livestock auctioneers who reel off numbers at breakneck speed. There's a real buzz in the air and it's hard not to get caught up in the excitement of it all, even if you're just an observer.

end of the scale, dryad's saddle protruding from a log like a broken dinner plate.

Identifying mushrooms is a complete minefield: one edible mushroom can look exactly like another poisonous one. 'You must be a detective,' Rose advises, 'checking for clues: the mushroom's dimensions, colour, smell, location; the cap, gills and spur print.' Chris adds, 'When you first start looking for mushrooms, don't go looking for your dinner. Spend time learning to identify them.'

Next up, seeds, roots and leaves from common weeds. I discover hogweed seeds have a wonderful aromatic flavour akin to cardamom, and wood sorrel, with its lovely fresh, lemony twang, makes an excellent garnish; and to my surprise, the haws from the ubiquitous hawthorn make for scrumptious jams, jellies and sauces. Rose and I agree that foraging, once a common practice, is now a lost art. 'It's a shame,' she observes, 'for when foraging, we're really engaging with nature and our world.'

Back in Hartington's kitchen, Chris cooks up a storm: marinated mushrooms on toast; partridge with elderberry jus and polenta, and a mouth-watering dessert using the haws and hogweed seeds we've collected. The countryside will never look the same again for me – and going for a walk in the woods may take a long time.

¶¶ FOOD & DRINK

You certainly won't go hungry in Bakewell, where every fourth or fifth shop seems to be a delicatessen, pastry shop, bakery, café or restaurant. There's also market food on Mondays.

Lavender Tearooms Hebden Court, 6 Matlock St, DE45 1EE ✆ 01629 814466. This cutesy café serves tasty food on floral china crockery. There's a lovely courtyard – and with blankets provided for those prepared to sit out on chillier days.

Original Bakewell Pudding Shop The Square, DE45 1BT ✆ 01629 812193. This is the real McCoy: Bakewell puddings, as they were originally conceived, served with custard or cream. In this building, the wife of the candle maker saw a business opportunity after the 'pudding accident' and set up her own trade alongside her husband, securing the recipe, baking and selling the puddings on the premises. You can order a take-away from the deli.

Rutland Arms Hotel The Square, DE45 1BT ✆ 01629 812812. Recently refurbished, this stylish hotel serves quality food in the restaurant – or bar (for more ambience). Not the cheapest place to eat in town, but you will be in good company: it's thought that Jane Austen wrote *Pride and Prejudice* while here.

🛍 SHOPPING

Bakewell is packed with little shops along the main shopping drag, a rectangle made up of Rutland Square, Market Street, Granby Road and Matlock Street, and along cobbled side streets that weave through the rectangle. Apart from the tempting bakeries, delicatessens and cafés there are plenty of kitchen stores, outdoor outlets and boutiques. Market day on Monday is the best day to come shopping with the many stalls in the square selling everything under the sun, from scented candles and soap to work tools.

EVENTS

There's something going on in Bakewell all year round, from craft and food fairs to carnivals and shows. Arts, crafts and food fairs are held regularly at Bakewell Town Hall, while the weekly market and monthly farmers' market attract visitors from far and wide. Keep an eye on ⌂ www.whatsonbakewell.co.uk for updated information.

April Bakewell Food Festival.

June Eroica Britannia (⌂ www.eroicabritannia.co.uk), is a retro-themed weekend of weekend of cycling, music and food based in Bakewell.

June/July Bakewell Carnival. Weird and wonderful events extending over a long week of fun. Check out the raft race and duck race on the Wye River, the Jack Russell races and Bakewell Pudding Fell Race, all combined with music, dancing and a carnival procession.

August Bakewell Show. At 200 years old, Bakewell Show is one of the oldest in the country. There are lots of animals (of course) alongside craft and food stands and food demonstrations.

November/December Christmas markets and Christmas Tree Festival in the parish church.

ART IN THE LANDSCAPE

Take a photography or painting course, inspired by the Peak District scenery, or simply walk through art and poetry.

1 Framing the Landscape with Yorkshire artist, Ashley Jackson. **2** Well dressings take place throughout the summer months in the Peak District – art and history created with petals and seeds. **3** Snow Stanza Stone by Yorkshire poet, Simon Armitage. **4** Sites of Meaning: a walk through poetry and words of wisdom on the boundary of Youlgreave.

LOCAL EVENTS

Open Gardens, well dressings, Wakes, arts and music festivals – all can be found year-round across Peak District towns and villages.

1 Saddleworth Rushcart Festival – the challenge of keeping balance on top of a moving haystack with just a kettle of ale for company. **2** Morris dancers are a frequent sight at Peak District festivals. **3** The Garland King lords it over his subjects as he rides through the streets of Castleton on Garland Day. **4** Beg, steal or borrow a hen and take part in the Hen Racing World Championship at the Barley Mow, Bonsall.

INDUSTRIAL HERITAGE

The Peak District is the birthplace of the Industrial Revolution and relics of this seismic shift in the nation's social and economic history pepper the landscape.

1 A ruined mill in the atmospheric Lumsdale, Matlock. **2** Masson Mills – one of the Arkwright mills. **3** The true meaning of 'horsepower' is demonstrated on special occasions by Friends of Cromford who offer regular boat trips on Cromford Canal.

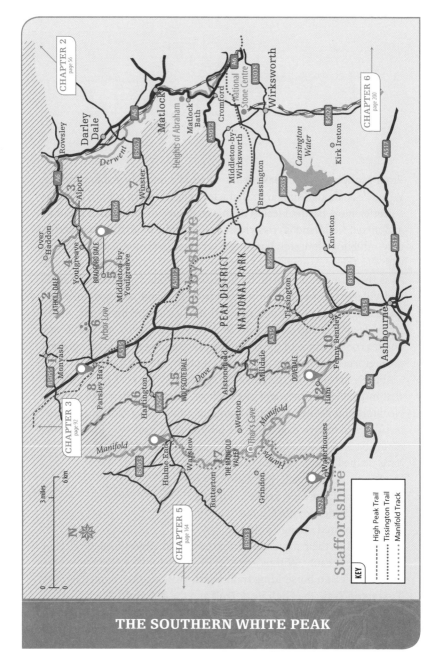

THE SOUTHERN WHITE PEAK

4

THE SOUTHERN
WHITE PEAK

From Monyash west of Bakewell to Dovedale north of Ashbourne, the White Peak, though similar in character to its northern counterpart, has a gentler, more pastoral feel to it. This landscape of flower-rich meadow and mixed woodland is criss-crossed with public footpaths too, offering easy rambling alongside burbling rivers and over undulating uplands, with just the occasional sharp climb out of the dales to test your mettle. As is the case further north, traditional limestone farmsteads, hamlets and villages are tucked into the folds of the land and are linked by quiet single-track lanes that rise and dip across the limestone. These riverside and upland settlements of duck ponds, greens, historical inns and tea rooms (some of these settlements retaining traditional butchers, greengrocers and grocery stores) are wonderful places to potter.

Above and below the surface of the southern White Peak is a landscape rich in geology, history and archaeology. Scattering these uplands are Neolithic and Bronze Age burial mounds and stone circles, the remains of ridge and furrow fields, and the hummocky meadows of lead works dating back to Roman times and beyond. In more recent times, quarries have shaped and reshaped the edges of the White Peak outside the national park, scarring the landscape before returning it to nature. Much of that industrialisation has disappeared along with the railway tracks, and in their place are leisure trails that wind through areas of outstanding beauty. Within a few miles of each other, there are three superb cycle and horseriding trails worth crossing the country for: the **Tissington Trail**, the **High Peak Trail** and the **Manifold Track**.

"Quarries have shaped and reshaped the edges of the White Peak."

On the southern reaches, just outside the park is **Ashbourne**, a particularly engaging market town that makes an excellent base for an exploration of this area.

WALKING & CYCLING

With so many **public footpaths** crossing the White Peak, the possibilities are endless using the ❋ OS White Peak Explorer map (OL24). From the tourist honeypots of Dovedale, Bradford and Lathkill to lesser-known dales such as Wolfscote, there's no shortage of riverside walking flanked by rocky crag, woodland or steep-sided grassland. You can combine walks on the dismantled railway trails with meadow footpaths for variety and interest. Likewise, plan circular walks to take in dales and uplands, preferably with a tea room or village pub along the way. Linear routes along the dales are possible, but require careful planning as bus services can be infrequent. Walking the southern White Peak section of the **Limestone Way** (the complete route extends from Castleton to Rocester in Staffordshire) is a great way to explore the area at a leisurely pace and takes in the historical villages of Monyash, Youlgreave and Tissington.

Three off-road **cycle trails** follow the line of dismantled railways through stunning scenery, all within a few miles of each other. From Parsley Hay, you can take in the **High Peak Trail** (almost 18 miles in length) as far as Cromford or the **Tissington Trail** that runs 13 miles southward to Ashbourne. Close by, the **Manifold Track** (almost 9 miles long) winds its way through deep-cut gorges, caves and soaring rock faces to Waterhouses. Plenty of quiet country lanes link all three trails for those who are happy to tackle the uphill gradients. In fact the whole of this area is riddled with narrow back lanes, mostly devoid of traffic and perfect for the road cyclist who relishes the challenge of a few ups and downs.

🚲 CYCLE HIRE

The Peak District National Park has bike hire outlets at Ashbourne for the Tissington Trail, Parsley Hay (serving both the Tissington and High Peak trails) and Middleton Top on the High Peak Trail. Limited opening times in winter – check the website for more details ⬢ www.peakdistrict.gov.uk/visiting/cycle.

ℹ TOURIST INFORMATION

Ashbourne Town Hall, Market Pl, DE6 1ES ✆ 01335 343666
Manifold Valley Visitor Centre Hulme End SK17 0EZ ✆ 01538 483741

Ashbourne Cycle Hire Mapleton Lane, Ashbourne DE6 2AA ✆ 01335 343156
Parsley Hay (south of Buxton on the A515) SK17 0DG ✆ 01298 84493 or 01629 816513.
Located at the beginning of the High Peak Trail.
The Manifold Track Cycle Hire Centre Old Station car park, Earlsway, Waterhouses
ST10 3EG ✆ 01538 308609

LATHKILL DALE TO WINSTER

Five miles southwest of the market town of Bakewell, **Lathkill Dale** is known for its crystal-clear waters and steep valley sides flanked by rocky crags. At the top end, you'll find the attractive grass-verged settlement of Monyash, while further east, the smaller upland village of Over Haddon lords it over the dale from its lofty position. The River Lathkill continues on to **Conksbury Bridge** and the picturesque hamlet of **Alport**, where it converges with the River Bradford to join the River Wye. Just west of here, you'll find the ridge-top village of Youlgreave offering tranquil riverside walks through meadow, woodland and limestone cliffs along the River Bradford. Continuing south, the historic village of Winster is

CHRIS GILBERT – PHOTOGRAPHER

✆ www.ravenseye.plus.com/ravenseye

Chris reels off the names of the hills, woodlands and villages stretching a ribbon outside the window of the Lathkil Hotel at Over Haddon. He points to a rise. 'Minninglow, up there on the horizon – I was there at dawn a few weeks ago taking a photograph with the mid-winter sun falling on the line through the middle of the trees.' I wonder about his bond with the Peak District landscape he loves to photograph. 'I grew up playing outside in the Fen countryside – so I love working in this landscape.'

We finish our coffee and walk down into Lathkill Dale. Chris spots a couple of dippers on the river and a buzzard catching an updraft

of air high above the concessionary path, but today he's focused on a particular weir further up the valley. We chat about his photography courses. 'It's teaching people to be there when something interesting's going on; opening minds to what's achievable.' At the weir Chris sets up his tripod, his eye constantly seeking out detail, comparison and interest. He focuses on the hard pebbles below the clear waters of the Lathkill, contrasting the liquid softness of the waterfall. Click. Ponder. Set up. Click. Assess. Adjust. Click.

Chris shows me his shot. It has a depth and breadth that pulls you right into this beautiful dale.

crammed with more than its fair share of handsome stone, mullion-windowed town houses and attractive mining cottages dating back to the 17th and 18th century.

1 MONYASH
Ⓐ Mandale Campsite (page 243)

At the head of Lathkill Dale, the village of Monyash feels as if it's still touching its past. The **Old Market Cross** on the green is a remnant of the settlement's long history, dating back to 1340 when the village was granted permission to hold a weekly market and a three-day festival to celebrate Holy Trinity. If you look closely at the base of the cross you'll find circular holes in the stone. They were created by the miners as they tested their newly sharpened drills on leaving the smithy opposite. The thriving mining community and blacksmith's are long gone, but the **Old Smithy** with all of its 250-year-old character still exists in the form of a popular café.

Monyash first appears in the Domesday Book as Manais, probably from the Celtic, meaning many waters, a reference to the numerous natural wells and meres (ponds) that once surrounded the village. Only one remains on Rakes Road at the edge of the village, **Fere Mere**. It's worth detouring to this little pool to seek out the warty great crested newts that bask in its shallow waters. On the eastern edge of the village towards Bakewell is the entrance to the glorious Lathkill Dale.

▌▌ FOOD & DRINK

Bull's Head Church St, DE45 1JH ℘ 01629 812372 ⊘ www.thebullsheadmonyash.co.uk. This lovely old stone building with contemporary décor serves flavoursome pub food and decent portions. The Bull's Head has a particularly nice beer garden for summer days.
Old Smithy Café Church St, DE45 1JH ℘ 01629 810190. With a café, bar and bistro, this rustic building filled with musical instruments and farm implements is a great place to come for breakfast, brunch or lunch. Portions are large and tea can be ordered by the pint – perfect for the hungry and thirsty walker or cyclist. Limited space inside and out may make it difficult to find a seat in busy periods.

2 LATHKILL DALE
Ⓐ Lathkil Hotel (page 242)

Lathkill Dale is internationally recognised for its ravine woodlands and flower-rich grasslands as well as its spectacular geological formations.

Its botanical and ornithological richness have resulted in its designation as a National Nature Reserve by Natural England. I've explored Lathkill Dale in spring and summer and returned on a snowy winter's day to remind myself why it is special. I started out this time from the dale head in **Monyash** where there's a small car park (for bus users, a service runs from Bakewell via Over Haddon to Monyash). Here the dale spreads out a grassy (in my case snowy) highway, the exposed rock just a scratch on one side at this point.

The broad valley is soon swallowed up by a narrow ravine though, reducing the way to a narrow, uneven path. This is a wild and rock-strewn place, with no sign of the River Lathkill initially. Part way down, the dale rock gives way to luminous green where water saturates weedy grass – the source of the River Lathkill. The water squeezes out of an inconspicuous rock next to **Lathkill Head Cave** here – except in dry periods. Soon scree and rocky bluff yield to woods, and the fast-flowing narrow brook broadens to a meandering river. The dale here is rich with wildlife: cowslips, orchids and the rare Jacob's ladder, coots, moorhens, trout, dippers and kingfishers. I didn't spot anything interesting on my winter ramble except a fistful of rooks darkening the sky, a solitary robin and a few mallards.

From here on, the Lathkill is dammed to create a series of still ponds that drop from weir to weir. At this point grassland gives way to woodland, noticeably softening the character of the dale. Signs warn of the mineshafts littering the path edges on this stretch of the walk. These reminders of Lathkill's industrial past are to be seen everywhere. Look out for the wooden footbridge leading to **Bateman's House** and its fenced off and gated mineshaft. Steps heading partway down the

RIVER LATHKILL – THE DISAPPEARING RIVER

'The purest and most transparent stream that I ever saw,' said writer **Charles Cotton** of the River Lathkill. He would have known: Cotton spent his days fishing the Peak District waters and wrote *The Compleat Angler* with Izaak Walton, the fishing bible of the 1700s, still renowned today. The angling guru claimed the river held 'the reddest and best trouts in England'. Nothing is ever perfect though – an almost two-mile section of river disappears in summer with the dry weather, seeping into the limestone and mines under the riverbed. When this happens, the fish are electrically stunned and removed to another location until the river fills again in the autumn.

mineshaft lead to a viewing point, revealing the bowels of the mine workings. Yet further down the dale, a steep path leads up the bank to the remains of **Mandale Engine House** and sough. **Mandale Mine** dates back at least to the 16th century.

Further on, a notice nailed to the tree reminds the walker that this is a concessionary path. The worn sign informs visitors that a fee of one penny is payable except Thursday in Easter week. Where a stone bridge spans the Lathkill beside an old mill and cottage, the road winds up to **Over Haddon**, perched on the top of the dale. If you just want to potter among the old industrial sites on the lower part of the dale only, this part of Lathkill Dale is a short walk from Over Haddon and has an easy-access path. If you have set out from Monyash, you can return to the village along the country roads that link the two villages or take the footpaths along the top of the northern side of the dale. Flagging down a bus is another option.

Lathkill is a wonderful place at any time of the year. As I crossed the snow-covered fields back to Monyash from Haddon Grove Road, the low sun lacing the copse in front of me, a hare ran along the base of the dry stone wall before bounding over it and disappearing over the other side. In spring, summer and autumn, the experience is different again, but just as magical.

FOOD & DRINK

Garden Tea Room Dale Rd, Over Haddon DE45 1JE 01629 810595 Apr–Oct (phone ahead to check if open). Fabulous cakes (gluten-free options) and great views, too, in this dog-friendly garden setting, all at affordable prices. Cash only.

Lathkil Hotel School Lane, Over Haddon DE45 1JE 01629 812501. This must be a contender for the hotel with the best view in the Peak District. Bag yourself a window seat in the cosy bar or restaurant – or head for the beer garden and marquee in the summer.

3 ALPORT

One of the most picture-perfect hamlets in the Peak District, Alport is a quiet backwater caught in the confluence of the River Lathkill and the River Bradford. There are no facilities in the village, but it makes an excellent starting point for some of the best, mostly level walks in the Peak Park through Bradford Dale and Lathkill Dale. In the hamlet itself, the 17th- and 18th-century stone mullion-windowed dwellings with their pretty cottage gardens and neatly trimmed hedges cluster round the burbling weirs of the River Lathkill. Add the narrow packhorse bridge to the mix, the old cotton mill with its waterwheel and the village's leafy surroundings, and you have all the ingredients for the country idyll.

From Alport along Lathkill Dale to Youlgreave

The best way to approach Youlgreave is on foot from the hamlet of Alport. Next to roadside parking on Alport Lane (the bus stop is just a short distance down the hill) there's an elegant creeper-covered house. Following the fingerpost, head down the lane at the side of the house and follow the pathway across meadows. This part of Lathkill Dale is a pastoral delight, surrounded by fields and woodland. Soon you will come to a handsome house on your left (used in an adaptation of D H Lawrence's *The Virgin and the Gypsy*), where the meadow pathway meets **Coalpit Lane**.

"Youlgreave retains a strong community – from the beekeeping group, village band, carnival and well dressing committee to the monthly cinema showings."

On the far side of the river there's a fetching summer house flanked by trees. Take the time to wander down to the little humpbacked bridge that crosses the River Lathkill. Retracing your steps, continue on up Coalpit Lane this time, turn left on to **Conksbury Lane** and on into Youlgreave. If you're returning to Alport, you can head straight down Alport Lane or follow the path along the River Bradford.

4 YOULGREAVE

⌂ **Thimble Cottages** (page 243), **YHA Youlgreave** (page 243)

Just south of Lathkill Dale, the village unfolds as a potpourri of housing styles – grand and modest; old and new. The main street sits on a broad limestone shelf, its buildings jostling near the ledge, while others spill down into the dale. Across the valley, meadows rise and dip to the sky, interspersed with patches of inky woodland. Despite attracting second-home owners and incomers, Youlgreave retains a strong community – from the beekeeping group, village band, carnival and well dressing committee to the monthly cinema showings – mostly happening in the black tin-hut village hall.

At the junction of Conksbury Lane, Church Street and Alport Lane, you'll find **All Saints Church**. The church was buzzing on my last visit, the parishioners setting up an exhibition to commemorate World War I.

They'd just installed several stained-glass panes salvaged by a local man, Charlie Waterhouse, from Ypres Cathedral and other surrounding churches destroyed by the Germans. These panes are a memorial to Charlie's brother, Rennie Waterhouse, who was killed in action in 1915. Alongside the Ypres glass is a beautiful pre-Raphaelite window behind the altar designed by the esteemed Edward Burne-Jones and made in the William Morris workshops. Also seek out a whimsical effigy of Thomas Cokayne, killed in 1488 as a result of a squabble while on his way to church. The miniature effigy doesn't refer to his size, but rather to the fact that the hapless teenager predeceased his father. Despite his dashing military attire, he cuts a humorous pint-sized figure with his dandy moustache and cockerel (referencing the family name) tucked behind his head. Across from the Thomas Cokayne memorial is a touching effigy of a medieval cross-legged knight, holding a heart in his hands, his dog curled under his feet.

The heart of Youlgreave

The narrow Church Street is lined with handsome Georgian houses and charming terraced cottages – along with the wisteria-covered **Old Hall**, engraved with the date 1656. On the left is the **Bull's Head Hotel**, an old coaching inn with a striking carved arched entrance. Just along from it is the **Youth Hostel** which has an unusual and attractive façade – once the village co-operative store.

Almost adjacent to it is a triangle of streets (the old market square) with the **Conduit Head** at its centre. This large, circular stone once held Youlgreave's private reservoir of water. Known locally as 'The Fountain', householders paid an annual sum of sixpence to access the water supply when it was first built. For centuries the villagers struggled up the steep-sided valley with water from the River Bradford. The water

WHAT'S IN A NAME?

Youlgreave, Youlgrave, Youlegrave? You'll find all these variations on signs in or around the village. The Highways Agency and the village have plumped for Youlgrave, while the Ordnance Survey mapmakers have opted for Youlgreave.

The 1086 Domesday Book recorded the village as Giolgrave, but there have been a staggering 50 or so variations over the centuries, including Yolgrave, Jalgrave, Yoleg, Isgrave, Igrave, Welegreve, Yolgreyve, Zolgrelf and Zolgrave.

was often contaminated, especially in the 'fever months' of July and August when the river was low, causing the deaths of many, especially children. Hannah Bowman took matters into her own hands. Founding the Women's Friendly Society, she set up a fund to have water piped from Mawstone Spring. Over one thousand yards of pipes were laid to the cistern in the centre of the village. After its completion in 1829, the village women congregated at the Fountain first thing in the morning, after the cistern had refilled overnight, and filled their pails. In 1869 the Fountain was

"Thimble Hall was once recorded as the world's smallest detached building by the Guinness Book of World Records."

upgraded and more pipes were installed, feeding water to various points in the village. The current annual **well dressings** (page 11) are located at the five village water taps. Youlgreave retains its private waterworks to this day, most of the water extracted from Bleakley and Harthill springs.

Notice the tiny whitewashed, one-up-one-down cottage in Market Place with its sagging slate roof. Aptly named **Thimble Hall**, it was once recorded as the world's smallest detached building by the Guinness Book of World Records. It's hard to believe this miniscule dwelling once housed a family of eight in the beginning of the 20th century, with no kitchen or bathroom, and a ladder to reach the top floor.

Down into Bradford Dale

Just past the Farmyard Inn, the last of the three pubs in the village, you can take the narrow pathway opposite Grove Place through the jumble of houses down into Bradford Dale. If you want to extend your village ramble, you can continue along the main street, taking the woodland path on the left. This will bring you on to a quieter section of the Dale with its Monet-esque fishing ponds. Turn left over the bridge and back in the direction of Youlgreave.

By the stone clapper bridge continue on along the wide, grassy banks of the river. This is a popular spot for visitors who come with all the paraphernalia associated with seaside outings: picnics and fishing nets, even deck chairs. It's the nearest thing you'll get to the seaside experience in this part of landlocked Derbyshire, with children, grown-ups and the occasional dog jumping into the deepest part of the river for a dip. If continuing on to Alport, cross Mawstone Lane, and head along the valley through meadow and on past limestone cliffs.

Walking & cycling with poetry along the Middleton & Smerrill boundary

What a wonderful way to explore the southern White Peak. This literary walk (and cycle) of undulating upland, rock-lined dales and burbling brooks, ancient site and modern-day industry can't fail to inspire. Combining words of wisdom and poetry, from The Bible to Wordsworth, modern-day wordsmiths and local residents, the words on the carved and sculpted stones reflect the beauty of this landscape and its long history.

🏃 The walk

❋ OS Explorer map OL24; start: Middleton-by-Youlgreave village square, 📍 SK196632; 5 miles; easy walking with just a few short rises; refreshments: Youlgreave

The Sites of Meaning trail combines a rural exploration of the Middleton and Smerrill Parish Boundary with a literary treasure hunt. To follow the trail, just print off the simple Sites of Meaning map (🖱 www.sitesofmeaning.org.uk) and use it alongside the ❋ OS Explorer map OL24 to ensure you find all the **Millennium Markerstones**. The focal **Village Stone** listing all 17 inscriptions is found in the **Village Square** picnic area, the texts radiating out from a circular centre roughly in the direction of their location.

The first individual inscriptions are found just outside Middleton on the bend of Youlgreave Road: **Roughwood Hollow Seat** and **Roughwood Hollow kerbstones** (📍 SK197638). From **Youlgreave**, head down into **Bradford Dale**, crossing the little clapper bridge. Turn right, passing a series of dammed fishing ponds. You'll find the next inscriptions at **Bradford Dale Bridge** (📍 SK200636) and the **Sheep Dip** (📍 SK199633) on the side of the Bradford Dale path. From here, detour left into **Row Dale** and the last inscription on the **Clapper Bridge** (📍 SK201633). Backtrack to Bradford Dale path and turn left to return to your starting point at Middleton-by-Youlgreave.

From here, head down Lowfield Lane where it crosses **Rowlow Brook** (📍 SK202626) to the next inscription. On the hill at **Over Rusden** (📍 SK199624) above the dale and Rusden Wood, the next one lies hidden in the grass. Follow the road to Elton next, until you reach the stone, **Smerrill** (📍 SK201617), on the bend just above **Smerrill Grange Farm**: two faces chiselled out of the rock corners and a mosaic of flowers interwoven with the words of Blake. Backtrack along the road to the **Holloway**, a dip between dry stone walls that leads to **Long Dale** (📍 SK191603) and the next inscription taken from a Nepalese teahouse menu. Continue on down the valley through a flat runway of meadow sandwiched between stone walls and mixed woodland. From here, the path follows the old **Roman Road** to the penultimate inscription from Heraclitus, **Balderstone** (♀ SK176611). Here two adjacent stone slabs mirror each other, including a reversed script. At **Friden Bends** (♀ SK175613), you'll locate the last inscription of the walk on a 'milestone'.

🚵 The bike ride

❀ OS Explorer map OL24; start: Parsley Hay, ♀ SK147638; 6 miles; moderately easy with undulating quiet roads, but will need to dismount on Green Lane; refreshments & bike hire at Parsley Hay (summer & w/ends only)

You can route march the country lanes for the last section of this literary hunt, but cycling is more pleasurable on the long road sections. It's possible to detour off the Sites of Meaning route to visit Arbor Low (page 142), just off Long Rake and up the farm track to Upper Oldhams Farm.

From Parsley Hay, leave the High Peak trail and cross the A515 on to The Rake (road) and turn right into **Long Rake**, where you'll find the next four inscriptions. The first, named **Arbor Low** (but some distance west off the actual Stonehenge site; ♀ SK151639), is situated close to the beginning of the road. The next is found at **Cales Farm West** (♀ SK165640) on the edge of a field. I didn't see the cranesbill mentioned on the cube-shaped stone, but the dried and faded Queen Ann lace (also mentioned) was thick in the meadow, crackling in the breeze on this late summer's day.

Continuing along Long Rake, the next marker-stone, **Cales Farm East** (♀ SK171640), lies on the edge of a field near Derbyshire Aggregates (stone and inscription sponsored by them), while the words of Youlgreave Primary children at **Long Rake** (♀ SK178639) are found in the dry stone wall at the forked junction of the road. Two stone gateposts at **Pen Close** (♀ SK186638) provide words of wisdom on the Youlgreave to Friden road. Turning right on to Green Lane, the track deteriorates to raised cobble, loose stone and muddy rut. I'd recommend wheeling bikes down the hill to preserve bones (unless you're a confident mountain biker).

The track passes by an old lead mine, a place of hills and holes, until it comes to a Latin inscription where Green Lane crosses the **Roman Road** – the name of the last inscription (♀ SK165623). The Latin inscription laments the fact that neither the Roman Road nor Green Lane has been maintained. The Roman road's no longer visible, but a long line of trees indicates its course. Green Lane soon intersects the High Peak Trail. Turn right here to cycle the last stretch of dismantled railway track, lined in summer with rose bay willow herb, harebell and granny's toenails, and back in to Parsley Hay.

5 MIDDLETON-BY-YOULGREAVE

This sleepy village just southwest of Youlgreave caught in a tangle of country lanes receives little traffic and only the occasional tourist – usually in the form of the rambler approaching from Bradford Dale. Among the farm dwellings and stone houses centred round a wide street and little green, you'll find the **Sites of Meaning Summary Stone** – and the starting point for a highly

"Among the farm dwellings and stone houses centred round a wide street and little green, you'll find the Sites of Meaning Summary Stone."

distinctive literary walk (pages 140–1). The Sites of Meaning was a millennium project dreamed up by the communities of Middleton and Smerrill Parish. Over seven years, local people, including artists, writers, photographers and businesses worked hard to bring the project to fruition. The end result: 17 sites are found along the parish boundary with inscriptions of sayings, poems, historic quotes and words of wisdom written by famous poets, writers and the local community. Poets and writers include William Wordsworth, W H Auden, Alexander Pope, William Blake, Heraclitus and Ralph Hodgson, as well as pupils from Youlgreave Primary School and Derbyshire Aggregates employees. The words are inscribed into natural and manmade stone landmarks: gate posts, kerbstones, seats, bridges and on road signs, as well as on especially commissioned sculpted art.

6 ARBOR LOW

As you look out from the prehistoric henge of Arbor Low (just off the A515 on Long Rake) the peaks fall away in waves to the horizon, mile upon mile in all directions. Our Neolithic ancestors seemed to have a knack for sussing out sites with breathtaking outlooks for such monuments as this, 1,200 feet above sea level. The farm track to the site doesn't hold much promise, but the circle of hewn stone across the meadow reveals itself as a place of mysterious beauty. Enclosed by an earthen bank and ditch, the site comprises about 50 limestone blocks surrounding the oval-shaped mound, with more monoliths at its centre. The stones lie flat on the ground, with no-one knowing for sure if they ever stood upright. Close by is the equally mysterious Bronze Age burial mound of Gib Hill. Arbor Low is reached by a farm track off Long Rake road.

7 WINSTER

🏠 **Brae Cottage B&B** (page 242), **Winster Hall** (page 243)

Sitting high above Darley Dale is the picturesque village of Winster, built on the wealth of its lead mining and claiming the highest density of listed buildings in the Peak District. From the tiny cottages clinging to the hillside to the elegant 17th and 18th-century houses lining the main road, this settlement is well worth exploring.

Jutting out on to Main Street is **Winster Market House** (⊙ Apr–Oct daily), built around the 16th century. Originally, the open arches (mostly bricked in now) were used by miners and street traders, with dairy products sold upstairs. Nowadays the upstairs space of this National Trust building is an **information point** with interpretive panels and a model of the village. At the west end of the village, the **Dower House**, a handsome double-fronted building behind ornate wrought-iron gates, sits across Main Street like a full stop, forcing the road to twist sharply right and left round it. The other building that shouts its pedigree is **Winster Hall**, a Neoclassical building complete with sash windows, corniced columns and balustrade. The **Limestone Way** runs along the edge of the village and there's a pleasant walk over to Birchover along grass-laced lanes and meadow paths. For old-fashioned village entertainment, visit Winster on **Shrove Tuesday** to watch the pancake race or in June or July in **Wakes week** for the Carnival Queen Parade, the tug-o-war game and other competitions, along with stalls and morris dancing. In July the **Secret Gardens of Winster** takes place, a good way to see the fine buildings of Winster up close and feel part of the local community. From here, head west into the heart of the White Peak.

🍴 FOOD & DRINK

Miners Standard Bank Top, DE4 2DR ✆ 01629 650279. Above the village, this 17th-century pub is an ever present reminder of Winster's mining past, and the attached B&B and campsite make it an attractive option for those who want to be within walking distance of a pub. Honest pub grub with more than adequate portions.

The Old Bowling Green East Bank, DE4 2DS ✆ 01629 650219. Cosy Peak District pub, serving traditional pub food with a range of options for vegetarians.

Winster Village Shop Main St, DE4 2DJ ✆ 01629 650683. Community owned, the village shop sells everything from a loaf of bread to beer and sandwiches. The shop has a small café area too with Wi-Fi access.

DOVEDALE,
THE MANIFOLD VALLEY & AROUND

Just outside the southern border of the national park, **Ashbourne** stands as the 'gateway to Dovedale and the Peak District' and is a vibrant market town sprinkled with historical detail and local colour. A few miles inside the national park to the north lies the much-loved **Dovedale** with its soaring limestone pinnacles, while the picture-perfect estate villages of **Ilam** and **Tissington** straddle the dale to the east and west. Much of this glorious landscape of deep-cut dale, upland plateau and gentle pasture can be seen from the superbly scenic Manifold Track and Tissington Trail. But there's also a quieter hinterland above the Dove and Manifold dales that shouldn't be forgotten: timeless Peak villages such as **Alstonefield**, **Wetton** and **Grindon** that sit serenely along the skyline.

8 PARSLEY HAY

Parsley Hay Station (just off the A515 Ashbourne to Buxton road) served the hamlet of the same name until the railway closed in 1963. Nowadays, the cycle-hire centre, kiosk (housed in the old station house) and outside picnic tables draw ramblers, horseriders and cyclists. It's a busy spot on the dismantled railway line as the departure point for the High Peak and Tissington trails.

The Istrian Kažun

A few yards from Parsley Hay car park on the High Peak Trail stands a circular building known as The Istrian Kažun, a dry stone shelter topped with a corbelled stone roof. Buildings such as this were erected in northwest Croatia in the 18th and 19th centuries to shelter those working the land. There are other versions of the Kažun found all over Mediterranean countries as well as further north, including Britain. The Kažun was a gift to the Peak District on Croatia's entry to the European Union in July 2013. It seems an appropriate present for this part of the country with its long tradition of dry stone building.

9 TISSINGTON

🏠 **Bassettwood Farm** (page 242), ⛺ **Rivendale** (page 243)

Whether you approach the estate village of Tissington from the B5056 or the A515, you know you're on to something special. And special

Cycling the High Peak Trail

OS Explorer map OL24; start: Parsley Hay, SK147638; 18 miles one way; easy, with small sections of steep gradients

Running along the trackbed of a long-defunct railway line opened in the 1830s to transport goods from Cromford Canal to the industrial northwest, the High Peak Trail certainly lives up to its name – from Hurdlow to Parsley Hay and on towards Longcliffe, it's like riding the crest of the limestone plateau with moorland, meadow and dale rippling out in endless peaks and troughs. Criss-crossing these uplands are the dry stone walls that are such a defining characteristic of the Peak District. The trail is superb, not just for the views, but also for its sense of space and big skies overhead. It takes you through a surprisingly industrialised countryside, ancient and modern; past the tell-tale pockmarks of ancient lead mines, centuries old limekilns, disused and active quarries scooped out of hillsides, and modern processing plants. **Refreshments** are available at the Royal Oak, Hurdlow (with bunk barn and camping), Parsley Hay, Middleton Top, The National Stone Centre, Black Rocks and High Peak Junction (note the kiosks on the High Peak Trail only open in summer & at w/ends).

The engineers overcame the problem of routing the trains across steep gradients by creating level sections of track between the inclines. By the 1960s the last trains had trundled through the High Peak and the track was lifted, a leisure trail laid in its place for the pleasure of ramblers, horseriders, and cyclists. Along the trail, information boards explain the crucial role of the railway in this industrialised landscape – from the brickworks at Friden to the quarries at Intake, New Hopton, Middleton Moor and Longcliffe.

Cycling southeast, you are advised to dismount at Hopton, and again at Middleton Top along with the section above High Peak Junction. Riding in the opposite direction, it's quite a challenge to cycle up the inclines, but there's no real shame in resorting to walking at this point. It's hard to believe that the heavy goods trains ever made it up these slopes, but it's all down to the engineering ingenuity of the time that the trains were able to ascend the five inclines from High Peak Junction to Buxton over about a thousand feet. First horses, then steam locomotives worked the level sections, while a stationary engine raised and lowered wagons filled with limestone and other heavy goods. To avoid the worst of the inclines between High Peak Junction and Middleton Top, you can rent a bike at the Middleton Top Countryside Centre and head northeast, but make sure you check out the Engine House and wagon before throwing a leg over the saddle. For those unfazed by the Middleton Top to High Peak Junction section, pause on the hillside above Cromford (the views over to Cromford Meadow and High Tor, with Matlock beyond, are magnificent) before plunging down through dank woodland to the junction with the Cromford Canal – and the end of the High Peak Trail.

it is – for Tissington is the quintessential Peak District estate village with its handsome Jacobean hall, its hillside Norman church, duck pond, cosy gritstone cottages, wide lawn verges and mature trees dotting the meadows surrounding the village.

From the B5056 you enter the village via Bent and Darfield Lane, but first you have to ford Bradbourne Brook. The river can appear worryingly deep, particularly after a spell of heavy rain, disconcerting for the driver – and for the passenger. But the cobble-bottomed ford isn't a problem if taken slowly. It's even more fun to splash through on a bike – or just to stand on the footbridge and watch the drivers nervously negotiate the volume of water. From here the lane climbs open farmland to the village.

From the A515, the approach is rather different, but equally delightful. Entered via a lodge through large stone gate-pillars, uneasy visitors may have the feeling that they're gate-crashing a private manor, a feeling enhanced as they continue along the lime-lined avenue. It's the overture to what lies ahead.

Seventeenth-century **Tissington Hall** is the centrepiece of the estate. Behind iron-wrought gates, steps lead up to the baronial stone building of mullioned windows, ornate chimney pots and a wide parapet hiding the roof. And if there was ever any doubt, the Fitzherbert coat of arms hanging above the door dispels any questions about the owner's pedigree. The gates are usually locked as Tissington Hall is still the Fitzherbert family's private home, but the hall is sometimes open for guided tours (www.tissingtonhall.co.uk Easter, bank holidays & Aug).

It's said that the unique Derbyshire custom of **well dressing** (page 11) originated in Tissington. And indeed, if you are only able to fit in one of the Derbyshire well dressings, Tissington is a strong contender with its half-dozen sites dotted around the village. But even if you're unable to attend the well dressings or visit Tissington Hall, it's still worth making a detour to this beautiful village. Take time to stroll around the village before you leave; enjoy its cottage gardens, lanes and jitties, taking in the tiny craft shop packed to the rafters with tempting wares as well as the traditional butcher's shop, once the village slaughter house (as it states above the door). For those who'd like to extend the walk, you can head out on to the Tissington Trail across the meadows, taking in a bigger loop.

"It's said that the unique Derbyshire custom of well dressing originated in Tissington."

FOOD & DRINK

Bassettwood Farm DE6 1RD ✆ 01335 350866. The farm is slightly off the beaten track above the village and down a long, pot-holed lane, but it's well worth the bumpy detour. The owners serve up simple home-cooked lunches on the little lawn outside the farmhouse (or in their living room when it's wet). You'll find some of the best cream teas here this side of Devon – and it's cheaper than Herbert's in the village. Before leaving, take a look at the animals – from the ornamental hens and pygmy goats to lambs and piglets.

Herbert's Fine English Tearooms DE6 1RA ✆ 01335 350501 🖥 www.herbertstearooms. co.uk ⊙ closed from Oct through the winter. It's all about the location. The old coach house run by Tissington Hall has a prime position in the village. Outside seating spills on to the wide grassy verge with views over to the church and duck pond. Inside, it's all vintage china and dangling chandeliers. Check out Herbert's classic, extra fine or sparkling cream tea – all at 'fine' prices.

The Tissington Trail

'Dream of noise and wheels and coal and steam' says the metal plaque screwed to one of the many bridges on the Tissington Trail, a 13-mile route for cyclists, horseriders and walkers from Parsley Hay to Ashbourne along a former railway line. And on a recent cycle, it wasn't hard for me to imagine the Victorian trains chuffing their way through this Peak landscape from **Parsley Hay** when my bike wheels spun through deep cuttings, under intermittent railway bridges, past the delightfully preserved signal box at Biggin, and on through the 600-metre tunnel on the outskirts of Ashbourne. The Tissington line was one of the last Victorian railways to be built in Britain. Opened in 1899, it supplied milk to London, while the quarries along the route provided limestone for transportation. The last train ran in 1967 when the track was lifted and the trail laid in its place instead.

The trail joins the High Peak Trail just south of Parsley Hay. You can start your ride from Ashbourne, or at the Parsley Hay end (just a few miles south of Buxton) as I prefer. The lively market town of Ashbourne is a great mid-point with plenty of lunch options before returning to Parsley Hay. Bikes can be hired at either end and you can do a there-and-back route along the dismantled railway. For a more varied circular cycle, you can ride cross-country over to the High Peak Trail – but beware of the greater gradients once off the dismantled railways. In the uplands there are wide-open views that spread out for tens of miles towards Staffordshire. As the trail drops towards Ashbourne, the landscape softens to leafy valleys and grassy farmlands. Whatever you do, stop off at Tissington.

10 FENNY BENTLEY

Just north of Ashbourne, Fenny Bentley straddles the A515 Buxton road. Passing through, there seems no reason to stop in this unremarkable village, but turn left up Ashes Lane and you will come to a wonderful church – **St Edmund, King and Martyr**. Since 1240, this tiny church has been rebuilt and renovated over the centuries, but it hasn't been diminished in any way. Insignificant looking on the outside, St Edmund's is one of exquisite beauty inside.

Perhaps the most interesting – and disturbing – feature in the church is that of the shrouded effigies of Thomas Beresford of Bentley Hall and his wife Agnes Hassall, the outline of their faces and bodies just visible through the 'creases' in the carved alabaster. In typical fashion their 21 children line the sides of the chest tomb – but untypically their bodies are shrouded in the same manner, like rows of potato sacks knotted at the top. Overhead is a painted Gothic ceiling, panelled in rich hues of red, green and gold, each section filled with the exquisite detail of the Beresford coat of arms, the bears referencing the family name (*Bere*), along with rays of sunlight and winged angels. Echoing the ceiling, the organ pipes are painted gold and red, while further panels on the wall depict saints, including St Anthony and St Katherine, each one accompanied by the objects that symbolise them. The richness of colour and detail is further reflected in the stained-glass windows of the church, with scenes from the Bible, its characters, the saints and memorials to the Beresford family. Before leaving this wonderful church check out the chancel screen, the oldest in the Peak District. Look out for the small fox and goose carving there, a satirical comment on William Rufus's extravagant gift to the Dean of Lincoln – at the expense of the local clergy, left poor by his disproportionate distribution of wealth.

11 ASHBOURNE

A handsome Georgian market town just south of the national park, Ashbourne has been dubbed 'the gateway to Dovedale'. It's a good base for the southern end of the White Peak. 'The thing about Ashbourne,' the helpful assistant at the TIC said, 'is that you need to slow down and take in its details. Look down the little yards and alleys to get a glimpse of the original medieval architecture behind the Georgian façades, and look up for some quirky features on the Georgian and Victorian buildings.'

This is good advice, it turns out. With every corner I turn, I'm sidetracked by a historical detail: a sun dial here, a head statue there; an interesting inscription; a Victorian boot scraper or lantern. It takes me an hour to reach St Oswald's church, a walk that normally lasts less than ten minutes from the market square.

The town of Ashbourne is a busy stopover and has been since medieval times when pilgrims walking St Non's Way rested up here – right through Georgian times when six coaching routes converged in the town including the London to Carlisle route. Ashbourne still bears that coaching legacy today. From the top of **Market Place** to the bottom of **The Shambles** (Victoria Square), there are more inns (past and present) than you can shake a stick at: Ye Old Vaults, the George and Dragon, the White Swan and The Horns, The Green Man and Black's Head (with its impressive gantry, painted green man and wooden black head sculpture – smiling on one side and scowling on the other).

The town has had its fair share of historical figures passing through too. Bonnie Prince Charlie declared his father James as King of England, Wales and Scotland here in 1745 as he forged his way south (although he only got as far as Derby before he turned on his heel). Queen Victoria also stopped off here to freshen up. Esteemed writers Samuel Johnson, George Eliot and Izaac Walton were also spotted knocking around town. Look out for the blue plaques.

While Market Place is mostly used as a car park these days, it's still retained for its original purpose on Thursday and Saturday, packed with stalls and goods. Along with the surrounding inns, there are cafés and restaurants aplenty to stave off hunger. The town has a healthy share of independent businesses and shops – borne out in names like Stepping

THE UP'ARDS & DOWN'ARDS

Ashbourne's Royal Shrove Tuesday and Ash Wednesday Football is an ancient tradition that's been going on for centuries. It's purported that the original ball was a decapitated head, tossed into the crowd following an execution. Nowadays the specially created cork-filled ball (to keep it afloat in the river) is carried through the town in a series of 'hugs', a bit like a rugby scrum. The Up'Ards and Down'Ards are made up of two teams north and south of **Henmore Brook**, their millstone goalposts set three miles apart at the demolished mills of Sturston and Clifton. Local shops and businesses wisely board up their windows before the scrum kicks off in town.

Stones Shop and Field and Stream of Ashbourne (sporting guns, fly fishing and country clothing). More shops are hidden down yards or side alleys. Continue west from St John Street into Church Street, passing by fine Georgian buildings and on towards an even older part of town. Here you'll find two rows of almshouses with stubby pencil chimney stacks, mullioned and lead-glass windows and wooden latched doors barely five feet high. Across the road is the original building of **Queen Elizabeth's Grammar School** (QEGS), founded in 1585. With its wonky walls bulging outwards, it hovers over the almshouses like a watchful headmistress.

St Oswald's Church

Just down from the almshouses and the original building of Queen Elizabeth's Grammar School is St Oswald's Church with 'the finest spire in England' – so George Eliot claimed. The church makes a statement straight off with its 12 ghoulish skulls supporting the pointed Gothic pillars on the gateposts by the entrance. Inside, the **Boothby Chapel** is filled with alabaster and marble effigies, chest tombs and wall memorials to the Cokayne, Boothby and Bradbourne families. There's no question about the importance of these old Ashbourne families with their stately demeanour and their grand attire – all ruffles, robes and armour. The sculpted lords and ladies, resting in majestic repose upon raised tombstones

"Don't miss the beautiful pre-Raphaelite stained-glass window of two sisters near the south entrance."

decorated with painted shields, battlements, angels and mythical creatures are impressive, but it's tiny six-year-old Penelope Boothby in her simple flowing gown who steals the show. The seemingly translucent Carrara marble figure sculpted by Thomas Banks lies on her side, 'asleep' in an innocent, childlike slumber: a picture of delicate perfection. There is something raw and touching about the effigy, enhanced by the painting of a younger Penelope on the floor beside the tombstone; and the inscription on the tomb that reads: 'She was in form and intellect most exquisite. The unfortunate parents ventured their all in this frail bark and the wreck was total'. Before you leave the church, take time to identify the head of the Green Man of Ashbourne on the church pillars, a little light relief after the sombre Boothby Chapel. And don't miss the beautiful pre-Raphaelite stained-glass window of two sisters near the south entrance.

ᵘ FOOD & DRINK

You are spoiled for choice in Ashbourne with its lovely little cafés and characterful pubs. Below are some of my favourites. Ashbourne markets are on Thursdays and Saturdays; the Farmer's Market takes place on the last Thursday of the month at the Town Hall.

Café Impromptu 14 Church St, DE6 1AE ⌀ 07733 242255. Always busy, so you may need to reserve a table in advance. The friendly, helpful staff serve carefully prepared, fresh and locally sourced food.

The Cheddar Gorge 9 Dig St, DE6 1GF ⌀ 01335 344528 ⊙ closed Sun. This characterful deli, housed in an 18th-century building, stocks scrumptious pies, tarts and cheeses (up to 80 in stock) along with other deli treats. There are only a couple of inside tables.

Whites of Ashbourne 6 Buxton Rd, DE6 1EX ⌀ 01335 345000. There's a limited menu but with some interesting choices served up in this tastefully decorated establishment. The camembert starter is particularly good.

EVENTS

There are some quirky events taking place in and around Ashbourne, the Up'Ards and Down'Ards apart. In June, the **World Toe Wrestling Championships** takes place at Bentley Brook Inn two miles north of town, while Ashbourne hosts its very own **Highland Gathering** along with the **Ashbourne Festival** (not to be missed). August sees in the more traditional **Ashbourne Show**. Check dates on ⌀ www.ashbourne.life.

12 ILAM

🏠 **Beechenhill Farm** (page 242), **The Izaak Walton Hotel** (page 242), **YHA Ilam Hall** (page 243)

Although Ilam sits by the River Manifold, most people associate the settlement with the River Dove and continue on to Dovedale (page 156) from here. The chocolate-box village of Ilam, west of Fenny Bentley, sits at the foot of steep-sided hills more reminiscent of the Lake District than the Peak District. The crinkle-crankle hills are actually coral reefs filled with holes and fossilised sea creatures – and coral, of course. Caught between Thorpe Cloud and Bunster Hill, lower Dovedale is probably the most iconic natural landmark in the White Peak and a fitting backdrop for this model village.

"The crinkle-crankle hills are actually coral reefs filled with holes and fossilised sea creatures – and coral."

Where Ilam Moor Lane meets Thorpe Road, there's a striking Gothic monument rising in tiers to the height of 40 feet like an elaborate wedding cake. This is **Ilam Cross**, erected by

ST BERTRAM

Bertram, Prince of Mercia came from humble beginnings, raised in a cave at Wetton. In his latter life, he returned to these simple shelters to reside as a hermit. A deeply religious man, Bertram travelled to Ireland to seek spiritual guidance, inspired by St Patrick. There he met an Irish princess and fell in love with her. The pregnant princess returned to Mercia with Bertram. As they neared Bertram's home, the princess went into labour. The child was safely delivered in Thor's Cave only to be mauled to death by wolves along with its mother while Bertram was searching for food. On returning, Bertram was overcome with grief and renounced his royal heritage, vowing to live out the rest of his days in simple servitude to God. A wise and holy man, people flocked to his retreat for spiritual guidance. His shrine at Ilam Church continues to draw pilgrims from all over Europe to this day.

Jesse Watts Russell of Ilam Hall in 1841 in memory of his beloved wife Mary 'to perpetuate the memory of one who lives in the hearts of so many in this village and neighbourhood'. The *Sheffield Mercury* called it 'an exceedingly beautiful stone cross, light and graceful; tasteful and delicate'. But over the decades, the stone eroded and the angels began to crumble, with the top layer, including its gilt cross, blowing away in a freak storm in the 1960s. It wasn't until 2011 that the section was restored to its former glory, along with the six carved angels. Look out for the **Ilam Imp**.

Further along the village is a row of **Swiss Cottages** and a matching spired schoolhouse, fable-like in appearance with their steeply pitched roofs, wooden shingled walls, oriel windows and fluted bargeboards. On the other side of the road, a path gently rises to Ilam Church and Hall. Take the left turning past Dovedale House and head towards the **Church of the Holy Cross** with its unusual crown-shaped annex. The church of Ilam is a box of delights. Start with the **Chapel of St Bertram**, where you will find the 13th-century tomb of the Saxon saint and hermit.

Sitting on top of St Bertram's chest tomb are the prayers of pilgrims, often moving reads. Squeezed into a corner beside the decorated organ pipes, there's a 17th-century alabaster tomb of Robert Meverell of Throwley Hall and his wife. They lie there in their finery, hands held in prayer – minus a finger or two. Above them the stoutly figure of their daughter kneels in prayer, while her equally portly children are lined up beside her, hands together in pious repose, although they have a look of scallywags who'd rather be climbing trees. At the entrance to the chapel, a **Maiden's Garland** hangs from the doorway. The curious-looking 'withered bits' are actually gloves, handkerchief and flowers made of paper, and would have been carried on the coffin of an unmarried woman and remained in church as long as no-one challenged the lady's virtue.

The main body of this Grade I church is also packed with interest. There are a number of stained-glass windows in vivid reds and blues, a beautiful wrought-iron chancel screen and polished pulpit of local stone. The font at the back of the church is Norman, carved in the naïve style of the period. The Ilam storyboards that surround the nave may look out of place among so much historical treasure. It's folksy and modern, but for me it's a laudable pictorial documentation of Ilam's history.

On the other side of the chancel from St Bertram's Chapel, the 19th-century **Pike Watts Monument and Mausoleum** is an impressive burial place, built by Jesse Watts Russell for his family. Taking centre stage is a grand monument of David Pike Watts, his father-in-law. Although Watts is on his death bed, he still has the appearance of the successful London businessman he was. At his feet, Jesse's wife Mary and their children gaze adoringly at the dying man elevated above them. To one side there is a bust of Jesse Watts Russell, the man responsible for rebuilding Ilam Hall, the church and village during his tenure, the village we can still see and enjoy today.

THE ILAM STORY

In March 2004 local artist Sue Prince made a visit to southern Sweden where she became intrigued by Swedish folk art, an art form that began in rural southern Sweden in the late 1700s. The Bonad paintings (wall hangings) were created to decorate the dark, smoky interiors of small farmhouses during the winter months. Back home, Sue and 11 other local artists created their own Bonad painting in the traditional Swedish style, using egg tempera paint (made with Ilam egg yolks and earth pigment) on a gesso of rabbit skin glue and chalk. They created 12 panels, 59 feet long in total, depicting the story of Ilam from 700BC, when Neolithic people built burial barrows on the hills surrounding Ilam through to the story of Bertram and on into present-day Ilam. The text along the top of the panels is from Burke's *Visitation of the Seats and Arms of the Noblemen and Gentlemen of Great Britain and Ireland* (not the snappiest of titles) and was quoted in the sale documents for Ilam Hall and Estate in 1910.

Ilam Park

National Trust

After Watts Russell sold the estate, Ilam Hall went through a chequered history. Much of the building was demolished, the present hall a pale shadow of its former self – but still a striking building for all that. Nowadays the hall is a rather lovely youth hostel, while the rest of the estate is managed by the National Trust. Near the hostel, you'll find the NT Visitor Centre, shop and tea room, while just a little further on is the **Italian Garden**, with superb views over to Bunster Hill and Thorpe Cloud. Some of the demolished stonework was rescued from the old hall and has been used to build a balustrade and planters in the garden. This is a fine place to claim a bench and enjoy a picnic.

A circular walk from Ilam through Dovedale

✳ OS Explorer map OL24; start: Ilam village, ♥ SK136508; 5 miles; fairly easy but for the short punishing climb out of Dovedale; refreshments: National Trust café at Ilam Hall & the kiosk selling drinks, snacks & ice cream at Dovedale car park

This walk takes in the best of Dovedale before climbing out of the valley and backtracking to Ilam along a wooded ridge. Where the path emerges from the trees into upland fields, the views across to the conical Thorpe Cloud, the Staffordshire Plains and the mountains of Wales (on clear days) are simply breathtaking. There's a chance to scoot up to the summit of Bunster Hill, if you still have any energy left over from the hike up the side of Dovedale, before tumbling down through fields into the lovely village of Ilam. There's a small amount of parking in Ilam and a limited bus service from Bakewell.

1 From Ilam Cross take the Thorpe road, with the river flowing on your right. Soon you will see a gate on the left. Cross the road and go through the gate into the field by the National Trust sign for Bunster Hill. Turn right and follow the track upwards past the NT sign and on to a broader track. Continue on in the same direction.

2 Go through the gap signed Public Footpath to Dovedale and continue through fields, watching out for the stiles over the dry stone walls. You'll pass farm buildings and the back of the Izaak Walton Hotel. Head downhill between trees, arriving at Dovedale car park. There's a chance to pick up a drink, snack or an ice cream from the mobile kiosk here.

3 Follow the path north along the River Dove from the car park, cross the stepping stones and continue on with the river now on your left for just under 2 miles.

🍴 FOOD & DRINK

Izaak Walton Hotel Ilam DE6 2AY ✆ 01335 350981. Walton stayed in the guesthouse here in the 17th century, spending many happy hours fishing on the nearby River Dove, the inspiration for much of *The Compleat Angler*. Along with fishing permits and accommodation, the Izaak Walton offers good food, locally sourced, in elegant surroundings with great views out to the countryside.

The Old Dog Spend Lane, Thorpe DE6 2AT ✆ 01335 350990 ☻ food served: Wed–Sat, Sun 12.00–16.00. Stylishly refurbished pub with flagstone floors, stone counters and roaring fires. The pub serves a simple lunchtime and evening menu.

The National Trust Manifold Park Tea Room DE6 2AZ ✆ 01335 350503. For a light bite in beautiful surroundings look no further than this NT-run café located in the grounds of Ilam Hall. Be prepared to wait at busy times. The views from the garden are particularly fine.

4 When you reach a wooden footbridge spanning the river, cross it and follow the path until you come to a three-way sign. Turn left here, following the fingerpost for 'Ilam 1¾ miles (steep ascent)'. The track does indeed climb steeply through trees up the wall of the dale.

5 At the top, ignore the stile and continue along the ridge of the dale, walking back in the direction you've come from. Taking care on the precipitous dale edge, you will eventually emerge from the trees and out on to a field with breathtaking views.

6 Drop down through the field to the wooden signpost and make your way along the track around the side of the farm, keeping your eye open for waymarkers. Head up to the gate beside the house and follow the farm track away from the buildings. Follow the bend left on the track and continue on, keeping the line of trees and stone wall on your right. Continue to follow the dry stone wall on your right through a field, until you see another National Trust sign for Bunster Hill. Go through the gate and turn right, still following the dry stone wall on your right as you drop downwards. Soon Ilam will come into view.

7 Drop down the side of Bunster Hill, following the grassy pathway into the valley. Cross the wall over a stile and continue on downhill towards Ilam. Take the wooden staircase over another stone wall, following the farm track past a pond on the right.

8 Soon you will come to the gate on to the road, where you began your walk through the fields to Dovedale. Go through it and turn right back into the village. Your walk is complete.

13 DOVEDALE

Of all the dales in the Peak District, it's probably safe to say that Dovedale is the most visited, and not surprisingly, for it's one of the most beautiful and dramatic valleys in the national park. At times, you're virtually queuing to get into the southern end of Dovedale. Persist though, the majority don't make it past the stepping stones at its southern end, while only a few stagger on to Lover's Leap. After that, it's primarily the more dedicated ramblers who pound the path. It's hard to begrudge the hordes who visit this iconic Peak District landmark, but if you want to avoid the picnickers and strollers, it's best to come outside peak holiday times. Even better, head out on to the hills above the dale or on into the significantly quieter Wolfscote Dale.

The spectacular southern entrance to the dale is bounded by the sheer-sided reef knolls (fossilised coral mounds) of **Bunster Hill** and **Thorpe Cloud** standing sentry at the dale's entrance. An ascent up the steep side of Thorpe Cloud turns the legs to jelly, but the drop down into Dovedale from the summit is a lovely approach to the River Dove. Otherwise, head up the valley from the car park. The **stepping stones** crossing the river are a delight for young and old alike while upstream the weedy river weaves rich shades of blues and greens. There's a good chance of catching sight of plump black-and-white dippers here, their tails bobbing up and down as they search for food in the water.

Soon the path climbs away from the river, up hewn steps (cut by Italian prisoners of war) to **Lover's Leap**. This is a great spot for a picnic – but only if you don't mind sharing it with others, as is the case most days. There are many romantic tales – tragedies and near-tragedies of heart-broken maidens throwing themselves off towering rocks, later dubbed 'Lover's Leap'. The story associated with this particular Lover's Leap has a happy ending: a young woman on hearing her lover had been killed in the Napoleonic Wars, leapt from the rocky premonitory, only for her fall to be broken by her long thick hair getting caught in the bushes. Luck was on her side. As she returned home the news reached her that her beloved, far from dead, was on his way to see her.

From Lover's Leap, the river squeezes through a ravine, so narrow in places that a boardwalk has been built out over the river. The section between Lover's Leap and **Ilam Rock** (a pinnacle that jabs the sky like a knife blade) is one filled with geological drama – from the rocky crags of the **Twelve Apostles** to the smattering of caves and arches that line the dale. After Ilam Rock, the valley widens, with the river meandering through grassy banks and woodland all the way to Milldale – and stuffed with wild flowers in spring and summer.

14 MILLDALE

The hamlet of Milldale is a quiet little spot on the River Dove, a short distance (and yet a world away) from the crowds that gather around the stepping stones further south. By the river a rustic **National Trust Information Barn** houses interpretative boards that tell the stories of Dovedale's geology, history and wildlife. In front of the barn, there's a tiny humpbacked bridge, so narrow that Izaak Walton (assigning himself to the character of the viator, or traveller in *The Compleat Angler*) wrote: 'What's here, the sign of a bridge? Do you travel in wheelbarrows in this country? This bridge was made for nothing else – why a mouse can hardly go over it, 'tis not two fingers broad!' As a result the bridge is still known to this day as the **Viator's Bridge**. Beyond the River Dove, the rest of the village is thrown topsy-turvy into the valley that drops down to the waterside. One of the little square stone houses sells snacks and drinks from the opening in the half door. Ring the bell if it's closed – you might just be in luck.

15 WOLFSCOTE DALE

North from Milldale, the River Dove meanders through Wolfscote Dale, another beautiful valley of rocky crags, grassy slopes and woodland, with a wide path that follows the curve of the River Dove. It's a gentler version of Dovedale, and as a result only receives a fraction of the latter's visitors. I've done a circular walk of this quiet and tranquil dale, taking in Wolfscote Dale from Alstonefield; then returned the following week to do the Dovedale section. For a thoroughly satisfying, though demanding, day's hike you can walk the entire Dovedale and Wolfscote Dale in one go, completing a circular route via Stanshope and Alstonefield across the uplands, a distance of around 13 miles.

16 HARTINGTON

🏠 **Charles Cotton Hotel** (page 242)

Sandwiched between the Tissington Trail and Manifold Track is Hartington village with its gracefully weathered stone buildings centred round a market square, green and duck pond. It can get really busy here, so come out of season if possible. While Hartington is renowned for its setting, few know of its long association with cheese. Hartington once produced 25% of the country's stilton at Long Clawson Hartington Dairy until it was sold in 2009. But this particular chapter of Hartington's cheese-making history continues with the recent opening of **Hartington Creamery**, all thanks to the entrepreneurial spirit of local cheese-makers who hunted down suitable barns in the parish to convert into a small-scale creamery. They now produce stilton and Peakland white and blue along with the Hartington bomber, Cheddleton and chives (from local farms around Leek), Dovedale blue and Staffordshire cheddar, on sale at the Old Hartington Cheese Shop.

ⅱ FOOD & DRINK

Devonshire Arms Market Pl, SK17 0AL ✆ 01298 84232. There's terrific food in this lovely old pub. There's also a restaurant attached to the pub, but the bar has a much better ambience, even if the punters are squeezed in together.

Old Hartington Cheese Shop Market Pl, SK17 0AL ✆ 01298 84935 ⅋ www.hartingtoncheeseshop.co.uk. Hartington Creamery cheeses are on sale from this cute barn-like building opposite the duck pond.

Charles Cotton Hotel Market Pl, SK17 0AL ✆ 01298 84229. Angler, poet and gambler Charles Cotton was Izaak Walton's fishing companion and co-writer of the fishing bible, *The Compleat Angler*. The hotel pays more than a nod to Cotton with its paintings, maps and fishing paraphernalia (plus organises fishing packages). Apart from the stylish surroundings and historical interest, the restaurant and (cosier) bar have a reputation for good food – locally sourced, organic and GM-free – along with carefully selected wines and local ales.

17 THE MANIFOLD VALLEY

🏠 **Secret Cloud House Holidays** (page 243)

The Manifold Valley, west of Dovedale, is often referred to as the 'little Switzerland of Staffordshire'. The lofty comparison of the Manifold to the Alps may not be very imaginative or accurate, but it's true to say this is a valley of distinctive English scenic qualities. The valley trail runs from Hulme End and finishes in Waterhouses. The steam trains that once chugged their way along the Manifold are long gone, but the resurfaced dismantled railway track is alive with cyclists and walkers. The trail winds its way through meadows, woodlands of ash, hazel and lime, and alongside the Manifold until the river disappears underground near Wetton Mill. Wild flowers and herbs thrive in the rich limestone soil, attracting butterflies and bees. The brown, peaty Manifold River is filled with trout and you might catch a glimpse of a kingfisher surveying the riverside.

Ecton Hill on the east side of the valley is of geological interest and is a Site of Special Scientific Interest (SSSI). Here, Ecton Hill Field Studies Association (EHFSA) organises field trips for students and other interested parties. Its strapline: '300 million years of geology, 3,000 years of archaeology and 300 years of social and industrial history', is quite a claim for this ordinary-looking hill. Certainly copper and lead have been extracted from the hill from Bronze Age times, and by the 18th century the Duke of Devonshire was making so much money from the

"'300 million years of geology, 3,000 years of archaeology and 300 years of social and industrial history'"

copper mines it paid for the magnificent Crescent in Buxton (page 113). Indeed the mines at Ecton Hill lay claim to a series of industrial advancements: the sinking of the deepest mineshaft in Britain, the first use of explosives in British mining and the building of an early Boulton and Watt steam engine, as well as the effective use of water power for mine pumping. The land on the hill is open access but if you wander up there, take care in this area of hills and holes. Be sure not to miss the **Ecton Engine House** owned by the National Trust, and watch out for NT public events offering visitors guided walks on the hill and a visit to the underground mine itself.

Before beginning an exploration of the Manifold Valley, stop off at the visitor's centre in the **old railway station** at **Hulme End** to arm yourself with information leaflets on the area. Then hire a bike for the gentle downhill cycle to Waterhouses – or lace up your walking boots so you can wander off-piste. I'd recommend both.

Thor's Cave

Why would a Norse god find himself holed up in rural England? A less romantic, but more likely explanation is that the name is a corruption of *tor* meaning hill. Either way, this cave is an extraordinary geological and historical SSSI. The crag that sits in landlocked Staffordshire in the northern hemisphere was once a tropical reef lying under warm shallow waters south of the equator. The steps to Thor's Cave bear evidence to this fact, the fossil crinoid stems and the odd brachiopod imprinted in the rock. The cave itself was created over thousands of years by wind and water. In time it was used by animals, then man for shelter. Excavated bones show that the caves in the area were used in prehistoric times by giant deer, bear and even mammoth. More recent finds (including stone tools) reveal Thor's Cave was used as a burial site in the Bronze Age and probably right through to Roman or Saxon times. Today the cave is occupied by nothing more exciting than modern *Homo sapiens* – holidaymakers and children who scramble over the rock. Before leaving, take in the spectacular views over the Manifold Valley and beyond, framed by the great mouth of the cave.

A walk through the Manifold Valley to Thor's Cave

❋ OS Explorer map OL24; start: Manifold Way Visitor Centre car park, Hulme End,
📍 SK102593; 7 miles; easy except for the stiff climb up to Thor's Cave & Wetton

This walk is one of charming diversity, taking in the Manifold Valley, a cave, an upland village and an area of ancient copper and lead mines. Refreshments at Wetton Mill (summer only) and Ye Olde Royal Oak, Wetton.

1 Head down the Manifold Track, crossing the gated road that meanders alongside the rust-coloured River Manifold.

2 Cross another road and continue through Swainsley Tunnel, following the two-mile road section that's open to traffic (although it's the bicycle that's king here, not the car).

3 Cross the little bridge to Wetton Mill if you're in need of refreshment. Alternatively you can spread a picnic out on the grassy slopes in front of the mill and dip your toes in the River Manifold, weather permitting. After Wetton Mill, the river goes underground in summer and all that remains is a stony riverbed. The valley becomes steeper and more dramatic at this point. From time to time, the rambler will catch a glimpse of **Thor's Cave** in the distance, soaring skyward.

4 You will see the Thor's Cave information board on your left. Follow the footbridge across the Manifold and take the take the well-defined path uphill. Turn right, signposted 'Thor's Cave' and continue steeply uphill. It's a lung-busting but worthwhile climb and, inside, the cave is cathedral-like. Watch your step on the slippery, foot-polished limestone.

5 On the way back down, take a right turning this time signed for **Wetton**. Climb steeply up through woods and meadows and into the village.

6 At the main junction in the village you can detour right down Main Street for more refreshments at **Ye Olde Royal Oak** where the British Toe Wrestling Championships

The Manifold villages

🏠 **Limestone View Farm** (page 243), **New Hanson Grange** (page 243) ⛺ **New Hanson Shepherd's Huts** (page 243)

While most visitors head straight for the Manifold Way, it's worth climbing out of the valley along the zigzagging, rock-edged lanes to the villages that sit on the uplands above it. Cycling will challenge the fittest here, but the rewards are worth the effort. Otherwise, you will need a car. Start with **Alstonefield**, the quintessential Peak village with its traditional stone houses gathered round the village green and **The George** pub with its spreading tree. From **Wetton**, another picturesque village,

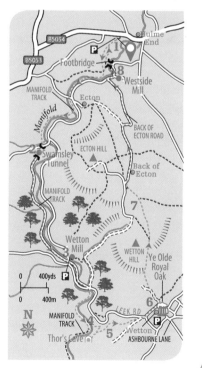

originated. The main walk continues by taking the left fork along a tarmacked lane; following this up out of the village, signed as 'public footpath only' and 'Back of Ecton 1½'. At the top of the lane, cross the stile on to National Trust land. Follow the wide grassy path downhill, skirting east of **Wetton Hill**.

7 Soon you will leave the NT land behind, crossing a boardwalk and up through meadows. Follow the footpath until it meets the road to **Back of Ecton**. From here, just keep to this quiet lane downhill for 2 miles to a T-junction near the River Manifold again where you turn right.

8 Shortly you reach **Westside Mill**. Take the footpath just beyond the buildings on the left then cross a footbridge that will take you through a meadow and back on to the Manifold Track. Follow the track right, back to the car park at Hulme End.

Cycling the Manifold Track

❄ OS White Peak Explorer map OL24 ; start: Water Houses, ♥ SK084502; 18 miles there & back; moderately easy; refreshments at Water Houses, Wetton Mill & Hulme End

The nine-mile trail follows the route of the dismantled railway, with a road section between Wetton Mill and Swainsley containing an illuminated tunnel around 100 yards long. As a scenic cycle route, it holds its own with the illustrious High Peak and Tissington trails. Bikes can be hired from Waterhouses (page 133), and a regular bus service runs to Waterhouses from Leek and Ashbourne.

At the other end of the Manifold Track, the sleepy hamlet of **Hulme End** makes an excellent base for an exploration of the Manifold Valley with its pleasantly sited riverside campsite, characterful B&Bs, and **Manifold Inn** serving traditional ales and pub grub. There's a handy village shop and the **Tea Junction** café by the trail (Hulme End SK17 0EX ℰ 01298 687368). From the hatted sheep by the entrance, to the engine shed design with a contemporary twist, this is a great place to start or end an outing along the Manifold Valley. Snacks and lunches are on offer, along with biscuits and preserves from the shop.

the road twists and turns and drops down Leek Road towards the Manifold, with spectacular views over to the great mouth of Thor's Cave and the Manifold ravine. Winter is best for views, when the thick roadside vegetation dies off. The road follows the river for a short distance before crossing it and climbing steeply again up to **Butterton**. Just before the village, you'll see the **Manifold Craft Barn** (Wetton Rd, ST13 7ST ℰ 01538 304604) on your right, a great place for all those who appreciate stylish ceramics, or would like to have a go at throwing a pot. Alternatively you can drop in for a cup of coffee and slice of homemade cake. Butterton is a 'Thankful Village' meaning it didn't suffer any fatalities in World War I. Head past the handsome St Peter's Church, with its pointed spire in this village at over 1,000 feet above sea level, on past the **Black Lion Inn** and down Pothooks Lane where Hoo Brook takes over the road for several yards (particularly impressive after heavy rain). Up and down, down and up and on to **Grindon**; like Butterton the soaring spire of the church dominates the village. Inside All Saints, there's a memorial to the Halifax Bomber crew who died when their plane crashed as they were dropping supplies to the villages cut off by snow drifts in 1947. Just outside the church gates there's a

Rindle Stone, a rindle being a brook that only appears in wet weather; the Lord of Grindon Manor placed the stone by the church to mark his ownership of the brook. The noticeboard by the church car park and picnic area describes Grindon as 'One of those high places which, as if heaving, towards it, seems to have more than its fair share of the sky'. This description just about sums up Grindon – and indeed the other upland villages around the Manifold.

FOOD & DRINK

The George Alstonefield DE6 2FX ✆ 01335 310205. A truly romantic pub set in a captivating location high above the Manifold Valley: lime-washed walls, log fire, candlelight and good food.

Ye Olde Royal Oak Wetton DE6 2AF ✆ 01355 310287. Above Thor's Cave, this traditional pub serves decent ale and food. There's an inviting beer garden for summer days.

THE PEAK DISTRICT ONLINE

For additional online content, articles, photos and more on the Peak District, why not visit ✆ www.bradtguides.com/peak.

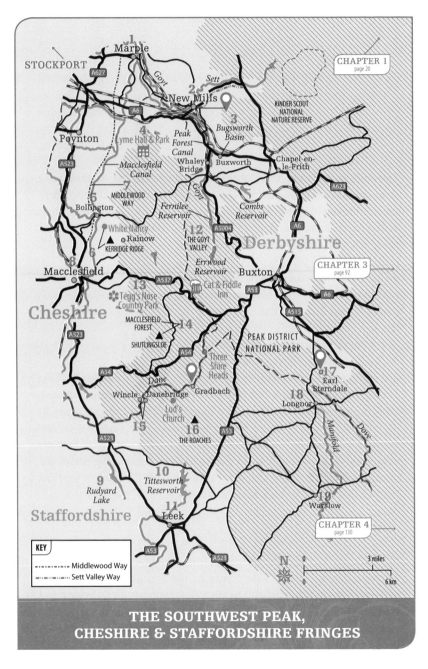

STOCKPORT

CHAPTER 1
page 20

1 Marple

Goyt

Sett

2 New Mills

KINDER SCOUT
NATIONAL
NATURE RESERVE

3 Bugsworth
Basin

4 Lyme Hall & Park
Peak
Forest
Canal
Whaley
Bridge

Poynton

Macclesfield
Canal

Buxworth

Chapel-en-
le-Frith

A623

7 MIDDLEWOOD
WAY

Fernilee
Reservoir

Combs
Reservoir

6 Bollington

Goyt

A5004

White Nancy
Rainow
KERRIDGE RIDGE

12 THE GOYT
VALLEY

6

Derbyshire

8

Errwood
Reservoir

Buxton

Macclesfield

13

A537

Cat & Fiddle
Inn

CHAPTER 3
page 92

A53

A6

Tegg's Nose
Country Park

A515

Cheshire

MACCLESFIELD
FOREST

14

SHUTLINGSLOE

A54

PEAK DISTRICT
NATIONAL PARK

Three
Shire
Heads

17 Earl
Sterndale

A523

A54

Dane

Wincle Danebridge

Gradbach

18 Longnor

Manifold

Dove

15

Lud's
Church

16

A53

THE ROACHES

9
Rudyard
Lake

Staffordshire

10
Tittesworth
Reservoir

A523

11 Leek

19
Warslow

CHAPTER 4
page 130

KEY

------------ Middlewood Way
··········· Sett Valley Way

N

0   3 miles
0   6 km

THE SOUTHWEST PEAK,
CHESHIRE & STAFFORDSHIRE FRINGES

5
THE SOUTHWEST PEAK, CHESHIRE & STAFFORDSHIRE FRINGES

Surrounding the long finger of the national park in the southwest is a string of mill towns, including New Mills, Macclesfield and Leek. These are a testament to Victorian enterprise and ingenuity: **New Mills** with its sweeping viaducts and great arched bridges; **Macclesfield** with its red-brick silk mills (now part of a fine museum trail); and **Leek** with its Arts and Crafts architecture (built on the wealth of its own mill industry). Between Macclesfield, Leek, Longnor and Buxton, there are some of the loveliest yet largely unexplored parts of the national park, an area with its own distinctive character: it is a mix of millstone

"There's no better place to go slow, whether its fishing on the River Dane, sampling beers in a local brewery, or conquering one of the mini-peaks."

grit and coal measures with sweeping ridges of open moorland falling away to pasture, carved out by wooded cloughs and fast-flowing streams. Within are isolated hamlets and villages, with unexpected treats to be found in the quietest corners. There's no better place to go slow, whether its fishing on the River Dane, sampling beers in a local brewery, weaselling and rock hopping on the Roaches or conquering one of the mini-peaks such as Shutlingsloe or Parkhouse Hill. It's a part of the Peak District that draws me back again and again.

WALKING & CYCLING

Riverside walks through verdant pasture, gorge and wooded valley extend along the **Dane Valley Way** in the southwest Peak District, passing through the delightful hamlets of **Gradbach**, **Danebridge** and **Wincle** and on to the **Three Shire Heads**, where three counties meet: Cheshire, Staffordshire and Derbyshire. By the **Packhorse Bridge** here, there's an opportunity for some 'wild swimming' in the series of

little pools. Some of the most spectacular walking is found around the
Roaches and Back Forest, where you'll find the mystical **Lud's Church**.
And in a Peak District distinctly lacking in peaks, you'll find some great
exceptions in the pointed **Shutlingsloe**, **Parkhouse Hill** and **Chrome
Hill**, all highly recommendable little climbs. Other bucolic long-
distance walks in the southwest take in the Goyt Valley Way and the
Sett Valley Trail.

For cyclists, the **Peak Forest and Macclesfield Canal**, along with
the dismantled railway tracks of the **Middlewood Way** (also good for
horseriding) and the **Rudyard Reservoir** route, offer easy, flat cycling
in pleasant surroundings. For something more challenging, pick up the
Cheshire County Council leaflet, **Riding the Ridges**, a circular route
taking in a mix of road, track and off-road cycling around Shrigley and
Rainow near Macclesfield. The 17-mile route starts and ends at Tegg's
Nose Country Park, winding its way past gritstone quarries along
narrow country roads and over rough moorland tracks, including the
demanding Corkscrew.

MARPLE TO LYME PARK

It's hard to believe that Marple is part of Greater Manchester and lies a
mere five miles southeast of Stockport on the edge of a densely populated
conurbation. But with the Dark Peak to the south and east of it, and
the countryside of the Cheshire plains immediately on its west side, its
character is more agrarian than urban. Southeastwards from Marple,
extending to New Mills and Buxworth beyond, the area is laced with
quiet waterways, soaring aqueducts and expansive bridges, along with
the remnant mills that stand as a legacy to the great Victorian engineers.

To gain a bird's-eye view of this landscape, where the Cheshire Plains
meet the Peak District, and conurbation meets near-wilderness, visit
Lyme Park, a stately home that sits on the edge of the moorland a
handful of miles inside the national park.

1 MARPLE

Gentrified Marple is an affluent suburb on the southeast fringes of Stockport, well facilitated with restaurants, cafés and shops – even a cinema – while retaining its traditional village ambience. But it is Marple Junction (the meeting point of the Peak Forest Canal and Macclesfield Canal), the Marple Locks (the second steepest flight of locks in the country) and Marple Aqueduct (the highest in England) that make Marple such a fascinating corner of the Peak District fringes. Indeed, most people come to this little town to watch the narrowboats navigate the 16 locks, potter along the canals and admire the lofty Marple aqueduct on the Peak Forest Canal with the River Goyt 100 feet below it.

Wandering south towards New Mills along the Macclesfield Canal, it's hard to believe the waterway almost faced closure in the 1960s. Nowadays it's busy with narrowboats, ramblers and strollers, particularly in the summer months. Past the town's scruffy riverside development, the corridor of green is only interrupted by old snake bridges and the occasional marina. At **Higher Poynton**, canal boats sit cheek by jowl with whimsical and romantic names. It's a place where life goes by very slowly indeed – and it's infectious, particularly on a warm sunny day, watching the boats plough the waterway with a drink in hand. And if the water's calling, it's possible to hire a boat for the day from Bailey's Trading Post.

¶ FOOD & DRINK

Bailey's Trading Post Near bridge 15 on The Macclesfield Canal, Lyme Rd, Higher Poynton SK12 1TH ✆ 01625 872277. Just a shack serving hot drinks and snacks with some outside seating by the canal, but a wonderful place to sit and watch the canal activity.

2 NEW MILLS

🏠 **Pack Horse Inn** (page 243)

New Mills is a spit-and-sawdust kind of place with no pretentions, though stamped with natural and manmade drama and sliced by deep incisions that cut through its very heart. Here the River Goyt and River Sett converge before the Goyt continues on its merry way towards Stockport, squeezing between gritstone rocks far below the town. It's a spectacular section of the Goyt Valley Way (pages 168–9). Before the 19th century, toll roads tipped horses and carriages down into the ravine, with packhorse bridges linking the rough roads that wound their way back up the other side. The Victorians added mills, railways, great viaducts and high-level bridges that simply spanned the top of the chasms. New Mills is a place with a long and impressive archaeological history, from its single corn mill to the expanse of cotton mills, print works, railways, roads and bridges, all linking the town. Most of the mills have been demolished or destroyed by fire, but that Victorian legacy, with its impressive infrastructure, is still very much intact.

A walk around town

Before exploring the town, head for the **Heritage Centre** on New Mill Lane adjacent to the bus station and arm yourself with leaflets, maps and trail guides. You can also get an overview of the town's history from the interpretive boards and a fascinating 3D model of the town as it was in 1884, when Union Bridge was under construction. Outside the centre, across the pebbled path, a viewing point gives a tantalising glimpse of the ravine and the Millennium Walkway far below.

A circular walk from
New Mills along the Goyt & Peak Forest Canal

✵ OS map OL1; start from New Mills Heritage Centre, ♀ SK000854; 5 miles; easy walking alongside river & canal; refreshments in New Mills

This is a longer walk around New Mills that takes in Torr Riverside Park, the Millennium Walkway, the River Goyt, several nature reserves and the Peak Forest Canal. The walk has fine views across from Goytside Meadows and the Peak Forest Canal to the town.

1 From the heritage centre head down Rock Mill Lane and turn right into Rock Street and continue on to Lower Rock Street. At the end of the cobbled street, turn right on to the path that leads down into the ravine. Cross the **Millward Memorial Bridge** over the River Sett, next to the picnic area, Archimedes screw and the ruins of Torr Mill and follow the path under the two-tiered **Queens Bridge**.

2 At the end of Goytside Farm, turn right (signed the Goyt Way) and cross the footbridge over the river. Go through the gate on your right into Goytside Meadows, a marshy meadow rich in wildflowers from April to October. Climb the hill up to the Peak Forest Canal, taking in the views of the multi-arched railway viaduct across the valley.

3 Turn right on to the towpath, past New Mills Marina, lined with narrowboats, and under

Make your way to Station Road, where the 1853 terraces housed the 'under-livings' (the poor who lived on the lower floors) with two storeys facing on to the main road and four to the rear on Station Road – typical of the houses that cling to the side of the valley. Just before the entrance to the railway station, turn left (signed Millennium Walkway) and follow the steep path down to the bottom of the ravine. Turn left again to reach the **Millennium Walkway**. Opened at the end of 1999, the 525-foot long elevated steel walkway is bolted to the retaining wall or supported by pillars on the riverbed. Built to link an inaccessible stretch of the Midshires and Goyt Valley Way in the squeeze of the ravine, the structure has won numerous awards for its innovative design.

On the other side of the river, **Torr Vale Mill** sits dramatically on a rocky promontory, the only surviving textile mill (dating back to the 1780s), but in a sad state of decay despite its Grade II listing. The path twists and turns with the meandering Goyt before grandly revealing views of the **Union Road Bridge**, a 94-foot wide, four-arched Victorian

the bridge, passing the **Swizzels Matlow** works, the scent of sweets wafting from the factory.

4 After just over a mile you come to another bridge. Turn right here on to a minor road, Lower **Greenshall Lane**. Follow the path downwards and veer slightly right on the crook of the more major road, Waterside Road. Follow the road.

5 When you come to the road bridge recrossing the Goyt, turn right on to the path signed Mouseley Bottom Wood and New Mills Centre. The path takes you through and past wildlife ponds, wetlands, woods and nature reserves. Keep to the path that hugs the river, following the Goyt Way signs.

6 Go through the gap next to a metal gate and head through another gap in a stone wall, leading into woodland. Follow the path alongside the gable of a stone building.

7 Turn left through woodland and enter a small park. Cross the road at the end and take the path leading down the Goyt Valley and Millennium Walkway. From here open meadow gives way to the narrowing rock-clad gorge of New Mills and the remnants of an industrial landscape. Millennium Walkway ends climb the ravine path back into town.

viaduct spanning the ravine at its highest point. Continue on to the site of **Torr Mill**, destroyed by fire. Here you'll find **Torrs Hydro** with its fish pass and reverse Archimedes screw turbine (known locally as Archie), providing enough energy to power 50 homes. This is an extraordinary location, caught between three imposing structures: Union Road Bridge, Queens Bridge and the railway viaduct.

"Horses once ploughed this steep pathway, taking supplies and goods to and from the mills."

Cross the **Millward Memorial Bridge** and bear right towards the base of **Queens Bridge**, passing under the impressive two-tiered arched bridge along the leat and on to the sluice gate. Retrace your steps back across the Millward Bridge, keeping right to follow the Sett River upstream. Horses once ploughed this steep pathway, taking supplies and goods to and from the mills. Take the left fork, passing under the railway viaduct, and continue uphill to the viewing point and on through the cobbled **Lower Rock Street**. At the corner of Rock Street and Torr Top Street, notice the plaque honouring the bravery of the Torr Top men who fought on the front line in France during the Great War. At the end of Torr Top Street, turn right on to Market Street and again on to High Street, lined with old-fashioned stores, some with Victorian frontage.

¶ FOOD & DRINK

Gioia Mia Café 41 Market St, SK22 4AA ✐ 01663 746893. The café and bistro serves a mix of English, Mediterranean and Middle Eastern food. Good service provided by the friendly owner in this popular little venue. Be prepared for a wait at busy times.

W Potts and Son 17 Union Rd, SK22 3EL ✐ 01633 744389. The old-fashioned bakery offers a large selection of freshly made bread, cakes, biscuits and sandwiches – everything needed for a picnic at Torr Riverside Park.

Pulse Café 34 Union Rd, SK22 3ES ✐ 01663 741468. Excellent value for money, tasty food and large portions served by friendly staff in this vegetarian café.

3 BUGSWORTH BASIN

Bugsworth Basin sits at the end of Peak Forest Canal, an inland port at the heart of a once industrialised landscape. Limestone and gritstone were transported here along the tramway from the nearby quarries before being taken by canal to Ashton Junction and the Mersey Canal. The 3D model by the waterside gives you an idea just how much the canal terminus was an industrial hub, with its canal-side cottages, wharf manager's house, warehouses and wharfs, lime kilns and public inn. With the arrival of the railways, the canal terminus was abandoned, slowly returning to nature. Left derelict for 40 years, the canal has been rescued by the Inland Waterways Protection Society and lovingly restored over the last 30 decades.

Wander round the various basins, crossing the horse transfer bridges and read the metal information panels that line the waterside. In summer this is a great place to have a picnic and watch all the waterside activity – or sit with a pint outside the Navigation Inn ($\mathscr{O}$ 01633 732072) where you might just catch a glimpse of vole, kingfisher or heron. You can also stride out along the Peak Forest Canal, the Peak Forest Tramway Trail, or up on to Whitehough, Eccles Pike or Cracken Edge. On leaving Bugsworth Basin, I caught a glimpse of a heavy-duty freight train hurdling across the bridge towards Manchester – a reminder of the reason for the demise of the canal.

4 LYME HALL & PARK

🏠 **East Lodge** (page 243)

SK12 2NR $\mathscr{O}$ 01663 762023 ⊙ variable opening times for house & gardens; phone or check website for details; National Trust. Note: The entrance to this National Trust property is only half a mile from Disley train station, where a complimentary bus takes those arriving on foot through the estate to the house – a great option as car parking is expensive for those who aren't National Trust members. Free access to grounds; house & gardens charge for non-NT members.

Sitting on the western tip of the Peak District National Park, Lyme Park is flanked by the Peak District hills, while below it the land drops away to the Cheshire Plains. It's a magnificent location for a stately home. Setting apart, there's a lot going on at Lyme Park throughout the year, from orienteering and themed walks to kite flying. Inside the house there's a dressing-up wardrobe of fine Edwardian attire – not just for children, but for adults too. 'It's amazing how people hold themselves differently when they are dressed in period outfits,' Cia, Lyme Park's general manager, said to me. 'The clothes somehow make them move and behave differently.' Whether you dress up or not, you'll leave Lyme Park with a strong sense of what it was like to live here from Elizabethan times right up to the 1940s when the Legh family packed up, departed and handed over the house to the National Trust.

The house

The arched gateway before the circular lawn and driveway draws the eye to the 'craziest Elizabethan frontispiece', as architectural historian Nikolaus Pevsner observed. It was certainly built to impress, with its columns and pediments, coat of arms and clock face, topped with a statue of Minerva. Go under the central bay to the altogether more understated, but lovely, Italianate courtyard. From there, steps lead into the house and the **Entrance Hall**. The asymmetrical entrance and fireplace is cleverly concealed by the strategic positioning of Corinthian columns.

"It's claimed the land was given to a branch of the Legh family in return for battle honours."

As expected this is a room created to make a grand entrance, with its full-length portraits (including Edward III and the Black Prince), Mortlake tapestries and magnificent fireplace surround. Look out for representations of the severed arm around the house. It's claimed the land was given to a branch of the Legh family by the Black Prince in return for battle honours when the Royal Standard was recovered together with the arm of the French man who'd seized it. A short flight of stairs takes you to the richly decorated **Drawing Room**. The dark panelled wood and detailed plasterwork contrasts the bright colours of the stained-glass windows, partly medieval. A hinged painting, the **Wyatt's Squint**, opens out to allow a peep through to the entrance hall below. The **Stag Room** (where the men congregated after a meal to smoke, gossip and make plans) leads on to the dining room and the **Ante-Room**, where the servants made ready the guests' meals. The most interesting item in the library is the **Caxton Missal**, a pre-Reformation prayer book. Don't miss the virtuoso limewood carvings attributed to Grinling Gibbons in **The Saloon**, rich in detail with references to the seasons, music, the arts and science. From there, take the grand stairway to the **Long Gallery**, where the ladies paced the floorboards in a form of gentle indoor exercise. The adjoining gallery demonstrates the family's love of hunting with pictures of horses and dogs and sweet-looking children. Of all the grand, four-poster bedrooms, the **Knight's Bedroom** is the most interesting with its wonky plaster over the mantel, ceilings and floors – along with the ghost stories. It's said a skeleton was found under the floor. There are also claims that a secret tunnel leads from the cupboard, via a priest's hole, to The Cage (a hunting lodge). No wonder it's said the room is haunted.

The gardens

At a height of almost 800 feet, the gardens would be moorland if they'd been left in their natural state. The daunting task of taming this wild landscape began around 1570, but it wasn't until 1643 that work began in earnest, with the arrival of Richard and Elizabeth Legh. By 1683, there were gravel walks, bowling greens, tennis courts, lawns, hotbeds and greenhouses. By 1860, Lord Newton had added the Italian garden, while the second Lord Newton created a rose garden in 1913. The garden fell into neglect during World War II, but since the estate was handed over to the National Trust in 1946, it has worked hard to return these delightful gardens to their former glory. This is a place to return to through the seasons, from the narcissi around **Reflection Lake** and the secluded **Rhododendron Walk** with its Killtime Ravine (called so because the staff hid themselves from sight when guests were in the grounds) in spring, to the **Rose Garden** in summer, along with the **herbaceous borders**, **Wyatt** and **Italian Gardens**. Don't miss the **Orangery** and the **Rough Cascade Waterfall**. From the gardens you can appreciate the 15-bay grandeur of the south front along with the statues of Neptune, Venus and Pan.

The estate

The house and gardens apart, there are approximately 1,300 acres to explore in the deer park, with several points of interest around the estate. A short walk up the rise from the entrance of the house takes you to **The Cage**, an old hunting lodge with wonderful views across to Kinder Scout. **Paddock Cottage** sits on a rise with expansive views over the Cheshire plains.

LIGHTS, CAMERA, ACTION!

Lyme Park has inspired directors and location scouts all over the country. The National Trust estate was chosen for an episode in the TV series *Red Dwarf, Timeslides; The Village* in 2014; and appeared in *The Awakening*. But perhaps the most memorable film scene at Lyme Park is the one in which Mr Darcy (aka Colin Firth) takes a dip at Lyme Park lake (to the west of the house) in the 1995 BBC TV adaptation of Jane Austen's *Pride and Prejudice* – setting pulses racing all over the country. If you're a Colin Firth fan, pick up the National Trust *The Only Way is Pemberley* leaflet, a walk that takes you to the film locations, following in the footsteps of Darcy.

On the eastern boundary, you'll find **The Lantern**, a three-storey viewing tower, or belvedere, complete with octagonal spire. It's said that if Lord Newton could see The Lantern from his breakfast table, he knew it was a good day for hunting. The **Red Deer Sanctuary** is home to a medieval herd of red and sallow deer, found next to **East Lodge** (see ⊘ www.bradtguides.com/peaksleeps).

"Bowstones is a fine vantage point for deer as well as birds such as curlew, skylark and lapwing."

Bowstones is also a fine vantage point for deer as well as birds such as curlew, skylark and lapwing. In the heart of the park, **Knightslow Wood** is used for den building – ideal for kids to let off steam, along with the **Timber Yard** and **Playscape**.

Lyme Park Estate has abundant scope for **walking**, with six- to ten- mile circular routes taking in the Middlewood Way, Macclesfield Canal, Bollington, Pott Shrigley and the Gritstone Trail. The park is also excellent for fell running, cycling and mountain biking, with enough gradients to get the heart pumping. The National Trust *Getting active at Lyme Park* leaflet gives detailed information on outdoor activity in the grounds.

BOLLINGTON TO LEEK

Sandwiched between the Cheshire Plains and the Peak District National Park are the historically rich mill towns of **Bollington** and **Macclesfield**, linked by the Middlewood Way and Macclesfield Canal, a delightful rural corridor offering cycling, horseriding and nature walks. Further south, the Arts and Crafts town of **Leek** has an enviable position with the Staffordshire moorlands to the east and the locally popular reservoirs of Tittesworth and Rudyard to the north. While outside of the national park itself, these fringe towns and waterways have retained the essential character of the Peak District.

5 BOLLINGTON

The small town of Bollington sits just outside the Peak District National Park south of Lyme Park and north of Macclesfield, tucked under the steep slope of Kerridge Ridge with the Peak District moorland rising in waves to the east. Once a thriving industrial settlement, the old mills and workers' terraced cottages of Bollington have become gentrified.

You can speed your way there by bus or car – or choose between three wonderfully Slow approaches: by bike along the Middlewood Way; narrowboat along Macclesfield Canal; or on foot along the superbly scenic Kerridge Edge before it drops steeply down into the town. In town, pick up a trail guide for the 'Majestic Mills' or for 'Yesterday's Folk', taking in Bollington's historical streets; then head to the **Discovery Centre** (☉ Wed, Sat & Sun) at **Clarence Mill** on the canal, where you can find out about Bollington's mill history, the development of the Macclesfield Canal and Middlewood Railway. You can finish with a bite to eat at the **Waterside Café**, if desired.

6 KERRIDGE RIDGE & WHITE NANCY

Reached by a legs-to-jelly 300-step slog from Bollington is the structure of White Nancy on Kerridge Ridge. Alternatively, you can take the woodland path with its tree identification interpretive boards. Even better – walk the entire Kerridge Ridge from Rainow.

Once on top, it's an easy stride along Kerridge, the views sustained along its length. On one side of the ridge, you can see the Cheshire Plains sweep across England to the Shropshire hills and north Wales (on clear days), while on the other side the soft curving lines of the Peak hills ripple up to the sky.

The ridge comes to a glorious full stop in front of **White Nancy**, built in 1815 as a summer house for the Gaskell family of Ingersley Hall below the hill (to commemorate victory at Waterloo, it's believed). Inside there was a seat running round the wall, with a large circular table cut from a single slab of stone in the centre, now blocked up. Nowadays, White Nancy's brilliant white rendering can be seen for miles around, high above the town of Bollington. Over the decades, the bell-shaped structure has seen many coats of paint and has been decorated to different themes – from a Christmas pudding to Father Christmas; an insignia for the Queen's Diamond Jubilee to a poppy commemorating World War I in 2014. Vandals can't resist adding their own contribution from time to time, the town wakening up to a 'Pink Nancy' on one occasion.

If you are returning to a start point in Rainow, take the steep stone steps down to Ingersley Vale, keeping right. You'll arrive in a cul-de-sac with a gushing weir and sprinkling of buildings beside the River Dean. From here a (mostly) slabbed pathway takes you across fields back to Rainow.

7 MIDDLEWOOD WAY

It may not have the drama of the Peak District National Park's dismantled railways, but this ten-mile traffic-free trail for walkers, horseriders and cyclists, with the Macclesfield Canal and Peak District foothills on one side and the Cheshire Plains farmlands on the other, is very pleasant.

Just outside Macclesfield Railway Station, you can pick up the trail from Gas Road. There are a few semi-steep gradients out of town as the trail follows alongside Silk Road, and after the bridge crossing there's a series of San Francisco's Lombard Street type loops (bypassing the steps) for cyclists, making the going interesting. Some more interesting ramps and rises and the trail becomes an obvious wide, flat dismantled railway just after the **Bollington Labyrinth** (a modern stone based on an ancient Greek unicursal maze). Soon after, **Bollington Viaduct** comes into view. Pause a while on the bridge to take in the views over **Bollington** and the surrounding area. With great foresight Macclesfield Borough Council rescued the structure from demolition by purchasing it for just £1: the town's gain. After Bollington, housing and business development gives way to open countryside. At **Poynton**, you can detour off the Middlewood Way into the wildlife-rich nature reserve at **Poynton Coppice** on one side, or over to the Macclesfield Canal on the other – and on to Lyme Park beyond if wished. It's worth stopping at **Nelson Pit Visitor Centre** to gen up on the history of the local area, the Middlewood Way and the Macclesfield Canal; leaflets outline eight circular walks from Nelson Pit. Further on, **Jacksons' Brickworks Nature Reserve** offers another tempting detour. The wildflower-rich meadows attract moths which in turn feed a healthy bat population. Drawing closer to Marple, the way can be muddy and wet, particularly in the winter months. From Marple, you can return back to Macclesfield along the Middlewood Way, or you can brave the towpath along the Macclesfield Canal. I'd recommend the latter for variation – with a word of caution: the path is narrow and bumpy in places with its surface of raised stones. But for me it's worth the more challenging cycle for the wonderful outlooks over to the foothills of the Peak District and for the buzz of waterside activity, particular in the summer months.

🍴 FOOD & DRINK

The Boars Head Shrigley Rd North, Stockport ✆ 01625 876676. On the Middlewood Way, this pub serves tasty food, particularly pies. Be prepared to wait in busy periods.

THE GREAT & THE GRAND

Medieval halls, stately homes, grand hunting towers and quirky follies litter the dales and uplands.

1 Chatsworth House and gardens – designed and built to impress. **2** Haddon Hall, possibly England's most romantic medieval manor house. **3** Lyme Hall with views across to the Cage, the estate's hunting lodge. **4** Solomon's Temple was built to keep the local unemployed occupied and out of mischief.

KEVIN EAVES/S

TOWNS & VILLAGES

Riverside hamlets, hillside villages and handsome market towns offer charming tea rooms, country pubs and independently owned shops.

HELEN MOAT

FRANK FELL/ROBERTHARDING/SS

DASCOTT (FLICKR)

· SOFT WORDS TURNETH AWAY WRATH ·

THE QUIET WOMAN

A FREE HOUSE

EARL STERNDALE

1 Matlock Bath – a 'little Blackpool' in landlocked Derbyshire. **2** Bonsall, historic village – and UFO capital of the world. **3** The Quiet Woman, a welcome stop for weary walkers in spite of its disquieting sign… **4** Bakewell's famous puddings. **5** Chatsworth's model village, Edensor. **6** Holmfirth of *Last of the Summer Wine* fame.

RICHARD BOWDEN/S

CHURCHES

The Peak District's churches are places of great beauty, stuffed to the gills with historical artefacts, church masonry, art and architecture.

1 Church of the Holy Cross in picture-perfect Ilam. 2 St Oswald's Church, Ashbourne. 3 The creations of Morris & Co are to be found in many corners of Leek, including All Saints Church. 4 One of the intricate bench carvings found in 'The Cathedral in the Peak', Tideswell.

TRAVELIBUK/A

HELEN MOAT

ARENA PHOTO UK/S

8 MACCLESFIELD

It may not have the romance of the ancient Silk Routes that crossed exotic far-flung places such as China, Kazakhstan, Mongolia and Russia, but down-to-earth Macclesfield has its very own Silk Road running through its heart. This town was built on the silk trade, and there are four museums in town telling that story. Before heading to the museums, stop off at the **information centre** next to the imposing town hall at Market Place to pick up a town map and attraction leaflets. Close by is **St Michael and All Angels**, an unusually warm and inviting church for a historical place of worship – with its circular seating and modern glass casing. The highlight of the church is the Savage Chapel with its richly

"St Michael and All Angels is said to contain the finest collection of alabaster effigies in Cheshire."

coloured stained-glass windows provided by Morris & Co. The church is said to contain the finest collection of alabaster effigies in Cheshire.

From St Michael's Church, head down through the pedestrianised thoroughfare to the **Heritage Centre and the Old Sunday School** (Roe St, SK11 6UT ✎ 01625 613210 ☉ Mon–Sat). The Sunday schools that sprung up all over Macclesfield were, in many cases, the only means for young factory workers to learn to read and write. Not only were the Sunday schools educational, but they also played an important social role in town as well. Continue along Mill Street to Park Lane from the Heritage Centre to visit the **Silk Museum** (Park Lane, SK11 6TJ ✎ 01625 612045 ☉ Mon–Sat), with its wide-ranging collections and hands-on display. It tells the story of the silk industry from the button makers to the great silk mills. In the same location, **Paradise Mill** (Park Lane, SK11 6TL ✎ 01625 612045 ☉ tours only, Mon–Sat at 11.45, 13.00 & 14.15) takes you back in time to the factory as it was in the 1930s. It was a working handloom mill up to 1981, operating in a time-warp in its latter years – using looms installed in 1912; even the office furniture is antique. You're shown the silk process from silkworm cocoons, unwoven silk and then spinning and weaving. Further out of town, **West Park Museum** (Prestbury Rd, SK10 3BJ ✎ 01625 613210 ☉ Tue–Sun) has a collection of Egyptian artefacts, donated by Marianne Brocklehurst, the daughter of a local mill owner, as well as works by local artist Charles Tunnicliffe. You can find out about the four museums at ⌂ www.silkmacclesfield.org.uk.

¶¶ FOOD & DRINK

Chesterfield Bistro 66 Chestergate, SK11 6DY, ✆ 01625 611103. Great food, well presented. Excellent value for money. Check out the Early Bird menu.

Rustic Coffee Co 2 Church Mews, Churchill Way, SK11 6AY ✆ 01625 423202. Good coffee, wide range of savouries and sweets, all served with a friendly smile.

Treacle Market Market Pl & Chestergate ☉ last Sun of the month. You can shop for everything from locally produced food and drink to antiques, crafts and home design – often to the sound of live music.

9 RUDYARD LAKE

🏠 Horton Lodge Boathouse (page 243)

Just off the Macclesfield to Leek road, Rudyard Lake is a bit of a misnomer as it's actually a reservoir. As you stroll along the waterside though, it does feel as if Rudyard is part of the natural landscape, tucked into thickly wooded hillsides and meadow. It's only the dam wall at its southern end that gives the game away.

Rudyard was created for purely practical reasons (to feed Caldon Canal) but soon became a fabulous playground for the Victorians once the railway track linking Manchester and Uttoxeter was laid in 1829. There were fleets of rowing boats, a funfair, brass band concerts and scores of tea rooms. The world's greatest trapeze artist, Blondin, who'd recently awed the world with his crossing of the Niagara Falls on a high wire came to Rudyard to repeat the feat, while Captain Webb, the first man to swim the English Channel, showed off his skills in the reservoir. By the end of the 1800s, there were up to 20,000 people visiting the lake each day; among them, a couple called John Lockwood Kipling and Alice Macdonald. They named their first-born after the lake – Rudyard Kipling, acclaimed author of *The Jungle Book*.

> *"Blondin, who'd recently awed the world with his crossing of the Niagara Falls on a high wire came to Rudyard to repeat the feat."*

Nowadays Rudyard Lake is a much quieter place, but is still a popular leisure centre for the townsfolk of Leek and further afield. **Rudyard Lake Steam Railway** (✆ 01538 306704 🖥 www.rlsr.org ☉ holiday periods & w/ends; see website or phone for winter operation), a steam-hauled narrow-gauge railway, runs along the eastern side of the reservoir; from its terminus you can continue on foot around the lake.

A walk around Rudyard Lake

This route is just under five miles, and waymarked with lapwing motifs. At the end of the lake, turn left along the northern shore. There's a good chance of spotting a kingfisher, heron or at least a moorhen in the reedy, shrubby vegetation, or waders such as curlew, lapwing, snipes or plovers, when the mud is exposed in dryer weather. Turning southward, the path hugs the shore before curving west through the estate of Cliffe Park with views of the classic Gothic house. Keeping to the track between the stone gateposts, continue on along Realcliffe Road through Realcliffe Wood, home to woodpeckers, nuthatch and jay; in spring and summer the woods are scattered with bluebells, wood anemone, wood sorrel and dog's mercury. Keep left to arrive back at Rudyard village, passing between Rudyard Villa and Spite Hall before heading left again down to the visitor centre at the water's edge.

The lakeside

The elegant converted boathouse is home to the small **Rudyard Lake Visitor Centre** (☉ Mar–Oct) with information panels on the history and wildlife of the reservoir. Next to it, the **Activity Centre** also has a shop and café with some outdoor seating. You can hire rowing boats and canoes, or launch your own for a fee. A restored captain's clipper, *The Honey*, operates guided tours of the lake in summer, a great way to view the attractive waterside homes and boathouses along the water's edge, including the Victorian **Lady of the Lake Boathouse**, with its ship's figurehead on the side of the chimney. The lake is also popular with anglers.

Cycling from Rudyard Lake to Leek

At just over four miles each way, the dismantled railway is an easy, level cycle ride. You can access the northern tip of the lake from **Beat Lane**, just off the A523. Follow the pot-holed track on to the lakeside path with views over Rudyard and the chalet houses that line the shore on the opposite side. Continue through the narrow-gauge railway station car park and on past pastureland to Leek. The route through the suburbs into the town centre is well-signposted. To vary the return trip, you can take the lanes west of Leek with notably more challenging climbs and descents. You could also start your cycle from Leek and ride out to Rudyard. Pick up a *Cycling in Staffordshire Moorlands*, Issue 4, from the information centre to help you navigate the streets leading to the trail.

¶¶ FOOD & DRINK

Cheap and cheerful food can be found at the **Hotel Rudyard** (the carvery being particularly good value; ✆ 01538 306208), the **Activity Centre Café** down by the lakeside or at **Platform 2 Café** at the narrow-gauge railway station (the bacon butties are a particular hit). If you're looking for something more special, head into Leek.

EVENTS

Check out the Rudyard Lake Festival in August or the Light and Sound Show on Bonfire Night, along with other events and free guided walks throughout the year. Watch out for the lake's own navy (model boats created by local boat makers Kittiwake Boats) and the annual dragon boat race.

10 TITTESWORTH RESERVOIR

Four miles north of Leek is Tittesworth Reservoir, its northern end just dipping into the national park. With the dramatic Roaches as a backdrop, it's a great place to walk and relax. Although it's a busy spot in summer, it isn't difficult to get away from the crowds by taking the five-mile trail circling the reservoir along the water's edge, through woods and on quiet country lanes, watching nature either on the waterside or in one of the two bird hides on the northeast and northwest banks. Abundant waders frequent the mudflats, time of year permitting: oystercatcher, plover and heron; lapwing, snipe and curlew.

The visitor centre – information point, gift shop and restaurant – is housed in an Alpine-style building, with a raised roof and ceiling-to-floor glass the width of the gable taking advantage of the waterside views. Here Tittesworth Waterview Restaurant (✆ 01538 300180) serves breakfast, lunches and snacks. If you prefer to have a picnic or a barbecue, there are plenty of green areas with seating dotted around the centre, along with a decent playground for children.

11 LEEK

🏠 The Daintry (page 243), **The Silken Strand Hotel** (page 243)

As I've discovered with so many mill towns on the fringes of the Peak District, you just have to dig a little deeper in Leek to uncover its treasures. Between the crumbling mills of this former industrial town, you'll find some fine architecture, design and craftsmanship, some heavily influenced by the Arts and Crafts movement. Many of the town's buildings were designed by local architects Sugdens in collaboration with silk dyer and printer Thomas Wardle and his friend and colleague, William Morris – along with the well-heeled town's industrialists that include the Nicholson family. The best way to get the most out of the experience is to pick up one of the **Leek Architectural Trail** guides from tourist information (page 166) and follow it around town.

The obvious starting point is Market Place, with its ancient **Market Cross** of 1671, cobbled square and handsome town houses. From here step through the entrance of the **Butter Market**, with its intricate wrought-iron grid set into the arch, and you'll find yourself wandering into a post-war Britain of haberdashery and collectables, an old-fashioned café, a fishmonger and a butchers. The streets surrounding Market Place are filled with individual shops sprinkled with the usual chains, earning Leek the title of second-best 'High Street' in Britain as voted by the *Telegraph* readership. Look up to appreciate the detail of the red-bricked Georgian and Victorian buildings mixed in with the black-and-white timber-frames – such as the **Roebuck Inn** on Derby Street

TIME FOR TEA

Church St ✆ 01538 398726 ☉ opening times vary due to other interests; it's best to check ahead

Hidden at the back of Parker House across from Market Square on Church Street, there's a tiny tea room. It's a fine place to pause on the town trail.

'Have you come to look at the clocks?' a waist-coated 'Mr Pickwick' asked my husband and I, albeit slim and spectacle-less and minus the top hat. We'd been funnelled down a narrow corridor, lured by polished wood and stained glass – and the need for a cup of tea. Behind the latched door there was a tiny room crammed with tables and elaborate gold-gilt clocks.

The kindly 'Mr Pickwick' – in reality proprietor Roger – helped me off with my coat; he is a Dickensian character from a bygone age – when chivalry and politeness were still valued. Tea and scones arrived, courtesy of his wife Jane, served on floral china and we tucked in to the chatter of ticking clocks. At three, the clocks burst into a riot of strikes and gongs along with the grand pronouncement of the Westminster chimes, all clambering for attention like a schoolroom of squabbling children. I exclaimed in pleasure to 'Mr Pickwick' who laughed and said, 'It's all a bit mad in here.' We settled down again to our scones and tea, the riot of chimes now a quiet, harmonious ticking – until the clatter began again on the half hour. *Time for Tea*, as it turns out, is more than just a café: it's an experience.

which dates back to 1626. Nearby is the cutesy **Getliffes Yard**, with its original Victorian cobblestones, glass dome and weaver's cottages, now housing boutiques and craft shops behind latched doors.

At the end of the main thoroughfare on Derby Street, you'll find the **Nicholson War Memorial** by the old cattle market, erected by Sir Arthur Nicholson, the son of the successful Leek industrialist, Joshua Nicholson. It commemorates Arthur's son who fell in the Great War, along with the town's fallen across both World Wars, and at 90 feet high, is one of the highest war monuments in the country.

On Stockwell Street, Arthur's father made his own mark in town with the **Nicholson Institute**, an imposing Queen Anne-style building, designed by renowned local architects, Sugdens, who were responsible for many of Leek's finer buildings. The institute is an impressive building, with its Renaissance-style tower and copper dome, containing a minimalist, homespun museum and art gallery. It's a low-key affair but it's worth venturing indoors for the wall paintings and beautifully crafted needlework made by the Leek School of Embroidery, hidden away in a corner cabinet. This was a building that attracted some of Europe's greatest thinkers and writers. Oscar Wilde, John Betjeman and D H Lawrence wandered these corridors. Adjacent is the old silk school, decorated with distinctive plaster reliefs in the style of cameo brooches. Close by is the 17th-century **Greystones**, Joshua Nicholson's home. William Morris and Thomas Wardle later saved this fine 17th-century house, with its gorgeous Arts and Crafts gate, from demolition.

"The Nicholson Institute is an impressive building, with its Renaissance-style tower and copper dome."

Where Stockwell Street becomes Church Street, you'll find the **Foxlowe Arts Centre** housed in an attractive Georgian building opposite the Market Square. The centre is fast becoming the place where it's happening in Leek, with its buzzing café culture, performance space, film, talks and live music. An elegant building both inside and out, it has echoes of Morris' Arts and Crafts movement in the ironwork, doorways and windows.

For anyone who appreciates the craftsmanship, colour and simple elegance of Morris and Arts and Crafts design, hinted at in Foxlowe House and in various places around town, head for Leek's churches. **St Edward Church** next to the Arts Centre contains Burne-Jones and

Morris stained-glass windows, along with examples of the Leek School of Embroidery. Detour to **All Saints Church** on Compton if you want to see more: the majority of the stained-glass windows in this Grade I listed building were created by Morris & Co, with more work from Leek Embroidery Society.

Tucked down side streets are the graceful homes of Leek's movers and shakers. Various members of the Sugden family lived on Queen Street, a mix of Georgian and Victorian houses set among older cottages and terraces. It's not difficult to single out the distinctive Sugden homes at 29, with their elongated chimney stacks, arched and pointed window, floral motifs and terracotta detail. Over on **St Edward Street** (considered Leek's finest road), further elegant Georgian and Victorian houses were home to the silk industrialists, including Thomas Wardle.

¶¶ FOOD & DRINK

For those who would rather quench their thirst than feed their soul, there's an alternative to the Architecture Trail in the *Real Ale* Trail (pick up a leaflet from tourist information). It takes in more than a dozen interesting, quirky and historical pubs such as The Engine Room, The Cock Inn, The Blue Mugge, The Cattle Market, The Roebuck, The Bird in Hand and Den Engel – a Belgian bar selling over 100 Belgian beers and a rotating selection of traditional English cask ales.

The friendly **Cupcake Café and Bakery** (7a Stanley St, ST13 5HG ✆ 07896 983194) offers breakfast, brunch and lunch, as well as snacks; the attentive owners are passionate about their business, while **George's Tradition** (52 Broad St ✆ 01332 226640) is the most popular chippy in town. Step back in time at Time For Tea (see box, page 181 for contact details and more info), an abundantly characterful, amiably genteel café seemingly ensconced in a more gracious, bygone era. For good pub grub, head for the **White Lion** (Macclesfield Rd, ST13 8LD ✆ 01538 398823) where good food is combined with attentive service.

SHOPPING

Leek has fine potential for browsing in markets. The **Butter Market** (along with crafts and collectables) is open for business on Wednesday, Friday and Saturday, while the **Outdoor Charter Market** takes place on Wednesdays. The **Trestle Market** is set up on Wednesday and Saturday and includes a craft and collectables market on a Friday and toy and train accessories on advertised Sundays. Along with the Saturday food market, there's an antique market and WI market (also Wednesday), an antiques and crafts market and a **Festival of Fine Foods** every third Saturday of the month.

THE GOYT VALLEY TO WARSLOW

Inside the national park, the southwest contains some of the quietest and most interesting corners of the Peak District: little frequented moorland, rounded hills, razor-sharp ridges, wooded dales, streams and fast-flowing rivers. From the industrial remnants on the moorland at **Tegg's Nose** above Macclesfield, to the sylvan, hill-clinging hamlets of **Wincle** and **Danebridge**, this is a landscape of wonderful diversity. For those who find hill walking, rock climbing, scrambling, weaselling and rock hopping too energetic, there are plenty of more leisurely pursuits, from fishing, birdwatching and bilberry picking, to local ice cream and beer sampling.

12 THE GOYT VALLEY
⋏ The Cat and Fiddle Inn (page 244)
Beneath the windswept, peaty moors the Goyt Valley is a manmade adaptation of the landscape in the form of a string of reservoirs flanked by sizeable forestry plantations, making for some rewarding, energetic walking along the waterside and up along the breezy tops. If travelling by bus, alight at the **Cat and Fiddle** and head down to **Derbyshire Bridge**. Alternatively, High Peak buses stop adjacent to **Goyt Lane** on the Buxton to Whaley Bridge road. You can link the two to return to Buxton. Along the River Goyt is a short wheelchair-accessible route that takes in boardwalk sections and a tumbling waterfall – particularly striking in winter when the water is abundant, or in late spring when the rhododendrons are in full bloom. Other walks circumnavigate **Fernilee Reservoir**, or take in the ruins of **Errwood Hall**.

13 TEGG'S NOSE COUNTRY PARK
Buxton Old Rd, SK11 0AP ✆ 01625 614279 ⏚ www.teggsnose.co.uk
On the twisty Cat and Fiddle Buxton to Macclesfield road, high above the mill town, a side road (at Walker Barn) dips south down to Tegg's Nose Country Park. From here, an hour-long trail gives you an all-round panorama, encompassing Wales and Liverpool on a clear day. Drop into the visitor centre and café and admire the stained-glass windows before picking up a trail guide. There are two options to consider: the short, flattish circular stroll (just under two miles) that rings the hillock of Tegg's Nose, and a longer, more arduous trail, that follows part of the

Saddlers Way, heading down to **Tegg's Nose Reservoir** before climbing steeply back up to the country park.

To begin the shorter walk, head out of the car park to the road and take the wide path off to the side of it on the left. The path crosses meadows with views of Macclesfield and the Cheshire Plains. You can pick out the older red-brick mills set in among more modern offices. After a short distance the trail climbs up towards the quarry face, with various information boards on Tegg's Nose industrial days. Quarrying began here in Tudor times and continued for the best part of 500 years. The site has returned to nature, but various pieces of aggressive-sounding equipment on display – a stone crusher and a swing jaw (for making blocks and slabs) – are a reminder of the park's industrial past. As the trail rounds the southern end of the hillside, Langley and its reservoirs come into view, with Macclesfield Forest stretching out across the hills and the pointed peak of Shutlingsloe behind it. Take the little path down to the viewpoint, where a map identifies the surrounding landmarks. Back on the trail, continue along the west side of Tegg's Nose before rejoining the path across the meadows to the car park. You can re-tank at the centre's tea room (and warm up by the log-burner on damp or cold days). The country park is wonderful at any time of year, but try and come between May and August when the mountain pansies spread yellow across the meadows.

Cheshire East Council, which manages the country park, offers a range of walks and activities, bookable online (⌂ www.cecrangers.eventbrite. co.uk). From birdwatching, bats and rocks, to star-gazing, poetry, wildlife and wild food (including jam making from the bilberries that grow on the slopes of Tegg's Nose), there's plenty to whet the appetite.

14 AROUND MACCLESFIELD FOREST & SHUTLINGSLOE

Seen from the hills above, the sloping swathes of green of Macclesfield Forest and glinting waters of the reservoirs along with the little village of Langley beckon far below – and it's certainly worth heading down the path (or the road designated a 'quiet lane') to have a closer look at this tranquil corner of the Peak District just south of the A537.

From **Trentabank Ranger Centre**, you can pick up a leaflet outlining a number of colour-coded trails through the forests, ranging from less than one mile to six, and view the close-up images of the nearby heronry on CCTV. The walks take in forest, reservoir, moorland and lane – and the **Trentabank Heronry**. To see the birds lording it over from their lofty twiggy thrones, the best time to visit is between February and July when the herons lay their eggs and raise the young. There are some 20 nests on the nature reserve making the heronry the largest in the national park. There's also the chance of spotting numbers of cormorants, mallards and great crested grebes that inhabit the reservoir, while in the woods you may glimpse red deer, badgers and pipistrelle bats.

From the forest access road at the top of Macclesfield Forest, you can head out over **Piggford Moor** to Shutlingsloe, dubbed the Matterhorn of Cheshire because of its pointed top. The comparison between the two peaks ends there: at a mere 1,660 feet, you won't need crampons or an ice-pick to scale Shutlingsloe's summit. Indeed a wide slabbed path leads to the top, with only a few deeply hewn steps to challenge the walker for the last few yards. The wind often sweeps across its exposed top, but it's worth battling the elements for the panoramic views, taking in Tittesworth Reservoir, the Roaches, Macclesfield and the Cheshire Plains to the winding Buxton Road with Shining Tor behind.

Several other notable features surround Macclesfield Forest. **Greenway Cross**, near Oaken Clough, is a stone way-marker with carved crosses placed there by medieval monks. Near the delightfully named **Bottom-of-the-oven**, the tiny church of **St Stephen** (the Forest Chapel) is known for its rush-bearing ceremony that takes place every August, when rushes, taken from nearby swamps, are laid on the floor or plaited into decorations. South of Wildboarclough, **Blaze Farm** (Wildboarclough SK11 0BL ☎ 01260 227229 ☉ Tue–Sun & bank holidays) has a farm park, nature trail, ceramic pot painting (☉ by appointment only), farm shop and tea room, but it's their delicious homemade 'Hilly Billy' ice cream (produced from the milk of their own dairy herd) that draws most people. On the north side of Wildboarclough, a picturesque riverside ramble along **Clough Brook** heads off from **Clough House**.

¶¶ FOOD & DRINK

The Cat and Fiddle Inn Buxton Rd, SK11 0AR ☎ 01298 78366. Not many pubs in the Peak District sell themselves as 'ski friendly' (alongside dog-, walking-boot-, rucksack-friendly) – the Cat and Fiddle can because of its lofty location, set in the highest reaches of the Peak District – and claiming to be the second-highest pub in the country. What the pub lacks in atmosphere is made up for by the views. Pub nosh at reasonable prices.

Peak View Tearooms Buxton Rd, SK11 0AR ✆ 01298 22103 ⊙ closed Mon & Tue. An alternative to the Cat and Fiddle, Park View Tearooms is a mile further west along the A537. Close to Tegg's Nose Country Park and Macclesfield with great views over to Shutlingsloe. At a height of 1,670 feet, the tea room is the highest in the Peak District. There are roaring fires in winter and outside seating for summer days – and an enormous cake selection for hungry walkers and cyclists.

The Leather's Smithy Clarke Lane, Langley SK11 0NE ✆ 01260 252313. A rural pub overlooking Ridgegate Reservoir in the village of Langley, yet a stone's throw from the town of Macclesfield. Traditional pub with well-cooked food. The game is particularly good.

Following Clough Brook along country lanes

Just below the Cat and Fiddle road and the wild stretches of moorland, there's an altogether softer landscape made up of leafy country lanes flanked by woodland, meadow and marsh, with verges laced with bracken and foxgloves in summer. Travelling from Buxton towards Macclesfield, take the first left after Peak View Tearooms and drop down to the **Stanley Arms**, taking another left turn immediately after the pub. From here, the road hugs **Clough Brook** as it tumbles its way towards Wildboarclough, thoroughly recommended for road cyclists and part of Route 70 on the Cheshire Cycleway. It must surely be one of the most beautiful country lanes in the Peak District and it's a shame it's not on a bus route. For walkers, occasional wooden or stone bridges take you over to meadow and the uplands beyond. Shutlingsloe can be approached from this side too. Before Sharpley, turn left to keep with the brook, crossing the A54 to reach Wincle and Danebridge.

15 WINCLE & DANEBRIDGE

From charming Wincle, with its picture-book spired school and hillside church, **Barlow Hill** road heads over the rise before dropping down to the River Dane and a settlement of houses that cling to the valley side. The houses north of the river are part of Wincle and find themselves in Cheshire, while the buildings south of the Dane are in Danebridge and in Staffordshire. It's a beguiling spot with its little stone cottages set in among mature deciduous trees and conifers on the hillside. The hillside road drops down to the River Dane where it meanders its way through wide flat pastures. Here you'll find Wincle Breweries and Danebridge Fisheries. It's worth detouring to both businesses – not least for the setting. Fishing and beer-tasting apart, this little corner of combined

Staffordshire and Cheshire has some of the finest walking in the Peak District: along the Dane Valley Way or through mature woodland and pine-scented forest to Gradbach, Back Wood and Lud's Church, and on to the Roaches. If you're in the area in May, take the public footpath just above the **Ship Inn** (on the same side) that heads across the meadows (following the line of planted trees) to woodlands carpeted with bluebell woods.

LORNE CHADWICK, FISH FARMER

⊘ www.danebridgefisheries.com

At Danebridge Fisheries, the River Dane splutters its way through the floodplain towards Danebridge. At the end of the lane, owner Lorne points out a headstone with the inscription: 'Your valley; My Dream; God's gift'. 'My dad spent a long, long time looking for the ideal site for his fish farm,' he says, 'and he finally found it here in the fast-flowing spring-fed waters of the River Dane'. We climb down steps to a wooden shack adorned with a lifebuoy. Inside, I climb over the dogs and plonk myself into one of the garden chairs as Lorne rummages through the fishing tackle and tools for coffee cups, while telling me about the badger that comes down on to the farm every day to feed on the fish waste.

Coffee finished, Lorne takes me to the ponds, where he throws fish food into the water. There's a feeding frenzy as the trout come to the surface, golden trout among the blues. 'We've got about 13 to 14 thousand fish per pond,' says Lorne. 'We give them a bit more room so they're not tail biting. It takes a little bit longer to grow them up to size and you can see that from the fact their heads are in proportion with their bellies and their backs are broader. They actually have more flesh – and look better. It's the reason local restaurants buy our fish.'

Lorne is passionate about introducing fishing to young children. 'We've three little catch-all ponds for the kids. The children have got two expressions when they're fishing: total concentration on the job and pure joy and wonderment when they catch a fish. Then the parents can set up the barbecue and cook the dinner they've caught while the kids play. I give them a trail map and off they go hunting for the animal statues or doing brass rubbings – and learning to recognise, say, the footprint of a fox or badger.'

Across from the junior ponds, the main lake is lined with anglers casting their lines, while a little wooden fishing hut sits between water and woodland. 'There's nothing like this place,' he says. 'When I'm walking with the dogs in this little ecosystem caught in the valley, or on beautiful days when the mist has just risen and the sun's cutting through it, it's magical – or like the morning when I nipped through a hedge to come face to face with a stag with its horns; terrifying and exhilarating at the same time.'

Wincle Brewery

Tolls Farm Barn, Danebridge, Wincle SK11 0QE ✎ 01260 227777 ✐ www.winclebeer.co.uk
☉ 10.00–16.00 daily.

Wincle Brewery started its life as a low-key affair in a redundant milking parlour on a local farm before relocating to a renovated stone barn by the River Dane with its state-of-the-art 15-barrel plant. The day I called in there was a steady flow of customers, mostly walkers passing through, delighted to have an opportunity to sample two in-house beers and a guest brew before choosing a pint. Outside there's a small grassy area and picnic benches where you can enjoy the peace and tranquillity of this beautiful valley alongside the fishing lake. It's a great place to sip one of the local brews – and if you don't drink beer the brewery also does coffee and cake. The brewery offers tours, demonstrations and beer tasting.

I love the way in which the names and sepia pictures on the bottles celebrate local stories and characters. Bad Bill refers to an ill-tempered bull that lives around the back, while Wibbly Wallaby pays homage to the escaped wallabies that roamed the Roaches for a time. The manic individual holding a large knife on the label of Butchered is a retired local butcher and Life of Riley references another retired local called… Riley – who's clearly having a good time. Other local, real-life characters include a haymaker, dry stone waller and woodcutter. Sir Philip Lee Brocklehurst of nearby Swythamley Hall is honoured with a beer, having accompanied the great explorer, Shackleton to the Antarctic, while Mr Mullins was associated with the estate when it was run by Indian mystic Maharisha Mahesh Yogias as a training centre for transcendental meditation. Old Hag with her gnarled face is Bessy Bowyer who lived in the cave house on the Roaches, while the equally wizened Old Oak can be found at nearby Whitelee Farm, said to be a stately 700 years old.

The beers taste good too, with the brewery describing the flavours as everything from 'biscuit and moreish', 'chocolatey and comforting' to 'refreshing, fruity and citrusy'.

⑪ FOOD & DRINK

Ship Inn Barlow Hill, Wincle SK11 0QE ✎ 01260 227217. A varied and imaginative menu, using fresh local produce where possible. Lovely beer garden with fine views over the Cheshire and Staffordshire countryside.

16 THE ROACHES

🏠 **Don Whillans Memorial Hut** (page 243)

🖊 www.theroaches.org.uk

Whether approaching the Roaches from Danebridge and Tittesworth, or from the A53 on the Leek to Buxton road, the Roaches rise dramatically

A walk from Gradbach through Back Forest to Lud's Church

❊ OS Explorer map OL24; start: Gradbach car park, ♥ SJ999662; 3 miles; moderately easy, but watch your step in the slippery Lud's Church; there are no refreshments *en route*

This circular walk takes in meadow, brook and woodland. There's a climb up to Lud's Church, but it's well worth the effort (although more so in spring and summer than winter). Bring a picnic and sit on one of the great slabs of rock overlooking the Dane Valley.

1 Turn right out of the car park and walk along the lane until you reach a right fork leading downhill through stone pillars to **Gradbach Mill car park**.

2 From this car park, follow the public footpath sign left on to a wide gravel path with the River Dane on your right for about 20 yards. Climb the steps on the left up to a gate and follow the footpath. Follow the path through a gap in the stone wall to your right, continuing in the same direction. The path joins a track rising to a sharp left bend.

3 Here, there's an obvious gap in the stone wall straight ahead. Go through, turn right then cross the **footbridge over Black Brook**.

4 Immediately over the bridge, follow the sign for Lud's Church that points straight ahead uphill, past a large beech and up steps. At the top, turn right, following the track through the forest of mixed deciduous and conifers.

5 After a steady climb, you will come to a rocky outcrop called **Castle Rocks** (good for a pit stop). Turn left at the junction, on to the footpath signed for Lud's Church.

6 After a few hundred yards, you will see the gap in the rocks to the right with steps leading up and into the cleft in the ground. This is **Lud's Church**. Take the main route through the chasm, exiting by steps at the far end and turning left to an unmarked junction. Take the board-walked path straight ahead (southeast) through woodland, following signs for Gradbach.

7 Near the end of the woodland ridge, take a left turn signed for Gradbach and Danebridge on to a lower path, keeping left and following yellow arrows.

8 This will eventually lead down to the Black Brook again. If you are up to fording the river, cross over the stones and climb up the stony lane, joining the road past the Scout buildings

out of the moorland like a dragon with its serrated hump. Along with **Hen Cloud, Five Clouds** and **Ramshaw Rocks**, they provide some of the best climbing and walking to be had in the Peak District.

From Roach Road, the path climbs through bracken to the saddle between the Roaches and Hen Cloud. If you want to bag a peak and

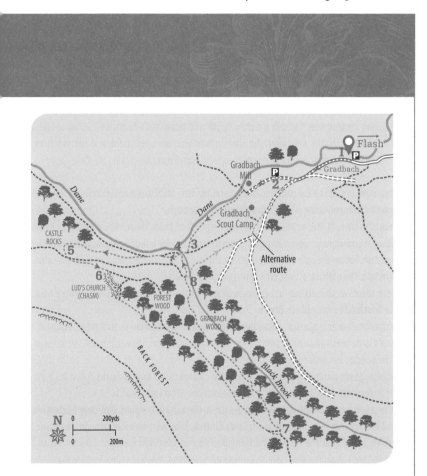

and back down to the car park. Alternatively, you can follow the signs for Gradbach back to the footbridge at point 4 on this walk, from where you can retrace your steps back to the beginning – this time keeping the River Dane on your left.

have a quick workout, it doesn't take long to climb Hen Cloud – and the views towards Tittesworth Reservoir and back across to the Roaches are stunning. Alternatively, if you take the first left path you come to, it will bring you to the base of the Roaches and the **Don Whillans Memorial Hut**, a strange Gothic building with arched windows, mock castellations and an annex that seems to grow out of the rocks. It's said the old crone Bessy Bowyer lived here, just inside the fallen rocks that had created a cave, from where she assisted smugglers and deserters on the Roaches. Rock Hall was built here as a gamekeeper's cottage for Swythamley Estate. Nowadays, the building belongs to the British Mountaineering Council and commemorates one of the greatest British climbers of the 20th century, Don Whillans, who forged many technically difficult new routes in Britain, the Alps and the Himalayas with climbing legends like Chris Bonington. Today the hut offers accommodation for individuals during the week and for groups at the weekend.

There's no better place in the Peak District to try a spot of weaselling and rock-hopping than on the rocks above the Don Whillans Hut. A rocky adventure playground, you can squeeze, crawl and scramble your way through the rock-strewn hillside, and hop from rock to rock. You don't need any specialist equipment, but care and a good dollop of common sense are required. Otherwise, there are weaselling courses on offer in the Peak District – along with rock climbing.

For non-climbers, a well-defined path runs along the top of the Roaches ridge, where strangely shaped and weathered rocks are twisted into corkscrews and pillars along the edge. Not far along the path, you will come to Doxey Pool, a beautifully rounded tarn on the humpback that catches the sky in its glassy surface on clear days and is said to contain a nymph within its depths.

The ridge path of the Roaches extends three miles. On a clear day, the views towards the Cheshire Plains and the hills of Wales are extensive. At Roach End, the path reaches the road. Turn left and follow the quiet lane back down to your start point. Alternatively, you can cross the road and continue on into Back Forest and Lud's Church to extend your hike.

¶¶ FOOD & DRINK

The Roaches Tearoom Off A53 (Leek–Buxton road), Upper Hulme ST13 8TY
✐ 01538 300345. Old-fashioned tea room serving sandwiches and cakes along with more substantial meals; all with wonderful views over to Tittesworth and beyond.

Lud's Church

Lud's Church isn't actually a church, but a **deep chasm** hidden in a quiet corner of Back Forest beyond the Roaches – a place you could easily walk right by without noticing. Although Lud's Church is a natural geological feature rather than a manmade place of worship, the cathedral-like space has a mysterious and spiritual quality to it. Descending into this chasm, it feels primeval with its towering columns of rock covered in moss, fern and lichen. Not much light penetrates this dark, moist place, yet it has an ethereal, magical feel to it. Lud's Church is associated with knights, princes and protesters and shrouded in tales of mystery and adventure, all mixed up with actual historical events.

Geologically, the landscape around Lud's Church is sliced with fractures that came about when a large section of Carboniferous grit and sandstone, rent by faults, slipped downhill towards the Dane Valley, resulting in the open rift.

Lud's Church was actually used as a place of worship by the persecuted Lollards. These followers of John Wycliffe, an early church reformer, used the secret location as a safe place to worship in the early 15th century. Some think the chasm was named after Walter de Lud-Auk who was captured here at one of the Lollard meetings. Others think the name could be associated with the Luddites, the protest group led by Ned Ludd who opposed the labour-saving machinery of the Industrial Revolution, also active in this area.

Then there are the great legendary figures of Britain's literature and history who supposedly used Lud's Church as a place of refuge: Robin Hood, Friar Tuck and Bonny Prince Charlie. What's more, as if this roll-call of legendary names isn't enough, Lud's Church has also been linked to Sir Gawain, one of the knights of Arthur's Round Table, and the Green Knight.

In one of the tales of Arthur's Round Table, the Green Knight, somewhat foolishly, came up with a bizarre 'beheading game', offering other knights the opportunity to take a free swipe at him with his own axe. There was a proviso as you can imagine: if beheaded, the Green Knight would be allowed to return the favour within a year and a day. Gawain, never one to shirk a challenge, accepted and beheaded the knight in a single blow. With that the Green Knight coolly stood up, collected his head, and politely reminded Gawain of his agreed appointment at the Green Chapel – Lud's Church.

Parkhouse Hill & Chrome Hill from Earl Sterndale

❄ OS map OL24; start: The Quiet Woman Inn, Earl Sterndale, ⚲ SK090670; 6 miles; strenuous ridge climbs, tricky underfoot, particularly coming off Parkhouse Hill (alternative easier route round the base of the hill); refreshments at the Quiet Woman

This walk takes in two thrilling ridge walks, Parkhouse Hill and Chrome (pronounced Croom) Hill, with short, sharp climbs to both summits. The descent of Parkhouse is particularly challenging – and neither of the ridges is recommended on wet days. You will be well rewarded though, if you do make it on to the summits – the views across the White Peak are second-to-none. For those who suffer from vertigo, head right, round the base of both peaks, returning by single-track road and meadow.

The return along a bridleway, through Hollinsclough and on along farm tracks through the valley (with great views over to the vertiginous Parkhouse and Chrome hills) is very pleasant after the rigours of the climbs. As you take in the ridges, you can quietly congratulate yourself on your bravery (or berate yourself for your foolishness).

1 From The Quiet Woman head up the side of the pub, following the fingerpost signed for Longnor. Cross the wall and turn left to follow it along the hillside and downhill. Cross a second wall and follow another Longnor fingerpost downhill, through a gate and on through a field towards a house.

Go through the gap beside the farm gate and turn right on to the farm track. At the end of the farm track, turn right on to the road.

2 Take the first left fingerpost pointing the way through fields to the base of **Parkhouse Hill**. Here there are decisions to be made: you can take the footpath skirting the base of the hill to the left, or you can head bravely up, following the worn path that winds its way up the steep side. Continue on along the ridge, watching your feet carefully. As you approach the last pinnacle, keep to the right of it (the path heading left leads down a sheer scree-covered path). At the bottom of the hill, you will meet a country lane.

3 At the cattle grid, follow the concessionary path signed and head up **Chrome Hill**, a longer climb than Parkhouse Hill, but less ridge-like on the ascent. As with Park Hill, watch your feet on the descent.

4 At the bottom of Chrome Hill, follow the path as it veers left along the base of the hill. Head through a gate on the right and follow the line of the dry stone wall and fence. At the next gate, follow the concessionary path up to the saddle of the hill. Head through the farm gate and follow the signposts through meadow until you come to a rough farm track. Cross it and continue over more meadow where you'll meet another farm track.

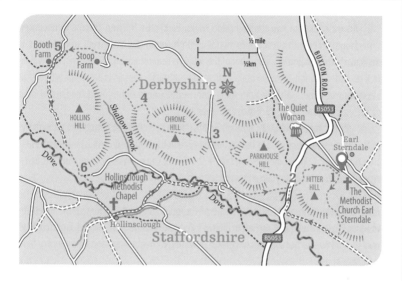

5 At the end of the farm track turn left on to the country lane and continue on to **Booth Farm**. Take the bridle path opposite the farm, bearing left of the road, and head downhill until you come to a signpost that leads away from the wide track and on to a narrow path.

6 Head down the path. Turn right to go through a metal gate, cross the little footbridge and turn left. The path rises up to the road, where a left turn leads to **Hollinsclough**. Turn left in the village and head down the road, taking the first left down a farm track (signposted). Turn right (signposted Glutton Bridge) where two farm tracks converge and follow it until you join another road. Bear right a short distance along the road before following the fingerpost that takes you along meadow at the base of **Parkhouse Hill**. Continue through fields until you reach the main road (where you started the climb to Parkhouse Hill).

7 Cross the road and go through the gate on the other side, bearing left up the hillside. Turn right before the path reaches the dry stone wall, making your way through small boulders. Go through the gate in the wall and on through a farm gate, heading for the church in **Earl Sterndale**. Go through a series of wooden gates behind buildings until you reach the **Quiet Woman** and your starting point.

Others say Lud's Church was named after a horse. The tale goes something like this: a huntsman, pursuing a deer on horseback, failed to notice the chasm. His horse Lud, quicker off the mark, bucked when it approached the chasm, throwing the unfortunate man to his death below. It's said the huntsman still roams the surrounding woods covered from head to toe in moss – hence the Green Man.

It's difficult to separate one tale from another and fact from mythology with regards to Lud's Church, but there is no doubt that it's a wonderfully atmospheric place.

17 EARL STERNDALE & AROUND

🏠 **Wheeldon Trees Farm Holiday Cottages** (page 244)

East of the Roaches, Wincle and Danebridge, Earl Sterndale sits in the hills, an unassuming farming village of church, pub and a smattering of dwellings. The settlement is surrounded by 'Postman Pat' steeply rounded hills and pointy peaks that bump along the otherwise flat Upper Dove Valley: High Wheeldon, Alderley Cliff, Hitter, Parkhouse and Chrome. There are two main reasons to detour to Earl Sterndale: for the character pub with its disturbing pub sign and name and for the wonderful walking country that surrounds the village.

If you enjoy the dizzying experience of a ridge walk, head for Parkhouse and Chrome (see walk, pages 194–5). If you prefer to feel your feet firmly planted on earth, there are pleasant walks along the floor of the valley – where you can admire the ridges from a safe distance. Nearby **Hollinsclough**, not much more than a hamlet, has no tourist facilities but is an agreeable place to wander through on a walk, with its faded bell-towered residence centre, Methodist church, school and handful of houses. Best of all is its backdrop in the shape of Chrome Hill, a wall of rock and grassy slope behind the village.

🍴 FOOD & DRINK

The Quiet Woman SK17 0BU ✆ 01298 83211. The 400-year-old pub, has two disturbing signs outside; both of a headless woman. On the first, the decapitated barmaid is walking along with a tray of drinks (quite a feat without a head). Both signs have the words written on them 'Soft words turneth away wrath'. This alludes to a story of the husband of an endlessly nagging wife who lost it one day and silenced her forever. Pretty sexist stuff, but don't let that put you off visiting this spit-and-sawdust pub where seemingly nothing much has changed over the centuries. The floors are tiled; the furniture plain and there's a bit of china hanging around along with a good old-fashioned coal fire. Outside, there's a little beer garden to the side with more seating out back, a good place to look out at the menagerie of animals including donkeys, hens, turkeys and ducks. You can buy all sorts from the character landlord: from free-range eggs to a bale of hay. Food is limited to the most basic pub fare – sausage rolls or pork pies, when available.

18 LONGNOR

All roads lead to Longnor – or at least four of them do in this backwater rural village straddling the crossroads, just south of Earl Sterndale. Longnor wasn't always the sleepy settlement it is today – as the signage to various hostelries and the cobbled market place indicates. Look to the board at the top of the **Market Hall** and it's not difficult to imagine a market square filled with animals rather than cars. A table of tolls payable at Longnor markets and fairs dates back to 1903. For sellers: 'for every stall not exceeding six feet in length four pence' – the same price for sheep or pigs, or a cart or carriage. A basket of eggs cost a mere penny, while cheese, chicks or poultry (not in baskets) cost two pence per score. As for buyers: 'for every horse, four pence; for every cow or bull two year old, two pence, and under two, one penny' (along with pig). But the best value animal in the market was the humble hillside sheep – at a halfpenny.

Take time to wander through this rustic village, up Chapel Road past the latch-door cottages that back on to the church graveyard and on round the village with its lovely stone buildings. There are still a couple of pubs and cafés selling food and drink – but alas, nowhere nowadays to pick up a sheep or a pig.

¶¶ FOOD & DRINK

Cobbles Tearoom (High St, SK17 0NU ✆ 01298 83166) is a sweet little tea room with great food across the board; the scones are particularly good. For something a bit more substantial, try **Ye Olde Cheshire Cheese Inn** (High St, SK17 0NS ✆ 01298 83218), a traditional pub with a collection of knick-knacks that makes it feel like a homespun village museum; friendly service, good beer and reasonably priced pub grub.

19 WARSLOW

Heading south again from Longnor, you'll reach Warslow, a down-to-earth village between Leek and the Manifold Valley. The B5053 that will take you to Warslow is a spectacular road, bumping its way along the moorland with extensive views on all sides.

There's little to hold you in Warslow itself, other than the **Partridge Inn** (serving a substantial, cheap-as-chips 'chippy menu') and **St Lawrence's Church**. From the outside it looks a very plain, uninteresting building, but once indoors you see five stunning Morris & Co windows, the colours and detail contrasting the whitewashed plainness of this little church. Local parishioner and respected Leek silk dyer and printer Thomas Wardle was a close friend and colleague of William Morris. Both men shared a passion for colour and design – as well as nature – and spent many hours together walking the surrounding moorland or fishing on the River Manifold. Behind the choir stalls, four exquisitely embroidered lectern drops are displayed on the wall, commissioned by Lady Harpur-Crewe to commemorate Elizabeth Wardle, Thomas's wife, herself a talented embroiderer.

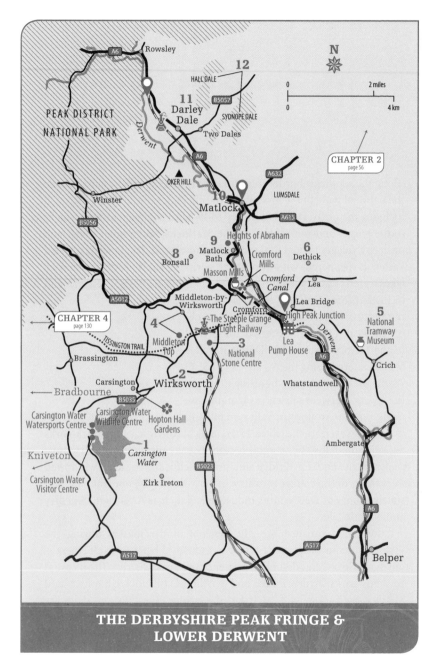

THE DERBYSHIRE PEAK FRINGE &
LOWER DERWENT

Map labels:

Rowsley

PEAK DISTRICT NATIONAL PARK

Derwent

12 HALL DALE

11 Darley Dale

B5057

SYDNOPE DALE

Two Dales

A6

OKER HILL

Winster

B5056

A632

LUMSDALE

10 Matlock

A615

Heights of Abraham

9 Matlock Bath

8 Bonsall

6 Dethick

Cromford Mills

Masson Mills

Cromford Canal

Lea

A5012

Middleton-by-Wirksworth

Cromford

7 High Peak Junction

Lea Bridge

5 National Tramway Museum

CHAPTER 4
page 130

TISSINGTON TRAIL

Middleton Top

4

The Steeple Grange Light Railway

3 National Stone Centre

Lea Pump House

A6

Derwent

Crich

Brassington

2 Wirksworth

Carsington

Whatstandwell

Bradbourne

B5035

Carsington Water Watersports Centre

Carsington Water Wildlife Centre

Hopton Hall Gardens

1 Carsington Water

Ambergate

Kniveton

Carsington Water Visitor Centre

Kirk Ireton

B5023

A6

A517

A517

Belper

N

0   2 miles
0   4 km

CHAPTER 2
page 56

6
THE DERBYSHIRE PEAK FRINGE & LOWER DERWENT

Along the southeast border this remarkably diverse area lies just outside the national park, but it contains all the character of the Peak District. It includes the gritty **Derwent Valley Mills** with soaring chimney stacks to the gorges and rocky bluffs of the **Matlocks**, and a quiet hinterland of sleepy villages tucked into the folds of farmland. The **Lower Derwent Valley** is peppered with industrial heritage: mills, canals, dammed lakes, rivers, leats, lynchpins and water wheels, evoking a seismic shift in Britain's economic and social landscape – the Industrial Revolution, when this corner of the Peak District witnessed the arrival of the factory system. The Derwent Valley Mills scattered along the A6 are a UNESCO World Heritage Site, recognising the part the Lower Derwent played in changing the world forever. Around the valley on hill and

"The Lower Derwent Valley is peppered with industrial heritage: mills, canals, dammed lakes, rivers, leats, lynchpins and water wheels."

in dale, however, are the tell-tale remnants of earlier ages: the pockmarks of lead mineshafts; the crumbling stone barns caught between dry stone walls; the rise and dip of ridge and furrow fields, and the long-windowed workshops of the cottage industry. In between are the opulent halls and stately homes of Derbyshire's industrialists such as Arkwright, Smedley and Nightingale.

Industrialisation also brought benefits to the masses during the Victorian era in the form of tourism. Industrial heritage aside, there is much else to see and do in this corner of the Peak District. The pleasure gardens, parks, hydro hotels and pavilions still adorn Matlock and Matlock Bath today with their faded elegance. The hills and dales are criss-crossed with public footpaths, including the glorious **Limestone Way**, while the market towns of **Cromford** and **Wirksworth** will tempt you with their arty cafés, boutiques and architectural heritage.

WALKING & CYCLING

From village ambles around the Matlocks to countryside rambles taking in woodland, ridge, dale and tor, there's something for everyone in this fringe area of the Peak District. **The Limestone Way** passes through Bonsall, while the Derwent Valley Heritage Way follows the Derwent Valley Mills World Heritage Site. These sections of the long-distance walks offer superb scenery as well as historical interest.

Cycling through the **Lower Derwent Valley** is flat and easy, although the A6 is busy. Alternatively, take the back roads that run along the hills either side of the main road, but be warned, the gradients are not for the faint-hearted. One of my favourite cycles is along the **Cromford Canal** from **Ambergate to Cromford**, a beautiful ride, best tackled outside of the summer months when the verge-side vegetation has died back. From **High Peak Junction** on the canal, you have the option to divert on to the **High Peak Trail**. Don't miss the trail around **Carsington Water** for heart-soaring hill and waterside scenery.

CYCLE HIRE

Carsington Sport and Leisure Carsington Water DE6 1ST ⊘ www.carsingtonwater.com/cycle-hire-information.
Middleton Top Cycle Hire Centre Middleton-by-Wirksworth, Matlock DE4 4LS ✆ 01629 823204. ⊘ www.derbyshire.gov.uk.

THE DERBYSHIRE PEAK FRINGE

West of the Lower Derwent Valley (just outside the perimeters of the national park) a fine area of wooded copse, sloping meadow and limestone wall hides ancient Bronze Age barrows and burial mounds along with the remains of a once-thriving lead mining industry.

TOURIST INFORMATION

Wirksworth Heritage Centre and Information Point 31 St Johns St, DE4 4DS ✆ 07802 725862 ☉ Fri, Sat & bank holidays
Matlock Peak Rail Matlock Riverside Station, Matlock ✆ 01629 761103
Matlock Bath The Pavilion, Matlock Bath DE4 3NR ✆ 01629 583388

The characterful mining villages here surround the more modern addition of **Carsington Water**, a hub for water sports, birdwatching, cycling and rambling. Close by, to the northeast, is the quirky, Bohemian market town of **Wirksworth**, increasingly gaining a reputation for interesting art and design. On the other side of the Derwent Valley is a sylvan landscape of gently undulating countryside, tucking small villages, hamlets and handsome country houses into its folds. While the Derbyshire Peak Fringe may lack the drama of the deep-cut dales and windswept moorlands in the White and Dark Peak, its gentle beauty and quiet serenity has a certain charm.

1 CARSINGTON WATER & AROUND

⋏ Pudding Room (page 244)

Carsington Water, Big Lane, DE6 1ST ✐ 01629 540696 ⏁ www.carsingtonwater.com
☉ summer 10.00–18.00 daily; winter 10.00–17.00 daily (except Christmas day)

On the B5035 between Ashbourne and Matlock, Carsington Water gleams a Mediterranean blue, specked white on sunlit days. This watery playground in landlocked Derbyshire has a strong pulling power for day trippers and holidaymakers in summer, when a cooling wind funnels through the valley. Visitors come here for the boating, cycling, walking and bird-watching opportunities – or simply to spread out the tartan rug, unpack a picnic and while away an hour or three.

While Carsington Water has been developed as a leisure facility, it was created purely for utilitarian reasons – as an emergency reserve of water for Derby and the East Midlands. The **Visitor Centre and Exhibition** with its interactive displays tell that story. Behind the centre there's a small courtyard of shops with **The Kugel** at its centre: one tonne of granite, revolving on a thin film of water, yet easily moved with the touch of a finger – a magnet for adults and children alike. Behind the centre, **Stones Island** (actually a small peninsula) takes you up a spiralled pathway of sculpted rocks, a modern take on the stone circle. Circular holes, like portholes, have been cut into the hewn rocks, capturing small segments of the reservoir and its surrounds. It's a fitting tribute to the Bronze Age burial mound and Roman lead workings that were excavated in the vicinity.

The reservoir itself is home to a host of local and migrating birds (more than 200 species), with their habitats of woodland, meadow, reedbed and island, and a supporting cast of butterflies and dragonflies.

Hides are dotted along the water's edge; you may spot a flock of lapwings, an elegant little egret or a gangly cormorant.

Before departing, stop off at the **Wildlife Centre** to find out more about Carsington Water's wildlife, and how its human custodians seek to encourage biodiversity. North of the Wildlife Centre and the Visitor Centre is the **Watersports Centre**, where you can hire bikes, sailing dinghies, canoes, kayaks, paddleboards and windsurfing boards; the centre offers taster sessions and training courses.

The villages surrounding Carsington Water

🏠 **Hoe Grange Holidays** (page 244) ⛺ **New House Organic Farm** (page 244)

Surrounding the reservoir are rural settlements with historical pubs and houses clinging to the hillside or gathered round a village green. They are all worth exploring. The old mining villages north and west of Carsington Water sit in a landscape pocked by lead mining: Brassington, Bradbourne and Kniveton, and closer to the shore, Carsington, Hopton and Hognaston, while on the other side of the reservoir Kirk Ireton has an elegant olde-worlde charm. The 111 bus service between Cromford and Ashbourne will take you to most of these villages.

Walking, it takes less than an hour to reach **Carsington** village from the visitor centre, along the edge of the reservoir and up a quiet country road; even less on a bicycle. You can quench your thirst after the uphill trudge at the **Miners Arms** (✆ 01629 540207). Look out for the old Saxon preaching stone on the village green, brought by an early visitor – a Northumberland monk who came to evangelise. The visitors continue to come, albeit tourists rather than missionaries.

Adjoining Carsington village is the hamlet of Hopton with the elegant Hopton Hall. While the house is private, **Hopton Hall Gardens** (Hopton Close, DE4 4DF ✆ 01629 540923 🖱 www.hoptonhall.co.uk) are open in January and February so the public can enjoy the profusion of woodland snowdrops, and again between June and August when there are fine displays of summer roses and cottage garden flowers. Much work has been done by the latest owners to restore the near-derelict gardens to their former glory, including the formal walled garden, the playful crinkle-crankle wall, ornamental ponds and flowerbeds, wildlife lake, arboretum and pinetum. The various parts of the garden are linked by the Badger, Beech and Woodland paths, along with the Laburnum Tunnel. You can finish off with a cuppa in the **Garden Tea Room** attached to the main house. The hall itself can be traced back to the 1400s and was home to the Gell family for 600 years. They hosted a long line of impressive guests including Oliver Cromwell, Mary Queen of Scots and Queen Caroline.

Brassington, less than three miles north of the visitor centre, is a popular detour with cyclists, especially those linking the Carsington Water Trail with the High Peak Trail. The village is reached from the B5053 with an uphill climb along Wirksworth Dale. The best time to visit is in the summer when the **Wickerman Festival** takes place – touted by its organisers as a 'festival of music, beer and general tomfoolery.' The willow Wickerman sits outside (yet another) **Miners Arms** on Miners Hill (✐ 01629 540222) over Wakes Week before being paraded through the village to a nearby field. At sundown the 30-foot figure is set alight, an impressive sight in the night sky.

Four miles south and straddling the Ashbourne road, **Kniveton**, a pretty Derbyshire village with its 13th-century church, feels timeless, surrounded by countryside boasting a couple of ancient barrows. On one of the Bronze Age burial mounds, a bronze dagger with an ivory pommel has been uncovered, along with an urn and amber ring (in the hands of the British Museum).

Kirk Ireton has an infrequent bus service from Ashbourne. If you're travelling by car from Carsington Water, you will need to wind your way through country lanes eastwards. The older part of the settlement dates back to the 17th century and continues to hold tight to its historical customs. Holy Trinity Church still carries out the ancient tradition of 'roping for the wedding,' with canny local children blocking the bride and groom's exit until they've paid a toll in silver. But the sense of history is strongest in The Barley Mow Inn on Main Street. The old sign on the tree at the end of the garden is the only hint that this old house is a pub. An inn since 1800, it feels as if little has changed in the three small, dark rooms of Jacobean wood panels, low beams, flagstone and oak floors. The proprietors (two sisters who don't suffer fools gladly) serve light ale from a jug they keep on the bar. Behind the counter, more ales are served directly from a row of barrels. It would seem The Barley Mow has always shunned modern ways: it was one of the last pubs in the country to accept decimalisation. Its 87-year-old landlady at the time didn't hold with the new money. If for no other reason, detour to Kirk Ireton to visit this pub caught in a time warp.

⦀ FOOD & DRINK

Barley Mow Inn Kirk Ireton DE6 3JP ✆ 01335 370306. Well worth beating a path to this miraculously unchanged village pub (page 223).

Main Sail Restaurant Carsington Water, DE6 1ST ✆ 01629 540363. Overlooking the reservoir, the restaurant with ceiling to floor windows and outside terrace has great views. The restaurant (which can get very busy) serves freshly prepared food – with particularly tempting cakes.

Red Lion Inn Main St, Hognaston DE6 1PR ✆ 01335 370396 ☉ daily with lunchtime & evening sittings. The pub serves restaurant-style food rather than the standard pub grub, with prices to match. Delightfully quiet village location, not far from Carsington Water.

2 WIRKSWORTH

At first glance the old mining settlement of Wirksworth, northeast of Carsington Water, looks like any other English market town, with its handsome town houses, square and bustling main street. The town's prosperity was built on lead mining, a local industry that extends back to Roman times, and possibly even earlier. The King's Field south of the town was opened up to anyone wishing to make their fortune in lead. As is often the case, the good times came to an end. While the lead mines closed down with the demise of the industry, the mining cottages have survived, connected by an extraordinary warren of narrow paths – known as jitties or ginnels – that criss-cross the hillside. You can explore many of these routes between The Dale, West End and Green Hill roads above Market Place (see box, page 209).

Wandering through the hillside of jitties is something like a scene from a child's book of fairy stories – it's not difficult to imagine fabled characters such as Wee Willie Winkie or the Pied Piper slinking between the high stone walls or ducking down cobbled alleyways. No wonder this quirky town, humorously dubbed 'Quirksworth' by Prince Charles, has become a magnet for artists, designers and architects. Wander the main street to find delicatessens, chic cafés and tea rooms, old-fashioned grocery stores, eco-shops and craft stores.

In contrast to the jitties, **St Mary the Virgin**, tucked behind St John Street on the east side of the main street, is a picture of ecclesiastical normality, enfolded by a lawned churchyard – the meeting point of at least five ancient pathways. Circling the graveyard of St Mary's is a footpath lined with historical buildings that reverently cluster around the church.

The historic centre

Moot Hall in Chapel Lane is as good a place as any to begin your exploration of Wirksworth. The building is not open to the public but the two bas-relief marble plaques set into the exterior are an interesting memorial to the town's history, depicting the miner's scales, a pick and trough. They were taken from the original Barmote Court at Moot Hall in Market Square, set up in the 13th century to collect taxes, settle mining disputes and check lead measurements. In 1814, the court was moved from Market Square (too many excitable miners disturbing the town's peace) to its present tucked-away site on Chapel Lane. It's not a particularly imposing building, but an important one, housing what's thought to be the oldest industrial courts in Britain.

"Not far from Elizabeth's house is a surviving wooden cruck thought to be part of a medieval cottage."

From Chapel Lane, head for Market Place and continue along St John's Street, where you'll come to the modest home of **Elizabeth Evans**, better known as Dinah Morris in George Eliot's renowned novel, *Adam Bede*. The Derbyshire settings for the novel are coded but recognisable: Derbyshire is referred to as Stoneyshire, Wirksworth as Snowfield and Ashbourne as Oakbourne – while the characters of Adam Bede and Dinah Morris are based on Samuel and Elizabeth Evans, George Eliot's aunt and uncle (Elizabeth Evans's gravestone is sited near the copper beech at St Mary's churchyard).

Not far from Elizabeth's house on John's Street is a surviving wooden cruck or crook (a curved timber frame used to support the roof of a building) thought to be part of a medieval cottage, now imbedded into a more recent brick gable. Beside it, a small but lively **farmers' market** takes place by the Memorial Gardens on the first Saturday of the month. It claims to be the 'friendliest market for miles,' and it certainly seems so. Wandering south along John's Street, you'll catch glimpses of St Mary's peering through the alleyways on the left.

St Mary the Virgin Church

St Mary's Gate DE4 4DQ ☺ 9.00 until dusk

Still heading south along the main shopping street, turn left down **St Mary's Gate** and aim for the spire. The Norman church, with Victorian improvements, is believed to be on the site of one of Britain's earliest Christian centres of worship. While the original church no longer exists, there are plenty of relics remaining. In the north entrance, you'll find the first of the whimsical **Anglo-Saxon stone carvings**. Among them is a large staring face and a tiny legless man above it, looking like a half-eaten gingerbread man.

In the **north transept** are two impressive alabaster chest tombs. The bas-relief of the distinguished gentleman sporting a moustache and pointed beard, and a long gown with ruff, suggests a person of great importance. And so he was: **Anthony Gell**, Wirksworth's most famous son, was the founder of the Free Grammar School (the local secondary school still bears his name) and the almshouses – both found on the circular path outside the church. The other is of his father, Ralph. In the chancel, there's another impressive painted gritstone tomb belonging to **Anthony Lowe**, his feet resting on a skull. Anthony Lowe was Standard Bearer (see the script below the Royal Arms) not only to Henry VII and Henry VIII, but also to Edward VI and Queen Mary. Not a bad list of names to drop on to your curriculum vitae.

In the south transept, you'll find some quizzical Romanesque carvings. There's a pair of legs on the run – the other half of the gingerbread man perhaps? Here you'll find the original **T'Owd Man of Bonsall**, a miner with pick and kibble (a metal bucket), representing Derbyshire miners.

But it's in the nave you'll find St Mary's *pièce de résistance* – the Anglo-Saxon carved coffin lid, or **Wirksworth Stone**, from around AD800. In 1820, there was great excitement when the stone was uncovered, two feet below the pavement in front of the altar, a perfectly preserved human skeleton beneath. No-one knows who was buried here, but the coffin lid is one of the finest Anglo-Saxon carvings in the country, with its bas-relief pictorial retelling of the gospels in comic-strip style.

The Dale, Green Hill & West End

On the other side of the main street from the church, terraced houses, cottages and courtyards crowd the hillside above Market Square, a legacy of the thriving lead industry. By the latter part of the 19th century, however, the town's mining was in decline. Limestone quarrying took its place, initially saving the town from economic doom. But Dale Quarry, locally known as the 'Big Hole', was to become less of a saviour and more of a monster by the mid-1920s: its massive stone-crusher filling the town with noise and dust. Business and home-owners simply upped sticks, leaving empty shells behind them to fall into decay

LOST IN THE JITTIES OF WIRKSWORTH

Climbing the narrow footpaths barely wide enough for a wheel barrow, never mind a vehicle, I have the feeling I'm all at sea in a land-bound fishing village. These so-called 'jitties' diverge and merge with each other, dipping and rising; twisting and winding towards the crest of the hill. In places they're so steep you're almost forced on to tiptoes.

To reach this otherworldly place, head up Dale Road, Green Lane or West End and cut across to the jitties; then ditch the map and take a random left or a right. I've come here many times, usually on the Architectural Trail of the Wirksworth Festival. But today the jitties are empty. I catch glimpses of bulging walls, impossibly narrow gables and sagging slate roofs. Lazy cats bask on the jitties' high walls, while disembodied voices drift over the limestone enclosures. The scent of Earl Grey tea and ripening apples wafts across the alleyways that are laced with Californian poppies and weeds. Old-fashioned neat-as-a-pin cottages, lived in for decades by local residents, sit comfortably side by side with the shabby-chic homes of the arty incomers; their peeling Farrow and Ball doorways, stained-glass windows and Arts and Crafts railings adding a touch of Bohemia to the jitties of The Dale and Green Hill. Gardens and patios are dug out of the hillside, sometimes dropping straight down to the slate roofs below them. In places the houses huddle round courtyards as if in conversation and in this magical place tiny 'puzzle gardens' are occasionally cut adrift from the houses they belong to by the tangle of pathways.

and ruin; Wirksworth was at risk of becoming a ghost town. But this particular story has a happy ending. With the help of the Derbyshire Historic Buildings Trust in the late 1970s and early 1980s, the people of Wirksworth threw themselves into the task of regenerating their town. Winning the prestigious Europa Nostra Award for architectural conservation in 1983 only gave impetus to the project, and since then Wirksworth has gone from strength to strength.

Wirksworth Festival

The liveliest time to visit Wirksworth is in **September** when the town hosts a programme of music, theatre, art and street entertainment during its festival. It is fast becoming one of the best rural arts festivals in the UK and is centred round a revived ancient celebration that takes place at St Mary's Church called the **Clypping (or Clipping) of the Church**. In accordance with this ancient tradition, the parishioners (and anyone else who cares to join in) link hands to encircle the church while singing a hymn before continuing their procession through the town.

The other main event of the festival is the **Art and Architecture Trail**. Over the opening weekend, Wirksworth throws open its doors to visitors to display the work of local, national and even international artists. Many of the festival volunteers offer tea and cakes in their living rooms and kitchens, and it really does feel as if you've been invited into the very heart of the community.

¶¶ FOOD & DRINK

Le Mistral 23 Market Pl, DE4 4ET ℘ 01629 810077. French sophistication: you can start the day with croissant and coffee and a newspaper, or have an evening meal with a good wine. The labyrinth of rooms and cellar all add to the French ambience. Try the *boeuf bourguignon* or the mushrooms in white wine sauce; both are very tasty.

Scrumdiddlyumptious 9 & 11 St Johns St, DE4 4DL ℘ 07940479563. The café lives up to its name with its sumptuous décor, cakes and ice cream, along with tasty vegetarian and non-vegetarian options. Don't leave without stocking up on treats from the old-fashioned sweet jars. Offering craft sessions too, it's unsurprising Scrumdiddlyumptious won the family-friendly category in the Derbyshire Food and Drink Awards 2013–14.

3 THE NATIONAL STONE CENTRE

Porter Lane, DE4 4LS ℘ 01629 824833 ⊘ www.nationalstonecentre.org.uk

Given the importance of stone in the Peak District, it's fitting that there's a discovery centre (along with a café and shop) devoted to the hard stuff right in the heart of quarrying country between Cromford and Wirksworth and beside the High Peak Trail. An indoor exhibition gives a brief history of the geology in the White Peak and wider afield. Among the rock exhibits is a fossilised shark's tooth, found here in 1990. Outside, it soon becomes apparent why: the Stone Centre stands on the site of a coral reef. As I stood shivering in front of one of the interpretive boards one damp winter's day, it taunted me with its words: 'You have arrived just 330 million years too late for your holiday in the tropical sun'. Behind the information board, there's a reef mound that once teemed with life but is now (as the board dramatically explains) a huge graveyard containing the remains of millions of fossilised sea creatures. Where there once was a seabed crammed with shellfish, sea urchins, sea snails, sea lilies, corals and sponges, there are now fossilised brachiopods, echinoids, goniatites

"'You have arrived just 330 million years too late for your holiday in the tropical sun'."

and crinoids. A highlight of the geo trail for me was the exhibition of dry stone walls, illustrating the diversity of stone and building techniques across Britain's regions from the Highlands of Scotland, Cumbria and Northumberland to the Midlands, Wales and Devon. For those who'd like to have a go at building their own dry stone structure, the centre offers one- and two-day courses on walling.

The Steeple Grange Light Railway

✆ 01246 235497 ⌖ www.steeplegrange.co.uk ☺ Sun & bank holidays from Easter through to the end of Sep, & Sat in Jul & Aug

Close to the National Stone Centre is an open-air, narrow-gauge railway that will take you on a 20-minute ride through superb limestone scenery. Check the website for special events.

4 MIDDLETON-BY-WIRKSWORTH & MIDDLETON TOP

Ⓐ **Ecopod** (page 244)

Just north of Wirksworth, **Middleton-by-Wirksworth** is a rough and ready mining village sprawling out across the White Peak uplands. Most visitors pass by on their way to the National Stone Centre, Middleton Top and the High Peak Trail. D H Lawrence spent a year just outside the village in a cottage perched above the Via Gellia (hounded out of Cornwall with his German wife for singing German songs and hanging out red underwear in their garden above the coast – allegedly sending coded messages to enemy ships in the Great War). There's a blue plaque on the wall outside Mountain Cottage marking his time there. On the Wirksworth side of the village and on the High Peak Trail (the bridleway running along a former railway trackbed; page 145), **Middleton Top** has a spectacular

> *"Middleton-by-Wirksworth is a rough and ready mining village sprawling out across the White Peak uplands."*

outlook from its lofty position. Apart from the tiny visitor centre and tuck-shop style café (along with bicycle hire for the High Peak Trail) is the restored **Middleton Top Engine House** (☺ Easter–Oct Sun & bank holidays), still complete with the original pair of beam engines, boilers and soaring chimney stack, all necessary for hauling the wagons up the steep gradients when the railway was still running. There's also a collection of railway paraphernalia, tools and other oddments.

5 THE NATIONAL TRAMWAY MUSEUM AT CRICH

🏠 **Cliffside House B&B** (page 244)

DE4 5DP ✆ 01773 854321 🖰 www.tramway.co.uk ☉ Apr–Oct. The attraction has tram exhibits & museum, tram rides, period shops & cafés, along with a woodland walk. See ad 4th colour section.

I jumped on a Berlin tram, but instead of creaking my way alongside the River Spree and smoggy city streets, I was ascending a steep hillside through wide-open English countryside.

This is National Tramway Museum, a few miles off the A6 in the Lower Derwent Valley along the B5035. It's a popular with history buffs, transport-spotters, retirees, families and just about anyone else who enjoys a good old-fashioned, fun day out.

Start your visit at **Town End Terminus** where the museum curators have done their best to recreate a pre-war British street scene. The carved stone façade of Derby's original assembly rooms (exhibiting the recent revival of British trams) sits side by side with the Red Lion, a Stoke-on-Trent Edwardian pub that was dismantled and taken to Crich to be recreated brick by brick. The Victorian street lamps and cobbled streets add to the feeling of nostalgia, further enhanced by the occasional classic car casually parked on the roadside. (Crich Tramway Village offers free entry to anyone who can add to the period set by parking their old-timer for a minimum of three hours.)

Jump on a tram and trundle up to **Glory Mine**, the last stop on the approximately mile-long hill. A trail leads out of the museum to **Crich Stand Memorial**, skirting the quarry. If the sight of British and European city trams ploughing the Derbyshire countryside seems somewhat surreal, so is the sight of this memorial tower perched on the edge of the limestone cliff like a stranded lighthouse in landlocked Derbyshire. At night, the flashing light of the tower can be seen for miles around. The memorial is to the Sherwood Foresters; the thousands of men who came from the counties, cities, towns, villages, hamlets and farms that stretch out far below. An honesty box at the bottom of the tower asks for a small donation. It's well worth it for the views that encompass five counties on a clear day.

The **depot** at the Tramway Museum below the hill has an impressive range of stock, mostly trams from British cities, interspersed with the odd European and North American model. They are a real mix of old wooden cars with ornate railings to more modern heavy-duty metal vehicles. To see how the trams developed from horse-drawn carriages to steam, diesel and electric street cars, head for the **Great Exhibition Hall**.

Before leaving, take a different tram up the hill, this time alighting at Wakebridge. Follow the path downhill through the **Woodland Walk** lined with sculpted forest creatures and objects: a giant woodland ant; the green man, an ogre drowning in rubble; mystical woodland creatures carved from branches and the ancient bound books shelved in the roots of a great tree stump – like something out of *Harry Potter*. There's also a stone maze with curved stone posts of stained glass, echoing Crich Stand Memorial on the hill above.

FOOD & DRINK

Cliff Inn Town End, Crich DE4 5DP ✆ 01773 852444. A proper local, no-frills pub serving good food and taking particular pride in its selection of well-kept beers. Inexpensive.

The Loaf Victoria House, The Common, Crich DE4 5BH ✆ 01773 857074 ☺ closed Mon. Artisan bakery, café and delicatessen. Eat in or take-away. Great breads plus a range of filling and healthy lunch options. Be prepared to wait at busy times.

IN THE FOOTSTEPS OF THE FAMOUS

The Lady of the Lamp **Florence Nightingale** spent long summers at her **Lea Hurst** home in **Holloway** (now in private ownership), actively involved in the local community, paving her future as a social reformer and founder of modern nursing. It was to Holloway she returned after the long, hard months tending injured soldiers in the Crimea. Further along the valley, writer **Alison Uttley**, Derbyshire's own answer to Beatrix Potter, resided on **Castle Top Farm**. One of the first women to receive an Honours degree from Manchester University for physics, she abandoned the rigours of science to write charming books for children that anthropomorphised the animals she observed in the Derbyshire countryside – in tales such as *Little Grey Rabbit, The Little Red Fox* and *Sam Pig*. Less frivolous, and of a more sinister nature, Uttley wrote a fictionalised account of the Babington conspiracy in *A Traveller in Time*. She was referring to the 'real-life' historical figure of Anthony Babington, who hailed from Dethick. Babington, not averse to risk, plotted the assassination of Elizabeth I while planning the rescue of Mary Queen of Scots from her perpetual imprisonment. Unsurprisingly, he was executed for his efforts. There's a touch of irony in the fact that the name Dethick derives from the phrase 'death oak', referring to the hanging of criminals. You'd have thought Anthony Babington might have predicted his own tragic end.

6 DETHICK & AROUND

Between Matlock and Crich the settlements of **Dethick**, **Lea Bridge** and Holloway surround the village of Lea, the villages sitting in a pastoral landscape of woodland, meadow, sloping valley and twisting country lanes. The area is outside the national park, yet its gentle beauty is comparable to anywhere in the White or Dark Peak. If you are arriving by public transport, the Matlock to Alfreton bus halts hourly in Lea Bridge and Holloway. The car park on Lea Road below Lea Bridge offers access to Cromford Canal and Bow Wood, and the villages.

Bow Wood bluebell walk

✻ OS Explorer Map OL24; start: Lea Bridge, ♀ SK431356; 3 miles; there are some short, sharp ascents & descents. Watch your footing along & coming off the wooded ridge.

Most counties in Britain claim to have the best bluebell woodland in the country – but this amble from Lea Bridge is exceptional on a number of fronts. In May, the forest and clearings will be carpeted with wood anemones as well as bluebells. Otherwise the best time to come is in October for the autumn colour. Outside of the bluebell season, continue along the ridge and down through fields to Cromford, where the views open out over the Derwent Valley.

1 Start at the public footpath sign on Lea Road, entering Bow Wood through the wooden gate at the foot of the lane behind the mills up to Splash Farm. Follow the path up through the woodland.

2 After about half a mile, by the Woodland Trust Bow Wood sign, take the right turn following footpath signs zigzagging up through the woods to a gap (and handy bench!) through a stone wall. Here there's a meadow between two woodland blocks. Follow the footpath across the meadow, down to a fingerpost and bear left past it for another ten yards.

3 Turn left at the next fingerpost up some steps, following the path steeply uphill with a low wall on your left. Stay on the path as it's signed right and follows a wooded ridge parallel to the Derwent Valley, with views over the stone wall to Cromford and Matlock Bath on the left and the ground dropping steeply through woodland on your right.

4 Where the vistas open out on the left for a second time, you'll find a path to your right, dropping sharply downwards off the ridge to a clearing. There are a few steep sections, but persevere. If you come in the bluebell season, you'll be rewarded with a carpet of blue-purple, sweeping down the hillside in a block of vivid colour. The vistas over to Holloway and Crich Stand are also worth the effort.

Dethick

🏠 **Manor Farm Bed & Breakfast** (page 244)

Just north of Lea, the village of Dethick consists of not much more than a church and three farms, one of which, **Manor Farm**, was home to the Babington family – and is now is under the ownership of Simon Groom (of *Blue Peter* fame) and Gilly his wife, who runs a successful B&B here. Indeed if you want to encounter Anthony Babington, book a night at the manor house and you might just experience the presence of the beheaded Tudor – so rumour has it.

5 At the bottom of the slope, the path swings round to the right and back through oak woods. Continue along the path, eventually passing the steps climbed earlier (3) but this time head on downhill, your path running between open hillside bluebell meadows (in season) with views to Holloway on the hillside opposite, then through a gate and further woodland.

6 At the end of the path, turn right on to the track that soon joins the paved road running behind the still working Lea Mills (John Smedley Ltd) at Lea Bridge and follow it until you reach Lea Road again and your start point.

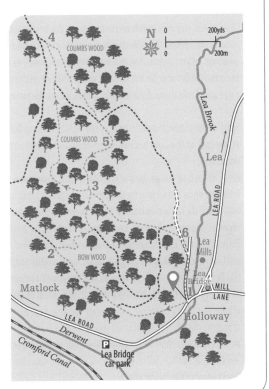

Next to the Manor Farmhouse is **St John the Baptist Parish Church** – explaining Dethick's village status in this tiny settlement. St John the Baptist was built in the early 13th century as a private chapel to Dethick Manor. Set high on the hillside and surrounded by fields, St John's was enlarged to its present size by Sir Anthony Babington in 1530. He raised the height of the chapel and added a tower to the west end, with a charming miniature lantern tower on top. Pick up the key from the dairy on Manor Farm and simply return it to its hanging place when you're done. The best way to approach this rural place of worship is on foot through Swinepark Wood from Lea Main Road through meadows that lead up to the church grounds.

Lea & Lea Bridge

If you are in the area in spring or early summer, don't miss **Lea Gardens** (Long Lane, DE4 5GH ☉ March to end of summer season ✆ 01629 534380 ⬧ www.leagardens.co.uk) created by mill owner, John Marsden-Smedley. From brilliant red, dazzling cerise and deep purple to the delicate shades of lemon, cream, pink and salmon, the rhododendrons, azaleas and camellias are a wondrous sight from late April to early June. Narrow paths criss-cross the woodland of Scots pines, oak, sycamore and birch, sheltering the plants crammed on to the hillside. If you're inspired by the planting, you can stock up at the adjoining nursery. Check the website for special events. The annual music day of jazz and folk music in June is a treat as you wander through the gardens with musicians tucked away in various corners – although the plants will be past their best.

Further down Lea Road, **Lea Bridge** sprang to life during the Industrial Revolution when entrepreneurs John Smedley and his associate Peter Nightingale (a direct ancestor of Florence Nightingale) built **Lea Mills**. The mill cottages with their tiny windows still stand today, while Smedley's Mill at Lea Bridge (Mill Shop, Lea Mills DE4 5AG ✆ 01629 530426 ☉ 10.00–16.00 daily) continues to produce quality knitwear; for classic clothing at factory-shop prices, the **mill shop** is worth checking out.

¶¶ FOOD & DRINK

There's a real dearth of places to eat in this corner of Derbyshire and apart from the **Jug and Glass Inn** (Main Rd, Lea ✆ 01629 534232) – the only pub to serve the surrounding villages – or Lea Garden tea room in season (see below), visitors will have to make their way to Crich, Cromford or the Matlocks, all within a few miles.

The owners of **Lea Gardens Teashop** (Long Lane, DE4 5GH ✆ 01629 534380) use local suppliers and produce and are known for their home baking. If you visit Lea Gardens on a warm, sunny day, grab one of the tables overlooking the woodland gardens: there aren't many tea rooms in the Peak District that can boast such a view of garden colour and tranquillity as this. The teashop remains open through the summer so you can still enjoy this tranquil outlook of woodland, dale and hill from the café – minus the colour.

THE LOWER DERWENT VALLEY

Around Cromford in the Lower Derwent Valley, there's a wealth of hugely important industrial heritage: the mills of Richard Arkwright (recognised as the father of the Industrial Revolution) and Cromford Canal. Further along the A6 to the north, the much-loved tourist towns of Matlock Bath and Matlock overlook the River Derwent, surrounded by rocky tor and dense hillside woodland. Beyond the busy centres of the Matlocks are quiet hillside villages, woodland gardens and returned-to-nature industrial dales, mostly only known to local people. There's much to explore in this part of the Derwent Valley.

7 CROMFORD

🏠 **Alison House Hotel** (page 244) **Cromford Station Waiting Room** (page 244)
⛺ **Birchwood Farm Campsite** (page 244)

Continuing westwards along Lea Road will eventually bring you to the intersection with Cromford, a gritty Midlands village flanked by rock-face, grassy slopes and woodland. From the other direction, the 'scenic' 6.1 Trentbarton bus tumbles down into town from Wirksworth and offers great views of Black Rocks and the surrounding countryside. Equally charming is the approach by train. From the railway station, just outside the village, turn right on to Lea Road and follow it until you reach St Mary's Church. Go through the gate on the right just past the church and follow the leafy, cliff-flanked riverside path up into town.

What Cromford lacks in chocolate-box perfection is made up for in character and history. Indeed it was the first purpose-built industrial village created to house the workers of the world's first successful water-powered cotton mill. No wonder Cromford is called the 'Cradle of Industrialisation'. When Arkwright arrived here, it was nothing more than a tiny mining settlement, the kind of place people passed through on their way to somewhere else. But this was soon to change. By 1771 the mill was completed, located on the edge of the village to take advantage of the waterpower from Bonsall Brook and Cromford Sough (a drain from the lead mines in the hills above).

The ex-miners from the village were not sufficient in number to fill Arkwright's factory, so the industrialist placed adverts in local papers targeting large families. **North Street** was created to house most of that initial workforce, the long rows of terraced houses built to an unusually high standard for labourers, with sash lead windows and solid doors. Notice the long windows on the top floor: here a continuous room extended across the entire length of the terraces, creating a single spinning room for the cottage frame workers not employed in the mill. At the end of North Street, **Cromford School** was built by Richard Arkwright junior. Under new legislation, the young factory workers would work a part-time system, spending part of the day in the factory and part at school. Turn left past the school and walk part way along the lane. Soon you will see a small path on the left snaking past the back end of the North Street houses. Walk down it and you will come to the **Cromford Sough**, affectionately named the Bear Pit by the locals. The path eventually leads back to the main street, **Cromford Hill**, lined with more Arkwright cottages. These tiny terraced houses, with equally tiny-paned windows, seem to mushroom out of the steep hillside pavements, reminiscent of the miniature houses that come with Hornby train sets.

You can also make the long steep climb up Cromford Hill to **Black Rocks** and the **High Peak Trail** (page 145) then down to **High Peak Junction**, before returning to the village along **Cromford Canal**; a fine circular walk. If you prefer to potter in the village, head for the bottom end of Cromford Hill, where the handsome **Greyhound Arms** brings a touch of class to Cromford. It was built by Arkwright to accommodate his patrons and mill visitors, as well as locals. Take time to head up **Scarthin**, a narrow lane shooting off from a corner of the market place. This lovely little street has a short promenade overlooking the **Greyhound Pond**, created for industrial rather than aesthetic reasons. You'll pass the **Boat Inn** and come to **Scarthin Books**, crammed with new and second-hand books from floor to ceiling in a warren of interconnecting rooms spread over three floors. It's not difficult to lose yourself in this world of books, curios and comfy armchairs. There's even a roll-top bath next to the toilet for those in need of a scrub. It's a shambolic kind of place, yet it somehow works in its organised chaos: the staff know their stock inside out.

🍴 FOOD & DRINK

Boat Inn Scarthin DE4 3QF ✆ 01629 258083. The pub next to Cromford village pond offers good-sized portions of well-cooked pub grub at reasonable prices.

Greyhound Arms 38 Market Pl, DE4 3QE ✆ 01629 822551. This 18th-century pub built by Arkwright serves a range of real ales and fairly standard food in fine surroundings.

Market Place Restaurant and Tapas Bar Terrace 16–18 Market Pl, DE4 3QE ✆ 01629 822444. English tradition meets Spanish living. On the outside patio, you can recreate your Spanish holiday with tapas and sangria – if only the proprietor could recreate the continental climate. Indoors, British favourites such as pie, steak, and fish and chips are served alongside Mediterranean dishes.

Scarthin Café Scarthin Books, The Promenade, Scarthin DE4 3QF ✆ 01629 823272. The café within Cromford's idiosyncratic bookshop is hidden behind a curved bookshelf and makes a great pit stop for vegans, vegetarians and those who are gluten allergic – or book lovers. Surrounded by books and odd artefacts, including stocks hung over the Aga, this is a place filled with character to match the rest of the bookshop (page 218).

Cromford Mills

Mill Lane DE4 3RQ ✆ 01629 823256; guided tours ✆ 01629 825995 🖑 www.cromfordmills.org.uk; free entry

The world's first successful water-powered cotton mill was built on this spot by Richard Arkwright in 1771, but problems with the water supply made it difficult to expand the textile industry here. After Cromford Colour Works abandoned the site in 1979, the complex fell into disrepair. There were plans to demolish the mills, because it was believed the site was contaminated with lead chromate. Newer development also compromised the original site. Following research and excavation, the historical value of the site was quickly recognised and Cromford Mills was given Grade I status. Bit by bit, the complex is being restored to its former glory. To find out more about Cromford Mills, take one of the daily guided tours. Otherwise have a potter around the mill buildings and over to the viewing platform above the weir. On site are a number of shops selling everything from local crafts to bric-a-brac. **Arkwright's Attic** is stocked with second-hand books, glass and tableware, while **Arum-Lilie** offers hand-printed textiles and pewter jewellery inspired by Derbyshire history, and an art gallery showcases local artists.

"The world's first successful water-powered cotton mill was built on this spot by Richard Arkwright in 1771."

WITH BRIAN BLESSED ABOARD BIRDSWOOD

One of Britain's most recognisable baritones booms out across Cromford Canal, welcoming passengers aboard *Birdswood*, the barge lovingly restored by the Friends of the Cromford Canal. As president of the organisation, Brian Blessed beseeches *Birdswood's* passengers to have a 'wonderful, magical, mystery' trip, and in a quieter, more understated Beatrix Potter-esque way, we do exactly that. It just so happens there's another Potter – Hugh Potter, volunteer and Cromford Canal enthusiast, acting as our guide today. As we putter along the canal, Hugh points out the canal's natural and industrial heritage. And it's an impressive one. A trip on *Birdswood* is the ultimate in going Slow – even the walkers on the towpath overtake us.

I arrive on a beautiful early summer's day, perfect for idling along the canal. As we cast off, I spot the old pike resting on the canal bed, while mallards dive for pondweed on the water's surface. I sense we're in for a treat. We slip between banks fringed with forget-me-nots, pink campion and May trees. White blossom drifts and settles on the surface of the water, while dragonflies dance and mate on the water's edge. Little grebes float alongside us, their chicks sticking to their mothers' sides like glue. Further on a coot sits on her twiggy island, where she's nesting. As we drift on, the still waters reflect the canopy of vegetation that lines the canal. It's a dreamy, lazy day.

Check the Friends of the Cromford Canal website for running times and departure schedules and for details of special events such as horse-drawn trips ✎ www.cromfordcanal.info/boat/boat.htm.

Cromford Canal

At the height of the Industrial Revolution, barges plied the canal stacked high with coal and limestone. Nowadays this sleepy backwater filled with plants and waterweed is the domain of coots, little grebes and moorhens. The canal once extended almost 15 miles to the Erewash Canal through four tunnels and 14 locks, but now ends just beyond Ambergate, a stretch of five miles. Today the industrial monuments that line the canal route blend comfortably with this wildlife oasis, an SSSI (Site of Special Scientific Interest).

Across the road from Arkwright's Cromford Mills (the driving force behind the canal) is Cromford Canal Wharf. In its hey day the wharf was a hub of activity, an area that took in the warehouse, weighing machine, sawpit, counting houses, stables and smithy. Most of the wharf buildings still stand today; along with the Grade II listed Canal Warehouse with its incongruous turreted gable – built on Arkwright's instruction to prettify the view from his proposed home, **Willersley Castle**.

Sir Richard Arkwright, having bought a large tract of land from the Nightingales, set out to build himself an elegant mansion worthy of his standing and position – Willersley Castle. As bad luck would have it, the house burnt down on completion and Arkwright had to wait a further two years to be rebuilt. Fate was to conspire against him yet again as the unfortunate Arkwright died just before he was due to move in. These days Willersley Castle is a Christian Guild hotel (Cromford DE4 5JH ✆ 01629 582270 ⌖ www.christianguild.co.uk/willersley) and conference centre, open for morning and afternoon teas in a lovely setting.

⅋ FOOD & DRINK

At Cromford Mill you have a pick of eateries including **Everything Stops For Tea** on Mill Lane and the **Mill Yard Restaurant**. Both are good, but for its lovely waterside location, I recommend you cross the road to Wheatcroft's Wharf.

Wheatcroft's Wharf Café (◯ Apr–Oct) opposite the Gothic warehouse makes for a great watering hole on the canal peninsula, surrounded by ducks, swans and Canadian geese. You might even catch a glimpse of the old pike that resides in the canal's depths.

High Peak Junction & Lea Pump House

From the canal end at Cromford Wharf, you can walk the two-mile towpath to **High Peak Junction**, where you meet the end of the High Peak Trail (page 145) as it drops down the inclined plane to meet the canal (or take the short walk across the bridge from Lea Bridge car park just off Lea Road at Lea Bridge). Stop at the **visitor centre** to stock up on information leaflets, maps and light refreshments. The picnic tables that line the grassy verge beside the canal are a prime spot for observing river life, from the swing bridge operator to the canal boat and waterfowl that drift past. You might even spot one of the water voles that inhabit the canal banks below, supported by local conservation groups, who work hard to keep this SSSI (Site of Special Scientific Interest) in tiptop condition.

Here at the junction, freight was transferred from canal to rail. It was the construction of the High Peak Railway that eventually brought about the demise of the canal: the railway faster and more efficient. Throughout the railway's life, this spot was a busy junction with its offices, workshops, forge, oil and lamp stores, engine shed and driver's mess room. The railway's active life may be over, but most of the buildings remain standing today alongside historical artefacts that include vintage railway equipment and tools.

Just a short distance away is **Leawood Pump House** (⚲ www. middleton-leawood.org.uk ☺ bank holidays & specified Sat & Sun), a fine example of Victorian engineering. To appreciate the sheer scale and craftsmanship of the pump house, attend one of the open days. The construction addressed the canal's low water levels by pumping water from the River Derwent into the canal many feet above it. The ingenious system connects the engine and the pump by means of a great beam. The steam cylinder is powered by a furnace that heats up to 800^0C and requires, by current costs, £250 worth of coal for a single day, while the plunger pumps four tonnes or 800 gallons of water with every stroke. Beyond High Peak Junction, the canal becomes a quiet idyll, perfect for walking and biking.

Masson Mills

Derby Rd, Matlock Bath DE4 3PY ✆ 01629 581001 ⚲ www.massonmills.co.uk. Museum open: ☺ Jan–Nov

Masson Mills, between Matlock Bath and Cromford on the A6 (walkable from both settlements and well served by buses), is mainly a retail outlet these days, set out over four creaky wooden shop floors (with a further basement floor housing a museum). The outlet shopping experience may not be for the Slow traveller, but it's worth dropping down to the **Masson Mills Working Textile Museum** and paying the small entrance fee in order to experience what it was like to work in one of the great mill factories. Entry to the museum is gained from the bottom floor at the very back of the mill. Go through the unassuming door part way along the bargain basement. Surrounded by bobbins, cotton reels and shuttlecocks, the little doorway doesn't look very promising initially. But instead of entering a small back room, it leads you, Alice-in-Wonderland like, into a vast industrial underground world of complex and intimidating machinery. If you arrive in time for one of the **guided tours** (☺ 11.00 or 14.00 Mon–Sat & noon & 14.00 on Sun), your guide will set the machines in motion, causing a deafening clatter. Further up, a carding machine (for cleaning and separating the cotton) called 'The Devil' is a terrifying sight, and was even more so for the women and children compelled to clean the machine while it was still in operation. Accidents were not uncommon. In this dark industrial underworld, smelling of cotton fibres, oil and dust, the visitor begins to have an inkling of what it was like for the Arkwright mill workers to spend their days labouring here.

8 BONSALL

A few miles northwest of Cromford is Bonsall – UFO centre of the world. This seems a strange accolade for a quiet Derbyshire village on the edge of the Peak District National Park. Since the new millennium there have been numerous sightings of strange lights and saucer-shaped objects hovering on the moors above the village. Welcome to Bonsall, a village that not only lays claim to unearthly sightings, but also holds the bizarre **World Hen Racing Championship** (see box, page 225).

"Bonsall not only lays claim to unearthly sightings, but also holds the bizarre World Hen Racing Championship."

Bonsall village tumbles down through High Street and Yeoman Street and on through the Clatterway before the road joins the wooded **Via Gellia** leading to Cromford. At the centre of the village, where High, Yeoman and Church streets meet, a striking market cross perches high on top of a circular plinth of stepped stones (11–15 deep depending on the slope of the road). John Wesley preached from these steps surrounded by old stone buildings still standing today, including the **Kings Head** (page 226). Just across the road, where the

COLLETTE DEWHURST, PUB LANDLADY AT THE BARLEY MOW

'Come in, come in,' Collette calls to me through the open window of the Barley Mow, a low-slung whitewashed pub found on the long limb of Bonsall's Dale Road that eventually elbows its way to Uppertown. 'This is a unique pub in a unique place with a lot going on,' Collette enthuses, 'with an annual World Championship Hen Racing competition, the Beer and Music festivals, along with the regular music sessions, French Club, Curry Night and Film Club (with free choc-ice).'

'Because we're off the beaten track, it's a destination.' As musicians, Collette and Dave have a good network of people to draw on for their weekly music sessions.

'On a Saturday night, when you've got a really great band and everyone's dancing, you feel a little bit proud to be part of the collective joy of this little place in the bowl of the valley.'

As we sit with our mugs of tea, I take in the curios that spill from the ceiling and walls, along with the hen ornaments and pictures and the references to UFOs. Collette talks about future plans: possible UFO weekends, the microbrewery Dave wants to develop, and longer term projects. 'I don't think I'll ever sell the Barley Mow though,' Collette comments. 'I'm very emotionally attached to the pub. It really sucks you in.'

Limestone Way is signposted, there's a carving of **T'Owd Man of Bonsall**, a replica of the original, now held at Wirksworth Parish Church (page 208). The T'owd Man is the earliest representation of an unknown Derbyshire miner, dating back to medieval times.

Off to one side of the square, **Stepping Lane** (more of a path really) heads out of the village. The steps, laid by German prisoners of war, lead on to the pock-marked fields of capped lead shafts and the Limestone Way. This countryside is rich in flora, particularly in spring and early summer, and is dotted with old stone barns now slowly being restored to their former glory, courtesy of heritage funding.

Continuing on down **Yeoman Street**, you'll wander past former miners' and weavers' stone cottages jostling for position with elegant Victorian red-brick semis and terraces, and the occasional handsome farmhouse. In the steepest part of the dale, one or two of the gardens have been dug over and flattened out on the sheer hillside, more typical of the terraced paddy fields of Nepal than the Peak District. I'd recommend taking a circular route around the village along **Dale Road** (past the Barley Mow pub), over **Uppertown** and back to Bonsall in order to see the best of this scattered settlement.

"St James' Church with its graveyard extending across the hillside and imposing spire is said to have the highest chancel in England."

From Market Cross, it's worth detouring up Church Lane to visit the striking **St James' Church** that perches above the village. It makes quite a statement with its graveyard extending across the hillside and imposing spire. The church is said to have the highest chancel in England.

Alternatively, head down the dale through the church grounds and out into the little park which will bring you back on to Yeoman Street further down. You'll come across another monument here where Dale Road and Yeoman Street meet, a **Victorian Gothic stone fountain** with its spire-like covering.

On your village amble, look out for the tiny stone workshops with long windows stretched out across the top floor on both sides. I spotted one on Dale Road and another next to the Market Cross. Besides working the lead mines, some villagers rented out knitting frames to make stockings from raw materials supplied by the hosier. At the height of the cottage industry there were over 140 knitting frame workers operating in Bonsall by the light of the long windows. With the arrival of

THE WORLD CHAMPIONSHIP HEN RACING COMPETITION

⊘ www.world-championship-hen-racing.com

You may not have a thoroughbred racehorse, but you could 'beg, steal or borrow' a hen to enter the prestigious World Championship Hen Racing Competition at the Barley Mow pub held on the first Saturday in August annually. This may sound like an April Fools, but the race is a very serious business (well sort of). The official World Championship Hen Races have taken place in this Derbyshire village since 1992, although the history of hen racing in the area goes back much further when local villages competed against each other using their fowl.

The hens are given sardonic names such as Korma, Kebab, Nugget and Drumsticks or more traditional country names like Flo Jo, Buffy, Jenny, Henry and Betty. Pruned and pampered, they're coaxed to run the 15-metre course with the promise of the best chicken feed at the end, shaken in a bag or rattled in a tin. The fowls are given three minutes to reach the finishing line. Any squabbles between the competitive, or more likely food-greedy, hens result in disqualification. Beware that red card.

The commentary is full of double entendre and hen jokes: 'That was a fowl!' 'Shame, he's beaked early.' 'Poultry in motion.' Some chickens ramble aimlessly, or even turn round and head back to the starting line. Others bolt through the course in a few seconds.

Hire a chicken, or just turn up on the day with your hen and register. Be aware though, it's claimed some of the competitors train their hens for months and put them through a rigorous exercise regime to keep them in tip-top condition. Otherwise, just sit back and enjoy the spectacle.

the Industrial Revolution, the villagers were forced to take the cobbled paths criss-crossing Masson Hill to Matlock Bath and Cromford and the factory mills.

Summer is the best time to visit the village. The **Bonsall Magical Open Gardens** (check the UK National Directory for annual dates *⊘* www.opengardens.co.uk) are indeed magical. From the terraced hillside garden and cliff-side woodland to the hidden courtyard and walled garden, you'll encounter temple, grotto, stream and waterfall. If you're unable to make the Open Garden day in June, there are always the village carnival and well dressings (page 11) in July, not forgetting the weird and wonderful World Championship Hen Racing taking place in August (see box, above). For details check the village website (*⊘* www.bonsallvillage.org) where Halldale Brook cuts through the steep-sided valley, quite gorge-like in places.

🍴 FOOD & DRINK

Barley Mow The Dale, DE4 2AY ✆ 01629 825685. An option for lunch (w/ends only). Otherwise stop by for a real ale or an evening meal. Good honest pub grub at reasonable prices in this event-packed pub at the heart of the local community. See also the box page 223.

Fountain Tearooms 1 Yeoman St, DE4 2AA ✆ 01629 824814. The Fountain Tearooms (plus B&B and holiday let) at the junction of Yeoman Street and Dale Road offer cooked breakfast options, an extensive lunchtime menu, as well as freshly made cakes in a lovely, contemporary room. There's more comfortable garden seating on the patio outside.

Kings Head 62 Yeoman St, DE4 2AA ✆ 01629 822703. This delightful historical pub dates back to 1677, and has a reputation for quality pies.

9 MATLOCK BATH

🏠 **High Tor Boutique Hotel** (page 244)

Continuing north from Cromford along the A6 you reach the holiday spa town of Matlock Bath. The Victorians called Matlock Bath 'Little Switzerland', but these days the town is more a 'Little Blackpool' with its rows of souvenir shops, amusement arcades and fish and chip shops. It even has its own illuminations (September and October). It's pretty riverside location and dramatic rocky backdrop draw visitors from far and wide.

The promenade running alongside the river gives the landlocked town a seaside feel. During the summer months, Matlock Bath is anything but Slow, particularly at the weekend. At times the nation's entire motorcycle population seems to descend upon its busy streets. On any given sunny day the main road will be lined with shiny metal speed machines, their leather-clad owners huddled over the bikes talking accelerator pumps, aerodynamics and anti-lock braking systems. Among the bikers, couples and families stroll along the main street, or sit on the promenade walls with ice creams and steaming chips.

However, outside of the summer season when the hordes have gone home you can have Matlock Bath all to yourself. Wander the tiny roads above the town or along the cliff tops to get a bird's-eye view of this quaint Victorian riverside town. Drop in on the lovingly refurbished **Fishpond** for a pint or a meal (page 228). While there, take in a gig: the Fishpond prides itself on attracting some of the best local, national and even international musicians, year round. Just across the road, the **Grand Pavilion** is an impressive statement of Edwardian grandeur, built at the height of the spa town's popularity. The edifice has struggled to survive in modern times, and with its future under threat, the local community stepped in to rescue this handsome Germanic-looking building. The 'Pav' (as it's known locally) was purchased at a snip, but millions of pounds will be needed. Unperturbed, the new owners opened up the multi-functional venue for visitor tours and events with the unashamedly cheeky marketing slogan: 'open, ambitious and still a little bit scruffy'. Despite the building's unfinished state, the Pavilion at the time of writing has managed to attract quality local musicians and artists, as well as a few regarded acts from further afield (check out events on the website ✍ www.thegrandpavilion.co.uk). Underneath the Pav, the **Peak District Mining Museum** (✍ 01629 583834 ✍ www. peakdistrictleadminingmuseum.co.uk ☉ Apr–Oct) gives an insight into the area's defunct lead-mining industry.

The Heights of Abraham
Dale Rd, DE4 3NT ✍ 01629 582365 ☉ Mar–Oct ✍ The attraction includes Woodland garden walks, 2 show caves, exhibits, viewing tower, playground & cafés.

It's time to take the **cable car**, season and pocket permitting, up to the Heights of Abraham. Sit back and enjoy this particularly Slow mode of transport. The cable car hovers mid-point, allowing you to drink in the views of the Derwent Valley, the riverside town of Matlock Bath and Cromford flanked by the rocky outcrops of the Black Rocks. You can also spot the Arkwright mills, Willersley Castle and Cromford Canal beyond.

At the top, take a guided tour of **Masson Cavern**, a lead mine later worked for fluorspar. Squeezing between the rocks, you get an inkling of the dark, damp and claustrophobic conditions the miners worked under, some of them children. In the **Great Chamber**, you'll be awarded for your efforts with a multi-coloured light show. There are a lot of steps and uneven ground, so wear comfortable shoes – and bring a jumper. It's cold down there. Further down the hill, **Rutland Cavern** has fewer steps. It's smaller than Masson Cavern, but its museum setup gives you a feel for the miners' existence. Check out the **Long View exhibition**, telling the story of Matlock Bath's development as a tourist town along with Heights of Abraham. Children can enjoy the hairy spiral climb to **Prospect Tower** with its 360° view of the surrounding area and the exceedingly long slide in the playground. For the best dining view in the Peak District fringes, grab yourself a table at the **Vista Restaurant** or **Terrace café**. They're both a cut above the average attraction eatery.

If you are planning to walk back to Matlock, leave the Heights of Abraham from the top entrance (page 230), pausing at the **Tinker's Mineshaft viewing platform** for yet more panoramic views of the Derwent Valley and surrounding area. If you happen to be visiting in July, August or early September, bring a bag as the bushes on the lane behind are laden with wild raspberries, and blackberries soon after.

FOOD & DRINK

The Fishpond Freehouse and Raft Restaurant 204 South Parade, DE4 3NR ☎ 01629 581529. This stylishly refurbished pub has its own in-house bakery, bar and restaurant (⊙ Wed–Sat & Sun lunch). The freehouse has a reputation for quality, locally sourced food and drink. The pizzas are particularly good.

Flavours Coffee Bar 190 South Parade, DE4 3NR ☎ 01629 580845. This contemporary coffee bar serves great food, snacks and decent coffee away from the main fish-and-chips drag – all with a friendly smile.

10 MATLOCK

🏠 **Riverside Guesthouse** (page 244)

Continuing north of Matlock Bath on the A6, you'll arrive at its sister town – Matlock, Derbyshire's county seat. While Hall Leys Park is the centre piece of Matlock these days, it was **Matlock Bank** (on the sunny side of the valley) that was at the heart of Matlock's tourism in times of yore. Smedley's Hydro (now **County Hall**) drew health-conscious Victorians to the then-fashionable spa hotel. The imposing building is still literally Matlock Bank's crowning glory with its metal crown perched on top of its central tower. Back in Victorian times, there was even a tram (long gone) that ploughed up and down Bank Road, saving legs and sore muscles from the near vertical street. The hydro and tram may no longer be part of the tourist scene, but Matlock still has oodles of old-fashioned charm, with its riverside park and **Victorian shopping**

MATLOCK AT CHRISTMAS

The **Victorian Matlock Christmas weekend** offers nostalgia in spades from its organ grinder to its 150 stalls. The weekend finishes with a glorious fireworks display. The **Boxing Day Raft Race** (in aid of the RNLI) has a range of conventional and homemade water vessels, all with varying degrees of water tightness, which make the four-mile journey along the Derwent from Matlock to Cromford; all to great comic effect.

street on Dale Road, while the area around County Hall still has some interesting individual shops and bars, not least the wonderful craft and events centre at the café-cum-pub, Designate at the Gate.

To get your bearings, stand on Derwent Bridge. Apart from the terrace houses that spread out along Matlock Bank, the eye is drawn along the green stretch of park beside the Derwent River and up on to the hillside above it with the Neo-gothic **Riber Castle** perched on the skyline. Lower down, **St Giles Church** sits on a rocky bluff that slopes up to **Pic Tor** and the town memorial. Looking to the end of the bridge and the junction with Dale Road, the countryside seems to rise straight up from the town.

Ambling through Matlock's parks & churches

Start your amble around Matlock at **Hall Leys Park**, surrounded on two sides by the town's shopping streets, Dale Road and Causeway Lane. Never has such a small parcel of land (originally just two fields) been so crammed with leisure facilities: tennis courts, a skateboard park, pitch and putt, bowling, an interactive play park and splash pool, boating lake, miniature railway, gardens, lawns and pavilion café. Head through Hall Leys and out the other end on to **Knowleston Place**. Enter **Knowleston Gardens** via the Monet-style bridge and take the path on the right squeezing between the River Derwent and the sheer cliffs of **Pic Tor**. Ignoring the path leading to High Tor, continue to a wrought-iron bridge on to the A6. Cross the bridge and the A6, climbing **St John's Road**, with the rocks of High Tor appearing like fangs in the sky.

Soon **St John the Baptist Church** will come into view, mushrooming from a wall of rough limestone. The church, built in 1887, has a fairy-tale quality to it with its oriel window and bell turret capped with a pyramidal lead roof. Its *raison d'être* is a dog called Vida. Its owner, Louisa Sophia Harris, built her own Anglo-Catholic chapel at the end of her garden after the vicar of St Giles in Matlock refused to memorialise her pet dog. Regarded architect Sir Guy Dawer designed the church, its furniture and light fittings, while artist Louis Davis, known as 'the last of the Pre-Raphaelites', was called upon to create the stained-glass window. John Cooke was responsible for the painted altar and George Bankart, expert in ornamental plaster work, modelled the embossed swallows and bands of roses and grapevines in the barrel-vaulted ceiling. It's a shame this enchanting church has to be kept locked because of vandalism. If you want to see the interior, contact Friends

A walk with a cable car ride – High Tor, Heights of Abraham & Masson Hill

✽ OS Explorer map OL24; start Matlock Bridge at Hall Leys Park, ♥ SK429360; 3 miles; one stiff climb up High Tor, then downhill all the way; refreshments at the Heights of Abraham

The walk takes in Matlock's 'Pleasure Parks' (page 229), a stretch of the River Derwent, High Tor and the cable car leading to Heights of Abraham (page 227). From the top entrance, a track leads downhill towards Masson Hill and Matlock. The views overlooking the precipitous gorge on this walk are never less than sublime.

1 From Matlock Bridge, walk through the park and out the other end into Knowleston Place, taking a right turn over the pedestrian bridge into **Knowleston Gardens**, and right again so that you're walking with the River Derwent on your right.

2 Take the left turn signed for **High Tor** and climb the path until you reach another signpost on your right. Go through the metal gate and climb the hill to High Tor. Victorian entrepreneurs (never afraid to employ a bit of hyperbole) sold High Tor as an 'exciting Alpine Route linking Matlock and Matlock Bath' and charged an entrance fee for the 'pleasure grounds'. They installed tennis and skittle grounds and opened a café: all gone now – and perhaps the better for it.

3 Towards the top of High Tor, go round the fenced off mining shafts of **Fern and Roman Caves**. Here you have a choice: you can take the path that gives the cliff face a wide berth, or you can take **Giddy Path** – nothing more than a narrow ledge cutting through the sheer rock face. The path is just wide enough to take both feet, but there's an old metal handrail screwed into the limestone to cling to, if you start to feel – well, giddy.

4 From here the path drops steeply towards Matlock Bath. Take a right turn through the woodland to the cable-car station.

5 Take the cable car up to the **Heights of Abraham** (charge includes entrance fee to attraction). Leaving the Heights of Abraham from the top entrance, turn right on to the

of Friendless Churches (⬧ www.friendsoffriendlesschurches.org.uk) or St Giles Church.

Retrace your steps down St John's Road, across the bridge and along the River Derwent, this time taking the right turn signposted for **Pic Tor**. At the crest of the hill there's a war memorial with fine views back across to Matlock. Head down the grassy path through the graveyard to **St Giles' Church**, a wonderful place of story and history inscribed

farm track and continue downhill along **Masson Hill** until you see a public footpath signpost on the right. Squeeze through the stile and follow the diagonal track through the field to **Masson Lees** farm on your left.

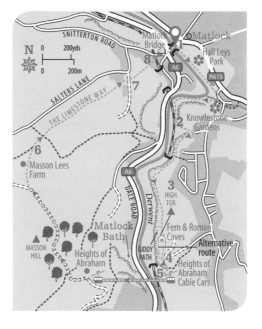

6 Go through the gate and join the path (part of the Limestone Way) following the line of trees downhill towards **Matlock**.

   At one point there's a muddy track through a field. Ignore it and continue to follow the line of trees with the concrete hut on your left. You'll head through a thicket before reaching a road.

7 Cross the road and continue down the hill with stupendous views of Matlock town below. Continue steeply down to **Snitterton Road**.

8 Turn right to reach **Dale Road** and the town bridge. Your circular walk is complete.

on limestone. Sagging Celtic crosses, engraved stones, tablets, grandiose monuments, cherubs and angels and toppled urns sit in among the long grass. The cemetery sits on a rocky promontory, the edge of the graveyard dropping tens of feet to Knowleston Garden below. It's a good place to come at the end of the summer with the edge of the graveyard thick with brambles – and juicy blackberries. St Giles (named after the patron saint of beggars and cripples) is a medieval church, restored and rebuilt over the centuries. Little remains of the original Norman structure, but the great ancient stone urn, retrieved after centuries from the rectory gardens, is a reminder of the building's long history. After viewing the church, slip out through the lych gate and down the steep cobbled path back to the park.

Lumsdale

Before leaving town, take time to explore Lumsdale, a deep narrow ravine of ruined mills beside a waterfall, just off the A615 in the direction of Tansley, tucked under a council estate and only known by local people in the main.

On the elbow of Bentley Lane off the Tansley Road, the path rises up the ravine past the ruins of Lumsdale mills. Under ivy, moss and lichen, you'll catch the remains of an industrial past: a gable here, an empty window there, a missing door, a roofless ruin, a right angle of walls instead of a rectangle, a pile of rubble. Climbing further up, there's the curved wall of an empty paint vat, a single surviving flue and a wheel pit with an empty lynchpin. Through an archway, there's the worn-away convex curve of stone where a millstone once ground. It's a place of strange decaying beauty. The first watermill was built here in the 1600s. By the height of the Industrial Revolution, there were at least seven mills crammed into this narrow dale. Standing on the pathway with the ravine dropping away beneath your feet, it's not hard to imagine the bygone aromas of the mill industry: ground minerals, the crunched bone of animal and the chaff of the wheat and the woven cotton; or to conjure up the grating millstone and the voices of mill workers in a once dust-filled air.

"Under ivy, moss and lichen, you'll catch the remains of an industrial past."

At the top of the dale, a waterfall spills 50 feet, the transparent pebbles of water bouncing into the air. Below, the stream is bracken-brown, while at the water's edge, great green and russet slabs of stone sculpt the valley like heavy, angular Russian monuments.

As you emerge on to open land above the ravine, you'll come to the only surviving mill pond of three. On my last visit, a black Labrador broke the glassy surface of the water with his snout, causing the inverted landscape to tremble. Mallards flew out of yellowed reeds and a flock of ravens rose up on the hillside in an echo – a truly atmospheric place, and a wonderful counterpoint to the bustle of Matlock town.

🍴 FOOD & DRINK

Matlock is very well served with restaurants and cafés, the majority of them centred round Hall Leys Park and Dale Road. Many of them source local produce with the food cooked on the premises.

Next to the park near Crown Square, **Bow Boutique and the Cosy Cup** (✆ 01629 580239) advertises itself as 'a quirky café full of cake, coffee and cuteness'; once you've filled up on cake, you can browse the hand-picked crafts, some created by local artists and designers. **The Café in the Park** (🖰 www.cafeinthepark.net) has seating on the terrace and promenade and offers lunches and snacks as well as hosting monthly themed bistro evenings from countries around the world. If you prefer to eat al fresco, head for the **Park Head Market at Hall Leys** every Wednesday. The stalls surrounding the Sunken Gardens in the park sell locally produced food: fresh bread from The Loaf, wine from the Derbyshire Winery, honey products from 'Dad's Bees' and organic fruit and veg from Garden Farm. **Cool River Café & Patisserie** (✆ 01629 580467) is another good option. The trendy café and patisserie is situated between Hall Leys Park and Dale Road.

On Snitterton Road, **The Green Way Café** (✆ 07502 289273) serves homemade vegetarian food.

Up on Smedley Street, the family-friendly, event-filled **Designate at the Gate** (✆ 01629 760033) has good-value one-pot meals. There's even a 'beach' in the garden.

Just outside Matlock, on Snitterton Road, **Matlock Meadows Farm: Ice-cream parlour, coffee shop and working farm** (🖰 www.matlockmeadows.co.uk) is definitely worth the detour for the farm's delicious real dairy ice cream, its milk supplied by the Holstein Friesian herd. Among the favourites are more unusual combinations such as Bounty, lime cheesecake, lemon meringue and stracciatella. For a taste of local flavour, try the Bakewell tart. Coffee and cake is also on offer. There's a small playground and petting animals for children.

Matlock's **farmers' market** takes place on the third Saturday of every month at the Imperial Rooms on Imperial Road. The market by the old bus station on Bakewell Road takes place on Tuesday, Friday and Saturday.

🛍 SHOPPING

Step back into retail history on **Dale Road** with a spot of vintage shopping. Names such as The Spinderella, Little Shabby Hen, Magpie, Unpolished Perfection and Vintage Rooms give an idea of the goods for sale on this regenerated Victorian street. And if that doesn't do it, the shabby-chic, vintage and retro goods spilling on to the pavements will. It's easy to get lost in the shops' tiny rooms crammed to the gills with distressed and recycled furniture, vintage clothing, vinyl records, collectables, retro goods, curios and one-off accessories. There are plenty of places to stop for a coffee, too.

11 AROUND DARLEY DALE

🏠 **Darwin Forest Country Park Lodges** (page 244)

For most tourists the A6 northwest of Matlock is an unattractive urban corridor through to the Peak Park. And indeed Darley Dale at first glance seems to have little in the way of interest, lined with offices, industrial units and blackened stone-built roadside terraces. But on the hillsides flanking either side of the A6 is a little-known landscape of settlements that cling to the slopes or lie stuffed into dales along with lost woodland gardens, babbling rivers, forgotten dams, hillside meadows and the moors that lie above.

"Take the Peak Rail steam train and travel the four miles alongside the River Derwent through meadows and flood plains."

A good introduction to the valley is to take the **Peak Rail steam train** from Rowsley South (📞 01629 734643 🖱 www.peakrail. co.uk) and travel the four miles alongside the River Derwent through meadows and flood plains, enjoying this slower, nostalgic form of travel. From the settlement of **Darley Bridge**, climb Oaker Hill to orientate yourself and to see the promise of what lies beyond the A6 (see walk, pages 236–8). On the crest of the hill, the Will Shore sycamore tree is immortalised in a poem by William Wordsworth (see box, opposite).

While in the area, drop in on the historic Norman church of **St Helens** at Darley Dale, where one of the country's oldest trees can be found. Estimated to be around 2,000 years old, the yew tree has an impressive girth – and is gnarled and wrinkled, as befitting an old boy (or girl). On the other side of the valley are the forgotten woodland vales of **Sydnope Dale** and **Hall Dale** in **Two Dales**.

12 Sydnope Dale & Hall Dale in Two Dales

Travelling along the industrial A6 corridor from Matlock, take a right turn on to the Chesterfield Road. Another right turn leads to Ladygrove Road, a quiet factory site of concrete, crumbling brick and corrugated tin. The site at **Ladygrove Mill** in Two Dales doesn't look promising, but there's something altogether more romantic in the valley above: a wooded dale of dammed lakes, babbling streams, weirs and flowering shrubs. **Sydnope Dale**, a forgotten garden woodland, once served the mill bought by the Dakeyne family to spin flax; the brook above ideal for harnessing the power needed for the machines. Weirs were

WORDSWORTH'S TALE OF TWO TREES

Tis said that to the brow of yon fair hill
Two brother clomb; and turning face from face
Nor one look more exchanging, grief to still
Or feed, each planted on that lofty place
A chosen tree. Then eager to fulfil
Their courses, like two new-born rivers,
they
In opposite directions urged their way
Down from the far-seen mount. No blast might kill
Or blight that fond memorial. The trees grew
And now entwine, their arms' but ne'er again
Embraced those brothers upon earth's wide plain,
Nor aught of mutual joy or sorrow knew
Until their spirits mingled in the sea
That to itself takes all – Eternity

William Wordsworth

The 'fair hill' in Wordsworth's poem refers to **Oker Hill**, a quiet, secluded corner of Darley Dale, yet only a stone's throw from the bustling town of Matlock. Two brothers, William and Thomas Shore, each planted a tree on Oker before going their separate ways to seek their fortunes, story has it. The brother who went abroad fell into poverty and died in obscurity. The sibling remaining in the local area prospered, lucky chap. Fittingly, the tree of the successful brother thrived, while the tree planted by the unsuccessful brother perished. Life's a lottery, they say, and so were Will and Tom's choices in trees and destinations.

The remaining sycamore tree, standing in splendid isolation on the horizon of Oker Hill, is a striking landmark in the area today. Two centuries earlier, William Wordsworth thought so too. Seeing the lonely sycamore on the crest of the hill from his lodgings, he asked his landlady about its origins; then penned the above poem. The rest is history – or folklore. You decide.

constructed and leats dug out. Smaller streams were dammed to create millponds. The Dakeynes went on to create three dams in all: Fairy, Fancy, and Potter, extending a distance of 96 feet. Follow the lane upwards and take a left turn across a bridge. The path follows alongside the first dam, the colour of tea diffused with light and fringed with rhododendrons in early summer. The path winds upwards through lichen, woodland shrubs and trees, revealing glimpses of Fancy and Potter dams below.

By train & on foot through Darley Dale

❄ OS Explorer map OL24; start Peak Rail car park, Rowsley South station, 📍 SK298602;
5 miles; fairly easy apart from the rise out of Matlock & the steep climb up Oker Hill;
refreshments: Matlock & Darley Bridge

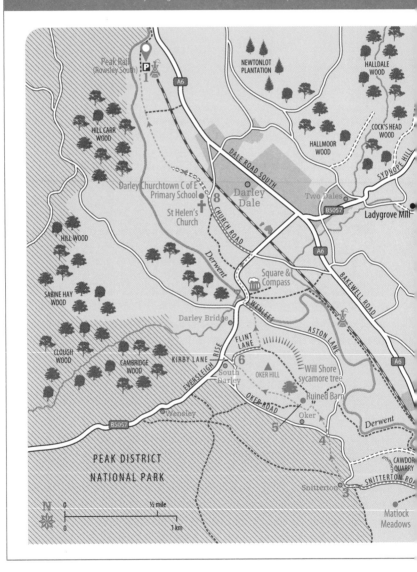

William Wordsworth felt the hamlet of Snitterton in Darley Dale worthy of an overnight stop – and the sycamore tree seen from his window on Oker Hill, worthy of his pen (see box, page 235). This five-mile walk takes in both, along with an ice cream parlour. The walk doesn't have the drama of the Dark Peak, or the striking beauty of the deep-cut White Peak dales, but this gentle landscape is delightful, skirting hamlets and villages via country lanes and riverside meadows. It's hard to believe the urban corridor of the A6 is within spitting distance. The walk kicks off by taking the Peak Rail heritage railway. Travelling to Matlock at the leisurely pace of the steam train and returning to Rowsley South on foot is the ultimate in Slow travel.

1 Take the **Peak Rail** steam or diesel train from **Rowsley South** to Matlock (see page 234), a memorable beginning for a walk.
2 Leaving the platform at Matlock train station, turn left up the footpath (away from Sainsbury's) to Snitterton Road. Turn right and continue until you see the sign for **Matlock Meadows** (see *Food & drink*, page 233). Follow the lane up to the farm for an ice cream, before backtracking and continuing on along Snitterton Road to the village of the same name. ▶

237

By train & on foot through Darley Dale (continued ...)

3 Where the road bends round on itself on the edge of **Snitterton**, follow the sign for Wensley and Winster that takes you along a hedge-lined footpath. At the end, you will encounter another metal sign. Follow the sign in the direction of Oker through fields until you hit Oker Road.

4 Turn left then cross the road and climb the stile into the steep-sided field that lies in the V between Oker Road and Aston Lane. At the top right-hand side of the field, climb the stile on to a farm track. Turn right and walk towards the ruined barn.

5 Where the track peters out, turn left and follow the sheep path up on to Oker Hill. Continue along the ridge past the **Will Shore sycamore tree** (see box, page 235) and keep on the ridge until it drops steeply down to the village of South Darley, with views across Darley Dale and to the distant Eastern Moors.

6 Through the gate at the bottom of Oker Hill, turn down Kirby Lane, before turning right along Flint Lane. Soon you will come to a public footpath sign on the left. Climb the stile and continue through fields until you come out at **Wenslees**, a country lane. Turn left, then at the end of the lane, turn right and cross the bridge at **Darley Bridge**.

7 Walk along Main Road until you come to the **Square and Compass** pub. This is your opportunity for a second pit stop, if needed. Continuing on, take a left turn on to **Church Road**. Follow the road until you come to **St Helen's Church**. Drop in to have a look at this historic church with its ancient yew tree.

8 Take the next left along a dead-end road, past the primary school. When the road runs out, continue straight on, over stiles and through flood pastures with the River Derwent on your left. Eventually you will see a right turn leading to the Peak Rail station. Follow the curve of the Derwent until you emerge in Peak Rail's car park.

Parallel to Sydnope Dale is **Hall Dale** (owned and managed by the Woodland Trust) where Halldale Brook cuts through the steep-sided valley, quite gorge-like in places. In the 19th century, this area was at the heart of a thriving local nursery trade, boosted by the Victorian passion for exotic plants. It explains the clumps of rhododendrons, laurel and yew lining the path today. Alongside the nursery specimens and planted conifers, there's also ancient woodland of larch and oak. The leafy archway into the upper section of the dale enhances the notion of woodland garden. You can combine the two largely forgotten dales of natural and manmade beauty to create a circular walk using the ❀ OS Explorer map OL24.

¶¶ FOOD & DRINK

There are a few pubs in and around this section of the A6 serving standard pub grub. For something more special, it's best to head into Matlock.

Espresso Deli and Coffee Bar 32 Lime Tree Av, DE4 2FS. Good for an alfresco lunch, or you can eat in. The deli offers a range of good-value specials and excellent pastries with coffee.

ACCOMMODATION

When choosing accommodation for the book, I've opted for places that are a little bit special in some way. They cover a wide spectrum: boutique hotels, country manors, homely B&Bs, farmhouse barn conversions and cottages, yurts, eco-pods, shepherds' huts, camping barns and campsites with breathtaking views. There's a Victorian boathouse, a converted railway waiting room and a hunting tower just to name a few of the more unusual properties. Some of them have been chosen for their historical links, imposing architecture and landscaped gardens; others for their cosiness, eco-friendly approach and helpful owners who pay attention to detail. In all of them, I've looked for accommodation that provides guests with good value for money. Throughout the book hotels, B&Bs and self-catering options are indicated by 🏠 and campsites are indicated by 🛆. For full descriptions of places listed here, go to 𝄐 www. bradtguides.com/peaksleeps.

1 THE DARK PEAK

Hotels
Losehill Hotel and Spa Losehill Lane, Edale Rd, Edale S33 6RF 𝄐 01433 621219 𝄐 www. losehillhouse.co.uk
Wind in the Willows Country House Hotel off Sheffield Rd, Glossop SK13 7PT 𝄐 01457 868001 𝄐 www.windinthewillows.co.uk

B&Bs
Cheshire Cheese Inn Edale Rd, Hope S33 6RS 𝄐 01433 620381 𝄐 www. thecheshirecheeseinn.co.uk
Ladybower Inn Bamford S33 0AX 𝄐 01433 651241 𝄐 www.ladybower-inn.co.uk
Rushup Hall Rushup Lane, SK23 0QT 𝄐 01298 813323 𝄐 www.rushophall.com. Also offers self-catering accommodation.
Sunny Bank Boutique Guest House Upperthong Lane, Holmfirth HD9 3BQ 𝄐 01484 684065 𝄐 www.sunnybankguesthouse.co.uk

Self-catering

Cross Farm Dunford Rd, Holmfirth HD9 2RR ✆ 01484 683664 🖰 www.crossfarmbarn.co.uk

Oaker Farm Holiday Cottages Losehill Lane, off Edale Rd, Hope S33 6AF ✆ 01433 621955 🖰 www.oakerfarm.co.uk

Campsites

Hayfield Camping and Caravan Club Kinder Rd, Hayfield SK22 2LE ✆ 01663 745394 🖰 www.campingandcaravanningclub.co.uk.

Swallowholme Camping and Caravan Park Bamford Station Rd, Bamford S33 0BN ✆ 01433 650981 🖰 www.ukcampsite.co.uk

Upper Booth Campsite Edale S33 7ZJ ✆ 01433 670250 🖰 www.upperboothcamping. co.uk

2 THE EASTERN MOORS

Hotels

The Maynard Main St, Grindleford S32 2HE ✆ 01433 630321 🖰 www.themaynard.co.uk

The Peacock at Rowsley Rowsley DE4 2EB ✆ 01629 733518 🖰 www. thepeacockatrowsley.com

B&Bs

Congreave Farm Bed and Breakfast Congreave, near Bakewell DE4 2NF ✆ 01629 732063 🖰 www.derbyshire-farm-accommodation.co.uk

Sladen House Jaggers Lane, Hathersage S32 1AZ ✆ 01433 650104 🖰 www.sladenhouse.co.uk

Self-catering

Gardener's Cottage Edensor ✆ 01246 565379 🖰 www.chatsworth.org

The Hunting Tower Stand Wood, Chatsworth Estate ✆ 01246 565379 🖰 www. chatsworth.org

Russian Cottage Carlton Lees ✆ 01246 565379 🖰 www.chatsworth.org

Swiss Cottage Stand Wood, Chatsworth Estate ✆ 01246 565379 🖰 www.chatsworth.org

Hostels

YHA Hathersage Castleton Rd, Hathersasge S32 1EH ✆ 0845 3719021 🖰 www.yha.org.uk

Campsites

Barn Farm Campsite Birchover DE4 2BL ✆ 01629 650245 or 07899 710018 🖰 www. barnfarmcamping.com

Chatsworth Park Caravan Club Site DE45 1PN ✆ 01629 582226

3   THE NORTHERN WHITE PEAK

Hotels

Monsal Head Hotel Monsal Head DE45 1NL ✆ 01629 640250 ⌕ www.monsalhead.com
The Old Hall Hotel The Square, Buxton SK17 6BD ✆ 01298 22841 ⌕ www.
oldhallhotelbuxton.co.uk

B&Bs

Merman Barn Bed and Breakfast Alma Rd, Tideswell SK17 8LS ✆ 01298 872033
⌕ www.mermanbarn.co.uk
Rambler's Rest Guest House Back St, Castleton S33 8WR ✆ 01433 620125
✉ enquiries@ramblersrest-castleton.co.uk

Self-catering

Brosterfield Farm Cottages Foolow S32 5QB ✆ 01433 630312 ⌕ www.brosterfieldfarm.
co.uk
The Wriggly Tin Wormhill, Millers Dale SKI7 85N ✆ 01298 872009 ⌕ www.wrigglytin.co.uk

Youth hostels

YHA Losehill Hall near Castleton, Hope Valley S33 8WB ✆ 0845 3719628 ⌕ www.yha.org.uk
YHA Ravenstor Millers Dale SK17 8SS ✆ 0845 371 9655 ⌕ www.yha.org.uk

Campsites

Greenhills Holiday Park Crowhill Lane, Bakewell DE45 1PX ✆ 01629 813052 ⌕ www.
greenhillsholidaypark.co.uk

4   THE SOUTHERN WHITE PEAK

Hotels

Charles Cotton Hotel Market Pl, Hartington SK17 0AL ✆ 01298 84229 ⌕ www.
charlescotton.co.uk
Izaak Walton Hotel Ilam, Dovedale DE6 2AY ✆ 01335 350555 ⌕ www.izaakwaltonhotel.
com
Lathkil Hotel School Lane, Over Haddon DE45 1JE ✆ 01629 812501 ⌕ www.lathkil.co.uk

B&Bs

Bassettwood Farm Tissington DE6 1RD ✆ 01335 350866 ⌕ www.bassettwood.co.uk
Beechenhill Farm Ilam DE6 2BD ✆ 01335 310274 ⌕ www.beechenhill.co.uk. See ad, 4th
colour section.
Brae Cottage East Bank, Winster DE4 2DT ✆ 01629 650375 ⌕ www.braecottagewinster.co.uk

Self-catering

Limestone View Farm Stoney Lane, Cauldon, near Water Houses ST10 3EP ✆ 01538 308288 ⌖ www.limestoneviewfarm.co.uk

New Hanson Grange near Milldale, Ashbourne DE6 1NN ✆ 01335 310258 ⌖ newhansongrangeholidays.co.uk

Secret Cloud House Holidays Limestone View Farm, Stoney Lane, Cauldon ST10 3EP ✆ 07845 939603 ⌖ www.secretcloudhouseholidays.co.uk. Yurts and glamping also available.

Thimble Cottages Youlgreave DE45 1UR ✆ 0781 7900841 ⌖ www.thimble-cottage.co.uk

Winster Hall Main St, Winster DE4 2DJ ⌖ www.winsterhall.co.uk

Hostels

YHA Ilam Hall Ilam DE6 2AZ ✆ 0845 3719023 ⌖ www.yha.org.uk

YHA Youlgreave Fountain Square DE45 1UR ✆ 0845 3719151 ⌖ www.yha.org.uk/hostel/youlgreave

Campsites

Mandale Campsite Haddon Grove DE45 1JF ✆ 01629 812416 ⌖ www.mandalecampsite.co.uk

New Hanson Shepherds' Huts near Milldale, Ashbourne, DE6 1NN ✆ 01335 310258 ⌖ www.peakdistrictshepherdshut.co.uk

Rivendale Caravan and Leisure Park Buxton Rd, near Alsop-en-le-Dale, Ashbourne DE6 1QU ✆ 01335 310311 or 01335 310441 ⌖ www.peakdistrictpods.co.uk/index.php

5 THE SOUTHWEST PEAK, CHESHIRE & STAFFORDSHIRE FRINGES

Hotels

The Silken Strand Hotel 64 St Edward St, Leek ST13 5DL ✆ 01538 371022 ⌖ www.thesilkenstrandhotel.co.uk

B&Bs

The Daintry 5 Daintry St, Leek ST13 5PG ✆ 01538 528051

Pack Horse Inn Mellor Rd, New Mills SK22 4QQ ✆ 01633 742365 ⌖ www.packhorseinn.co.uk

Self-catering

Don Whillans Memorial Hut Upper Hulme, The Roaches ST13 8UB ✉ rockhall@stockies.plus.com ⌖ www.donwhillanshut.co.uk

East Lodge Lyme Park, Disney, near Stockport. Check the National Trust website for details.

Horton Lodge Boathouse Rudyard Lake ✆ 01244 357116

Wheeldon Trees Farm Holiday Cottages Earl Sterndale SK17 0AA ✆ 01298 83219 ⌂ www.wheeldontreesfarm.co.uk. See ad, 4th colour section.

Campsites
The Cat and Fiddle Inn A537 Buxton Rd, Macclesfield SK11 0AR ✆ 01298 78366 ⌂ www.catandfiddleinn.com

6 THE DERBYSHIRE FRINGE & LOWER DERWENT
Hotels
Alison House Hotel Intake Lane, Cromford DE4 3RH ✆ 01629 822211 ⌂ www.alison-house-hotel.co.uk
High Tor Boutique Hotel Matlock DE4 3PS ✆ 01629 580440 ⌂ www.hightorhotel.co.uk

B&Bs
Manor Farm Bed & Breakfast Dethick DE4 5GG ✆ 01629 534302 ⌂ www.manorfarmdethick.co.uk
Riverside Guesthouse Riverbank House, Derwent Av, Matlock DE4 3LX ✆ 01629 582593 ⌂ www.riverbankhouse.co.uk

Self-catering
Cliffside House B&B and holiday lets Wakefield, near Crich DE4 5HD ✆ 01773 856338 ⌂ www.cliffsidehouse.com
Cromford Station Waiting Room Cromford DE4 5JJ ✆ 01629 580067 ⌂ www.cromfordstationwaitingroom.co.uk
Darwin Forest Country Park Lodges, Two Dales ✆ 01629 732428 ⌂ www.darwinforest.co.uk
Hoe Grange Holidays Hoe Grange Farm, Brassington DE4 4HP ✆ 01629 540262 ⌂ www.hoegrangeholidays.co.uk. See ad, 4th colour section.

Campsites
Birchwood Farm Campsite Wirksworth Rd, Whatstandwell, near Matlock DE4 5HS ✆ 01629 822280 ⌂ www.birchwoodfarm.co.uk
Ecopod The pod called Hidden Holly is found in a hay meadow between Middleton-by-Wirksworth and Middleton Top ✆ 07929 616282 ✉ craig.banks@hotmail.co.uk ⌂ ecopodholidays.co.uk
New House Organic Farm, Kniveton DE6 1JL ✆ 01335 342429 ⌂ www.newhousefarm.co.uk
Pudding Room Carsington Water DE6 1NQ ✆ 01629 540413 ⌂ www.thepuddingroomderbyshire.co.uk

INDEX

Entries in **bold** refer to major entries; those in *italic* refer to maps.

INDEX OF ADVERTISERS

BEECHENHILL FARM

A lovely B&B and two distinctive cottages on our organic farm at Ilam near Dovedale.

Our award-winning, eco-friendly organic farm is perched on a south-facing hill above the pretty village of Ilam on the Staffordshire–Derbyshire border in the Peak District National Park. Amenities include a wood-fired hot tub, sauna and Wi-Fi. We also have a resident folk artist, and creative activities to take part in. We are passionate about food, quality and customer service. This is a relaxing place to stay and we want you to enjoy your time here so that you visit us again and again.

Beechenhill Farm
Ilam Moor Lane, Ilam,
Ashbourne, Derbyshire, DE6 2BD

www.beechenhill.co.uk
Tel: 01335 310274
Email: stay@beechenhill.co.uk

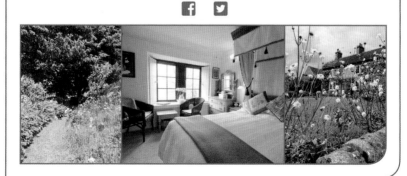

HOE GRANGE HOLIDAYS

A cosy, peaceful retreat in The Peak District.
Stunning scenery with wonderful walks from the door.

Hoe Grange Holidays
Brassington, Matlock,
Derbyshire, DE4 4HP

www.hoegrangeholidays.co.uk
Tel: 01629 540262
Email: info@hoegrangeholidays.co.uk

CRICH TRAMWAY VILLAGE

Crich Tramway Village, home of the National Tramway Museum, is situated in the heart of the Derbyshire countryside. Let our vintage trams transport you along our period street. Don't miss the Woodland Walk, exhibitions, tearooms, shops and pub.

Crich Tramway Village
Crich, Matlock,
Derbyshire, DE4 5DP

Tel: 01773 854321
Email: enquiry@tramway.co.uk

www.tramway.co.uk

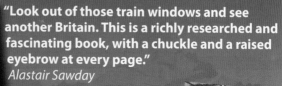